THERE AND BACK

Commentary by a Former Foreign Correspondent

by BARRIE DUNSMORE

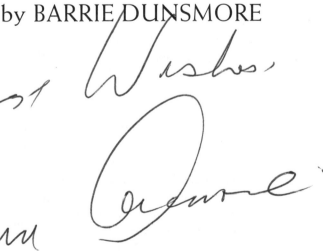

Published by Wind Ridge Publishing, Inc.
P.O. Box 752
Shelburne, Vermont 05482

ISBN: 978-1-935922-06-3
Library of Congress: 2011936815

Cover photo: November 9, 1989, Berlin Wall

AUTHOR'S NOTE:
The pieces herein were first published in my regular column in the
Rutland Herald & Barre-Montpelier Times Argus, with some notable
exceptions. "Howard Dean's Run for President" and "Fundamental
Anger" were first published in the *Burlington Free Press.* "A Triumph
of Realism" was first published in the *New Leader* magazine. I wish
also to thank Vermont Public Radio for permission to use the
following commentary: "Peacemakers," "Reagan's Role in Soviet
Union's Demise," "Remembering Yeltsin and Halberstam," "Moral
Values of Kerry Supporters," "Can Tiger Still Play?" "Remembering
Peter Jennings," "Hurricane Katrina's Effect on the Media," and
"From Facts to Opinions." This commentary can be heard via
podcast at www.vpr.net. I want readers to know that with the
exception of minor edits for clarifications on a few of the items, no
changes in substance were made from the original broadcasts and
published versions.

THERE
AND BACK

Commentary by a Former Foreign Correspondent

by BARRIE DUNSMORE

 Published by Wind Ridge Publishing, Inc.
Shelburne, Vermont 05482

DEDICATION

This book is dedicated to my family, to whom I will be forever grateful
for their love, their forbearance, and their inspiration —
my daughters Leeanne and Campbell, and son Tim
my grandchildren Meredith, Paige, Alex, and Malcolm
and to my beloved wife Whitney.

ACKNOWLEDGMENTS

I wish to express my deepest gratitude:

To Wind Ridge Publishing, Inc. for investing in their belief that my work would be of national interest;

To Emily Copeland, my principal editor at Wind Ridge Publishing who took my nearly four hundred disparate commentaries of the past decade, reduced them to seventy, created a conceptual framework and turned it all into a coherent book that faithfully reflects my thinking;

To Randal Smathers, executive editor of the Rutland Herald;

To my editors over the years at the Rutland Herald and the Barre-Montpelier Times Argus: David Moats, Steven Pappas, and Anne Galloway;

To Betty Smith, the head of the Commentary Series at Vermont Public Radio;

Finally, to my many friends and colleagues at ABC News, in America and throughout the world, thank you for an extraordinary thirty years; they far exceeded my wildest dreams.

TABLE OF CONTENTS

Part II: And Back

AND BACK:

FOREWORD

The day after the marriage of Prince William and Kate Middleton, an event that drew an estimated three billion television viewers, an editorial cartoonist captured the sheer idiocy of the current obsession with instant social networking. "Do you, William, take this woman...." reads a balloon over the Archbishop of Canterbury's head. Simultaneously the Archbishop is tweeting "I have just asked William if he takes Kate..." and an array of balloons over the tweeting fingers of sundry members of the congregation announce that "The Archbishop has just asked William if he takes Kate..."

We will never know how and by whom the estimate of three billion television viewers was achieved, but even assuming a margin of error in the 50 percent range, who (among those who cared) could possibly have been left unaware of the interplay on the altar? What was the point of all the imaginary twittering rendered in the cartoon, and all the real tweeting by which millions of banal observations on the subject were exchanged? But then, barring the occasional North African or Middle Eastern revolution, neither substance nor relevance appears essential to the Twitterholic. The perceptive reader (and who else would have bought or be considering the purchase of this book?) will have inferred already that I consider the social media a very mixed blessing indeed. Volume does not equal quality. Immediacy is no substitute for substance.

Quaint as it may seem these days, even broadcast journalism once considered good writing, careful editing, and the application of context to be essential ingredients of a story. The news events we covered were selected (by us, our assignment editors, or producers) because of what we perceived to be their importance or relevance to our audience. In part out of arrogance, but also it must be said, because we devoted a great deal of time and effort to the task, we thought ourselves better judges than our audience of what news fit into that category. We gave American television viewers what we thought they needed to know, not necessarily what they would have selected for themselves. If you would gauge how much things have changed in this regard, consider only the television news time devoted in the early months of 2011 to the emotional meltdown of actor Charlie Sheen.

While I would have written the introduction to this book out of friendship for its author alone, I do so with great enthusiasm because Barrie Dunsmore is a throwback to an era of broadcast journalism I shared. When Barrie was a foreign correspondent for ABC News in Europe and the Middle East, I played a similar role in Southeast Asia. In the late 1960s and early 70s, the ABC bureau in Saigon alone routinely served as base for six or seven correspondents. But ABC also had bureaus in Hong Kong, Tokyo, Cairo, Tel Aviv, Beirut, Moscow, Rome, Paris, Berlin, and London. We must have had almost thirty foreign correspondents in those days; and they knew something about their territory. That did not count the "stringers," or part-time ABC reporters, who filed dispatches from Africa and Latin America. Suffice it to say, those days, and the time and attention paid to foreign news, are long over. The conditions produced by the events of those years, however, remain very relevant to the interests of the United States.

The years that Barrie Dunsmore spent overseas, combined with the subsequent years that he spent as ABC's Senior Diplomatic correspondent, give him a sense of history that illuminates his columns and commentaries. That these have only been available (until now) to the already enlightened citizenry of Vermont has been an unfortunate oversight, remedied at last by this collection. Rather than being just a chronological sampling of his writing, the book is presented in two sections. The first reflects Barrie's thinking on major world events based on his personal experiences as a foreign correspondent. The second deals with the important news of the past decade in this country, as a foreign/diplomatic correspondent might interpret it. In this way we get to see a progression of his thinking on some subjects—and at least once he actually admits he was wrong.

I've mentioned already that Barrie is my friend. (We were BFFs before it was fashionable.) But I rejoice in the publication of this book because it is full of so many attributes missing in much of today's quasi-journalism. Here you will find context, insight, thoughtful reflection, and a bracing anger, based not on ideology but on impatience with fools and their mindless nattering.

— Ted Koppel

There

Part I

THERE: Reporting on the Middle East and the Former Soviet Union

British Army Private Alexander Lyon, a Glasgow bus driver with a wife and two small children, was killed by a German sniper's bullet in the waning days of World War I. His son died in the flu pandemic that struck the world shortly after the war ended. In 1922, Lyon's widow Nellie and her eight year old daughter Margaret went to seek a new life in Canada.

May Homersham, the daughter of an undertaker, found a job as a tobacconist's assistant on the Strand in London as the new twentieth century began. She too would eventually emigrate to Canada where she married Bob Dunsmore, a prairie homesteader whose great-grandfather was an escapee from Ireland's potato famine. May and Bob's first born child Wilbur would meet Margaret "Daisy" Lyon in Saskatchewan. They married amidst the Great Depression and the seven year drought—the "dirty thirties"—which would profoundly shape their lives as it did millions of others. Daisy and Wilbur's first born son Glenn died at ten months. Their second son Barrie came on the eve of World War II.

As a toddler during the war, I was often taken to watch the troop trains rolling through town. I vividly remember envying the soldiers—not because they were going to war but because they were going to places like Glasgow and London—"the old country" from whence my family had come. And so, after a decade of broadcasting in Canada, culminating as a reporter/anchor with the CTV Network's flagship station in Toronto, I made my move to attain my dream job—foreign correspondent.

In 1965, with considerable help from my friend Peter Jennings, I was hired by ABC News. This turned out to be a thirty year, all expenses paid ticket to see the world. The original plan was that after a few months to become acclimated at the network headquarters in New York City, I would go to cover the Vietnam War for a year or two. I was completely fine with that but fate intervened. Jesse Zousmer, the vice president of ABC News and a former colleague of Edward R. Murrow was killed in a major airline crash. This set off a series of personnel changes. When the dust settled, I was headed not to Saigon but to Paris as the "roving" correspondent.

In those days, much of the news was in the Middle East and ABC had no full bureaus in that region, so that's where I would spend a big part of my life over the next decade—for nearly three years working out of Paris and seven out of Rome. I covered the major events of the period including the June 1967 War, the September 1970 Jordanian Civil War, Egyptian President Gamal Abdel Nasser's sudden death and extraordinary funeral also in September 1970, and the October 1973 War. I flew on the diplomatic shuttles with then Secretary of State Henry Kissinger that kept that last war from becoming a major U.S.–Soviet confrontation. I often interviewed most of the key players: Israel's Menachem Begin, Golda Meir, Moshe Dayan and Yitzhak Rabin, Egypt's Anwar Sadat, Jordan's King Hussein, the PLO's Yassir Arafat. While I have sometimes disagreed with the policies of the leaders on each side, I developed a genuine affection for most of those I met on both sides of this seemingly endless conflict. My profound wish that they could all live in peace remains constant.

In 1975, I was brought to Washington where my focus remained on international affairs. When President Jimmy Carter decided to engage in Middle East diplomacy, I went along. But I also wanted to broaden my capabilities. I began to steep myself in the arcane subject of arms control so that I could report intelligently on the long standing negotiations to reduce strategic nuclear weapons. Those talks took me to Moscow a number of times with several secretaries of state on whose planes there was no shortage of Russian and arms control specialists more than happy to share their knowledge with me. This new expertise would get me assigned to all U.S.-Soviet summit meetings during the Reagan and Bush I presidencies.

When I returned overseas to London as senior foreign correspondent in late 1984, my new interest in Russian-American relations turned out to be timely. While I still visited the Middle East when major stories developed, I began spending extensive periods of time in Russia. I eventually got to watch Soviet President Mikhail Gorbachev in action at home and to see firsthand just how significantly the Soviet Union was changing. I started going to Hungary, Poland, and East Germany to examine their incipient revolutions. And so in 1989 I was prepared and present when communists lost power in Warsaw and Budapest—and then at the seminal moment when the Berlin Wall came down, signaling an end to the Cold War. That was the biggest news event of my career—and the subject of one of my favorite columns.

1

Middle East

February 6, 2011

Egypt in Revolution?

Former presidents Jimmy Carter, Gerald Ford, and Richard Nixon were walking slowly in the funeral procession of Egyptian President Anwar Sadat. I was about twenty paces behind them in a line that included former Secretary of State Henry Kissinger and then Israeli Prime Minister Menachem Begin. Suddenly about a dozen men whose dress uniforms identified them as members of the Egyptian Presidential Guard stepped in front of the Kissinger/Begin group, forcing us all to stop. The guards un-slung their rifles and assumed the high ready position: barrels pointed slightly upwards and directly toward us.

Immediately, American and Israeli security agents tensed up and began barking into their radios. I remember noting Kissinger's face was ashen, as I'm sure was mine. That's because less than seventy-two hours earlier, another unit of this same presidential guard had killed Sadat because he had dared to make peace with Israel. Now the Prime Minister of Israel and the famous American diplomat who had helped to bring about that peace were virtually in their gun sights (not to mention numerous American dignitaries and yours truly, who was one of the three pool reporters on the plane from Washington carrying America's official delegation to Sadat's funeral). For a few moments, probably no more than thirty seconds, I actually feared my then fifteen years of covering this area and these people was about to come to a dramatic end.

But just as suddenly as they had blocked our passage, the guards re-slung their rifles to their shoulders, moved to the side and allowed us to continue. None of the officials or the security people I subsequently spoke to knew what had happened. There were theories but no explanations. As events in Cairo have unfolded in recent days, I have not been able to shake the memories of Sadat's assassination and funeral and the involvement of Islamic fundamentalists in the Egyptian military. That said, understanding America's relationship with Egypt over the past four decades begins with Anwar Sadat.

Sadat broke with the Soviet Union and established a new strategic relationship with America. He went to Jerusalem and became the first Arab leader to make peace with Israel. Before he did this, Egypt was considered the one Arab country that could threaten Israel's existence. And the Middle East was widely considered to be the most likely of all the world's hot spots to set off World War III. Sadat profoundly changed the military balance in the Middle East and by so doing eased the tensions of the Cold War. For this he was gunned down by Islamic extremists in his own army.

Sadat's vice president, Hosni Mubarak, was standing right beside him that day. He was wounded but survived and for the next thirty years has been the beneficiary of America's gratitude for the foreign policies of Sadat, which Mubarak followed more or less faithfully. (That gratitude is still shown in the annual $2 billion in aid to both Egypt and Israel for having made peace in 1979.)

Mubarak was a dictator, although when it came to repression he was not in the same league as Iraq's Saddam Hussein, Iran's Shah, or the theocracy that replaced him. For years, while Egypt stagnated politically and economically, Mubarak shamelessly raised the specter of Islamic revolution every time there were calls for reform from human rights advocates in numerous American administrations. Then suddenly, when crowds in Tunisia demonstrating for freedom and democracy were surprisingly able to topple their tyrant, they ignited a revolutionary flame in Egypt, fanned by the Internet, Al Jazeera, Facebook, and Twitter. At the outset, I admit that I did not believe that Mubarak's rule could apparently be so quickly undone by a historically apathetic population.

If you were to take a poll among the American reporters and commentators covering the events in Egypt, I would guess that 90 percent of them think that rather than daily shifting his position, President Barack Obama should have immediately openly embraced the demonstrators and urged Mubarak to leave town ASAP. But as justified and credible as this broad cross-section of Egyptians calling for Mubarak's departure may be, the American president must consider many questions.

Some related examples:
- In the beginning, revolutions for freedom from oppression are intoxicating. But how often is the idealism of the disorganized street protesters hijacked by professional revolutionaries? Think Citizen Robespierre, the Bolsheviks, or Iran's Islamic Revolutionary Guard. How might Egypt's revolution end?
- The Muslim Brotherhood of Egypt has been active and often banned in Egypt since its inception in 1928. With current support of about 20 percent of Egyptians, the Brotherhood is really the only organized opposition movement and could be

expected to exert its influence, especially in the event of a power vacuum. It has forsworn violence and has been denounced by Al Qaeda. But in general, the Brotherhood opposes Israel and supports fellow Islamists Hezbollah in Lebanon and Hamas in Gaza. If it were a force in any future government, would it not press to end all cooperation with Israel, if not the peace treaty itself?

• The key to the immediate future is the Egyptian army. It struggled successfully to stay neutral in the bloody street battles between anti-Mubarak demonstrators and paid pro-Mubarak provocateurs. Since Colonel Gamal Abdel Nasser led the revolution of 1952, the army has been the nation's most respected institution. Currently, its upper ranks are populated with West Point trained generals who have strong ties with the Pentagon. But where does it actually stand today?

What has already happened in Egypt has profoundly shaken the foundations of the Arab world and the long standing American policy in the region which accepted the promise of stability and security in exchange for limited human rights. Those days would appear to be numbered, if not gone, thanks to the courage of ordinary Egyptians in places like Cairo's Tahrir (Liberation) Square. But what happens next remains very much an open question.

Author's note: This column was published five days before President Hosni Mubarak stepped down. There are to be elections in the fall of 2011. The roles of the Muslim Brotherhood and the Army in Egypt's future remain unclear. In August 2011, having been charged with the murders of many protesters, Mubarak made a televised court appearance—from a hospital bed behind bars.

February 20, 2011
Social Media and Revolution

I do not text or tweet. I have no Facebook page. I use my cell phone to make calls, not take pictures. I am computer literate, but hardly fluent. I primarily use the Internet for research and email. I do watch 24/7 cable news, including Al Jazeera in English when I can find it. But at best, for many I must seem like someone with an acute case of old-fartitis.

But despite my limited personal use of the "social media," I've been around long enough to recognize their transformative value. In fact, as we all take a break after the breathless moments of the new Egyptian revolution, I'm about to make a radical claim on behalf of the new communication technologies including social media—which may be obvious but is rarely mentioned.

There has been no shortage of news and analysis about the important role social media played in the non-violent overthrow of a thirty-year dictatorship by the Egyptian masses. But most of this has focused on how they were powerful organizing tools in bringing Egyptians of all walks of life together to achieve this historic success. I would not dispute this—but I would argue they were all this and much more.

To illustrate my point, let's revisit three events in relatively recent history.

- In Syria after many years, the conflict between the secular Baathist regime of then-President Hafez Assad and the Syrian Muslim Brotherhood reached a climax in February of 1982. Previously the Brotherhood had nearly succeeded in assassinating Assad, and he responded by executing about a thousand Brothers being held as political prisoners. The showdown occurred around the city of Hama, when 12,000 government troops with tanks, artillery, and air support surrounded this Brotherhood stronghold, and demanded its surrender. Considering the recent executions, this was out of the question. Over the next three weeks the army virtually leveled the city, killing from 20,000 to 40,000 people. Snippets of what had happened eventually came to light but there were no witnesses and no pictures. Once again, a murderous suppression had succeeded in virtual secrecy.
- In the spring of 1989, China, like most of the countries of the communist bloc, was coping with disparate groups generally

against the government's authoritarianism and calling for economic and democratic reform. Gatherings of intellectuals and students began in April in Beijing's Tiananmen Square and continued for seven weeks, over time drawing 100,000 demonstrators. From its inception, the People's Republic of China had zero tolerance for internal opposition. In the 1960s during the Cultural Revolution, Chairman Mao had shown no mercy in dealing with perhaps millions of perceived political opponents. But in 1989 the authorities hesitated, allowing hundreds of the world's journalists to descend upon Beijing to witness these rare events in Tiananmen and elsewhere in China. By the time the regime decided to act, first by expelling the journalists and shutting down all communications satellites—and then clearing the square of protesters with tanks and armed troops—it was, in a sense, too late. Even though by historical Chinese standards, the estimated casualty count of between 800 and 3,000 people killed was almost minor, never before had there been such widespread international condemnation of the PRC for its excessive use of force against its own unarmed and peacefully protesting citizens.

• By the autumn of 1989 the Iron Curtain had been sliced open by the Hungarians and the Austrians, allowing tens of thousands of East Germans to use that breach to escape their Stalinist oppressors. For many weeks in Leipzig, East Germany's second largest city, people had been gathering every Monday in a church in the old city square for a prayer meeting to protest the regime's emigration policies. In the beginning there were only a few hundred protesters. By late September there were tens of thousands, peacefully marching around the city's main thoroughfare. Like all Western journalists, I was forbidden to go to Leipzig but ABC News, among others, had numerous locals who shot video coverage of the protests with small cameras we had given them. After a huge anti-government rally on October 2, Erich Honecker, the long-time Communist party chief, decided this could not continue. He ordered that the next Monday's demonstration should be forcefully stopped. On the night of October 8, thousands of troops were trucked into the city to reinforce the State security police. Riot control weapons and a large number of Kalashnikov automatic rifles were issued. Hospitals were placed on alert with extra doctors, nurses, and blood supplies. Ambulances were ready in the side streets. Seventy thousand demonstrators had gathered by Monday afternoon. The stage was set for a bloodbath.

But not all Politburo members were on board. At the last minute, the number two man Egon Krenz cancelled Honecker's orders. Krenz, who was in fact plotting to overthrow Honecker, worried that a bloody crackdown on unarmed citizens would spell doom for his political future and for the regime. We later learned that before countermanding Honecker, Krenz consulted with the Soviet ambassador in Berlin who argued strongly against a "Chinese solution."

So went the evolution of repression in the 1980s. Fast-forward to February 11, 2011, when Egyptian President Hosni Mubarak resigns. In my view, the most important point in the seventeen-day revolt was the day the Egyptian military pledged not to attack protesters as long as they remained non-violent. The generals knew the whole world was watching. Mubarak should have resigned right then, because unless the military put down the revolution, he could not survive.

Throughout the ages, from the Roman Caesars to the twentieth century's Hitler, Stalin and Mao, the most appalling massacres and atrocities committed against millions of civilians have been all too frequent. But that is changing, thanks to the new communication technologies and the social media of the twenty-first century. Today, perhaps for the first time in human history, few tyrants will be able rule through the mass slaughter of their political opponents and get away with it for very long.

Author's note: Protests in Libya began February 15, 2011 and NATO airstrikes started March 18. After six months, a stalemate continues in what became a civil war. In Syria, President Bashar Assad used massive force against protesters in Damascus and elsewhere. By early August, thousands have died in Libya and at least 1,600 Syrian protesters have been killed.

January 10, 2009

Trip to Yemen

It may say something about Yemen that it has never produced another person as famous as its beautiful Queen of Sheba, who dazzled Israel's King Solomon with gifts of gold and spices 3,000 years ago. My own connection with Yemen is a little more recent, although at the time it didn't seem to me that much had changed in three millennia. My story begins (as journalistic exploits often do) in a bar. But this was no ordinary bar. It was the bar at the St. Georges Hotel in Beirut, at the time the most famous and elegant watering hole in the entire Middle East. Its patrons included representatives from virtually every intelligence agency in the world including the CIA, the KGB and Mossad, an assortment of Lebanese government officials and warlords, various members of the Palestine Liberation Organization, diplomats from everywhere, and of course a substantial contingent of the international news media.

It was early February 1967, and much of the talk that evening was about the reports that Egypt had been bombing some obscure villages in Northern Yemen with poison gas. Since 1962, Yemen had been the battleground for a proxy war between Egypt's President Gamal Abdel Nasser and Saudi Arabia's King Faisal. Nasser had sent 50,000 Egyptian troops into Yemen to support the rebels who had ousted the Yemeni King Mohammed al-Badr. Faisal saw this as a direct threat to his own country so of course, backed the monarch-in-exile. The fighting had bogged down. But there was still a lot at stake, as this was actually a struggle for the future leadership of the Arab world between leftist revolutionaries and ultra-conservative, traditional monarchies. If Nasser was using gas to intimidate the royalists and break the stalemate, it was a big story.

The shortest way to get to royalist-held Yemen was through Saudi Arabia and I knew that normally Saudi Arabia was basically closed to foreign journalists. However, I learned that evening that the Saudis would issue visas to reporters at the airport in Jeddah. They would also provide transport to the Yemen border. As it happened, it took much negotiation, but I, my French crew, and an Arabic speaking American reporter were finally allowed into Jeddah and after a week, the Saudis put us on an old DC-3 aircraft and dropped us in the middle of nowhere in the desert near the Yemen border. After several hours I spotted a small dust cloud on the horizon which seemed to be moving toward us. It was not Omar Sharif on a camel (as in that famous scene in Lawrence of Arabia). It was a new Pontiac with huge tires, driven by an impeccably manicured and pedicured Saudi in flowing white robes who greeted us with a smile and in perfect American English said, "Hi. What the hell are you guys doing here?" It turned out the new governor of the province of Najran was a Saudi prince, recently graduated from UCLA.

We spent the night in a nearby oasis and were awakened in the morning by the sound of explosions, which we soon determined were bombs being dropped by the Egyptian Air Force. Fortunately, they were not laden with poison gas and they skipped across the sand dunes without doing any serious damage. However, I will always remember how I began my twenty-eighth birthday on February 13, 1967. After this little bit of excitement, the four of us and a dozen Yemeni guides began the trek into Yemen. We were headed for the royalist outpost of Ketaf, the village which reportedly had recently been attacked with poison gas. Here is some of what I wrote at the time.

"From [Najran] only camels, donkeys, and your own stamina can take you into Yemen. Even in winter the temperature often exceeds one hundred degrees. The first obstacle is a 6,000-foot mountain range. This is child's play for the Yemenis but hell for a Paris-based correspondent." The trip took several days, during which the camel carrying some of the television equipment died of exhaustion. As hot as it was in the daytime, it was freezing at night. But finally, the village appeared on the horizon. "As you approach [Ketaf] its mud-brick towers stretch above the thorny trees that are the only evidence of vegetation. From a distance it is impressive. Up close, it is depressing. A shallow grimy little gutter winds its way around crude dwellings and down dusty alleys. This serves as a sewer. It has been dug so that it can be hit from the windows of the buildings and stains along the outside of the towers identify the local restrooms."

There was absolutely nothing about this place to link it with anything more recent than the middle ages except the old rifles the men carried, although these were not their weapons of choice. As I reported then, "Every man and boy wraps himself with a highly decorated bandolier. Nestled carefully at his waist is his most prized possession—his jambiya—a razor sharp, curved knife, carried in an ornate sheath, which he brags can disembowel a man with one swish. You believe him." I also came to believe the Yemenis that they indeed had been bombed with poison gas by the Egyptians. In addition to the

villagers' credible detailed descriptions of the attack, we also found:
- One hundred new graves containing one or more bodies, which we noted when they opened several up to prove the dead had been recently buried.
- Carcasses of camels, sheep, and dogs littering the streets showing no external wounds. A Red Cross Pakistani doctor who had arrived to treat survivors who told us that they all had lung problems consistent with gas poisoning.

The poison gas attack was later confirmed by independent investigators—a conclusion accepted by the U.S. Government.

So what, you might ask, has all of this to do with the current problems in Yemen?

In the forty-some years since, life has continued to be unkind to the Yemenis. The population has quadrupled to 24 million. It remains the poorest country in the Arab world and unemployment is about 40 percent. Tensions based on the 1960s civil war remain. There is rebellion in the north and a secessionist movement in the south. Al Qaeda has set up shop in the middle. The current president, Ali Abdullah Saleh, has squandered most of Yemen's limited oil revenues, including spending $120 million on a mosque to promote his son as his successor. His control of the country is very shaky. Saudi Arabia is still paying many of Yemen's bills, this time, not to stave off Nasser but Osama bin Laden's progeny. So, when I saw a headline this past week which read, "Yemen Near-Perfect Haven for Terrorists," I thought, sounds right to me.

Author's note: Pro-democracy demonstrations began in Yemen in early March 2011. After six months, Yemen's future remains bleak and uncertain.

March 6, 2011

Pinning Down Muammar Gaddafi

Is it Khaddafi? Ghaddafi? Gadhafy? Qaddafi? Kadzafi? When the man himself was asked, Libya's "brother leader" of the past forty-two years said he didn't care how it was written in the Western world just as long as it was spelled correctly in Arabic. (Explanation: any Roman alphabet spelling of Arabic is a transliteration. So, the hard guttural sound at the beginning of his name is variously written as "k," "g," "q," and with or without an "h." All such spellings are acceptable.)

Since he led a young officers' revolt to overthrow the monarchy of King Idris in 1969, figuring Colonel Muammar Gaddafi out is far more complicated than the spelling of his name. I don't mean to imply that Gaddafi is a misunderstood patriot or benevolent dictator. He is a despot. But over the years, deciding if he is a buffoon or a psychopath has been a challenge.

At times like these, I find myself sifting through the memory banks for clues to understanding the present. As many reporters, in addition to watching him in action I had my own personal encounter with Gaddafi. It was in the fall of 1984, two years before President Ronald Reagan ordered the bombing of Libya and four years before Pan Am 103 was blown up over Scotland by Libyan terrorists. ABC News was planning a series of programs and reports on major events or movements which had shaped the world in the forty years since the end of World War II. After serious negotiations, Gaddafi agreed to talk to us about Pan-Arabism, the movement begun in the late 1950s by Egypt's Gamal Abdel Nasser whose mantle Gaddafi had hoped one day to assume.

But people like Gaddafi are notoriously hard to pin down—as are the where and the when of the interview. Some random memories:

- After arriving in Tripoli, our team was then told to go to Benghazi. On the Libyan Airways domestic flight there, some of the passengers were live chickens. Also on the flight, a young Libyan identified me by name and claimed when he lived in America he always watched ABC News.
- After a day in Benghazi we still knew nothing. We did get a tour of some excellent Roman ruins nearby.
- We spent a night in something like an army barracks. The producer and camerawoman and the sound tech and I were given

four cots in one room, with clean sheets, but no other bedding
or towels. In the morning the women showered while wrapped
in their sheets because male guards were watching them.

- We were eventually driven to a desert encampment and taken
into a large, ornate Bedouin-style tent. When Gaddafi arrived
he was wearing traditional garb and was accompanied by four
tall, beautiful, professionally coiffed young women, dressed in
perfectly tailored camouflage jump suits and carrying automatic weapons. This was Gaddafi's personal guard.

- At the outset I made my pitch for him to do the interview in
English. For several minutes I went through all the reasons
why this would be best for him. Finally, he looked directly at
Eileen O'Connor, my young and attractive producer, and said,
"I will do it in English—for you."

Apart from a brief tirade against President Reagan, there was no
hot news in the hour-long interview. Basically, Gaddafi defined Pan-
Arabism as the way for all Arabs to come together to modernize and
shed the shackles of British, French, and now American colonialism
along with the conservative Arab monarchs who did the colonialists'
bidding. It was clear Gaddafi was in awe of Nasser and saw himself as
an eventual successor.

I have since concluded that Gaddafi's dream died when Nasser
suffered a massive heart attack at age sixty-two. Gaddafi had been in
power barely a year and had only just begun to hitch his star to Nasser
and the Pan-Arab movement. So try as he might to arouse Arab
nationalism and to offer himself as the new Nasser, he was doomed
to fail. The fact was that some unknown young army officer from a
small place like Libya—which in spite of its oil wealth was considered
provincial and had little influence in the Arab world—had virtually
no chance to become the leader of Pan-Arabism.

With Nasser gone, Gaddafi tried to buy his way into political and
economic union with Egypt. Egyptian President Anwar Sadat was
happy to take his money but was not about to give him the launching
pad to greater glory that he so clearly sought. After failing to achieve
union with Egypt, Gaddafi turned to spending his oil money on terrorists groups from the Middle East to Ireland and became an arsonist
and a fire-fighter in Africa's myriad disputes. But after many years, he
had little to show for these efforts, either.

Then, rather recently, having devoted much of his life to achieving power outside Libya, Gaddafi began taking surprising steps to

secure his power within. In 2003 Libya accepted responsibility for the bombing of Pan Am 103 and agreed to pay more than two and a half billion dollars in compensation to the families of the victims. Gaddafi then admitted that he had been developing a nuclear weapons program and agreed to its dismantling under international supervision. When in response, Western countries, including the U.S., normalized relations most Libyans cheered the end of decades of isolation. Libya's economy then began to boom as international investments poured in, mostly filling the Gaddafi family coffers.

A forty-two-year dictatorship is a long one, so when first Tunisia and then Egypt ousted their dictators, Gaddafi might seem a logical next domino to fall. But in a lifetime of confrontation, Gaddafi has never hesitated to use lethal force and now cares little what the world thinks of him. So I am not surprised to hear him say he will fight to the "last drop of blood."

March 20, 2005
Lebanon: Fools Rush In

One of the United States' enduring myths is that when pitted against an expert, a good person with sound instincts and common sense will usually prevail. It's based on a widespread belief that the expert gets paralyzed by detail while the non-specialist will not be distracted by useless information and can get to the heart of the problem. I concede that there may be times when this is true, but not when it comes to conducting American policy in the Middle East.

I raise this issue because *Newsweek* magazine's recent cover story on the Middle East's moves toward democracy contains the following paragraph: "People have often wished that the president traveled more over the years. But Bush's capacity to imagine a different Middle East may actually be related to his relative ignorance of the region. Had he traveled to the Middle East and seen its dysfunctions, he might have been disheartened." The story goes on to correctly point out that the current situation in the region remains very uncertain. Still, the myth is perpetuated that a lack of knowledge and expertise might actually be an asset. In fact, one reason the region is in the mess it's in today is because European and American leaders have historically known little or nothing about the Middle East but persisted in interfering in its politics anyway. The British and French bear much of the responsibility for today's problems by the way they divvied up the Ottoman Empire after World War I. But the United States has made its share of blunders too—especially when it comes to Lebanon.

When I returned to Washington after a decade as a foreign correspondent working mainly in the Middle East, I would soon discover that Americans, even a major candidate for president, understood very little about the region, particularly about Lebanon. In 1976, I was assigned to cover Democratic Senator Henry "Scoop" Jackson's presidential campaign. Though he's little remembered now, Jackson was Jimmy Carter's toughest opponent and won several primaries. In the spring of '76, the Lebanese Civil War was just picking up momentum. One morning, the senator surprised us all when he departed from his stump speech and began talking about the Christians being under grave threat in Lebanon. He implied that the United States should be prepared to take action as it had done in the past. (Jackson was strongly pro-Israel and some Israelis at the time were making that point.) As I was the only reporter present who happened to be fresh from the Middle East, I asked if he meant we should send in the U.S. Marines, as President Eisenhower had done in 1958 (in a Cold War move). With the Vietnam War barely over, Jackson apparently realized that suggesting a new American military adventure was not the way to get elected president, so he waffled, eventually suggesting we should raise the issue at the United Nations.

That night on his campaign plane the senator came to sit beside me and asked me to tell him about Lebanon. I began by explaining how Lebanon's political system was based on a delicately balanced, unwritten agreement reached at the time of its creation in 1943. Under this deal, known unofficially as the "Confessional" system, the president would always be a Maronite Christian; the prime minister, a Sunni Muslim; the speaker of the national assembly, a Shiite Muslim. Political power and its spoils would be split roughly six to five, in favor of the Christians. In the best of times, this was a fragile arrangement—and these were not the best of times. After a civil war in Jordan in 1970, the Palestinians had moved their operations to Lebanon, and began terrorist raids into Israel from Southern Lebanon. This brought Israeli retaliation, which in turn inspired the Syrians to get involved. The Syrians have always behaved as though Lebanon was a province of Syria, which at one time it was.

I also told the senator that the Christians in Lebanon were under less of a threat from the Muslims than from each other. Christian leaders were like mafia dons who thought nothing of killing each others' family members, including wives and children, in wars over turf. This had nothing to do with religion. It was about business—usually illegal business—such as who was in control of the ports where millions could be made in smuggling operations. Jackson didn't say much about Lebanon after that, not because of anything I said, but because it was not a vote-getter.

But a few years later, when the situation in Lebanon was pretty much as it had been in 1976—only worse—President Ronald Reagan did get very much involved. By 1983, the civil war was raging. The Israelis had invaded in '82 in an alliance with the Christians and had remained in force around Beirut. The Syrians had deployed about 30,000 troops, mainly into the Bekaa Valley in the East. And Iran had sent in Revolutionary Guards in support of the Shiite Muslims of the South. By this time, the downtrodden and docile Shiites had formed Hezbollah (Party of God) with a strong militia that often used terrorism as a weapon.

It was into this steaming Lebanese cauldron that Ronald Reagan, having supported the Israeli invasion, introduced the U.S. Marines as part of a multi-national force to try to bring some stability and to get the Palestine Liberation Organization and Yasser Arafat out of the country. But it wasn't long before the United States was seen as being on the side of the Lebanese Christians and the Israelis—against the Muslims—in the ongoing civil war. On October 23, 1983, a smiling driver of a Mercedes Benz truck filled with 12,000 pounds of dynamite slammed his vehicle into the Marine headquarters in Beirut, killing 241 American servicemen. Reagan quickly decided to redeploy American troops to ships offshore and by early spring, the ships had sailed away.

To this day, groups like Al Qaeda cite this episode to their recruits, as proof that America has no staying power and can be rolled by well-placed acts of terror. By the way, Hezbollah, the Shiite's party and militia, with help from Syrian intelligence, is now believed to have been responsible for the Marine barracks attack.

If you're still with me—congratulations! This is a very twisted road and it's easy to get lost. But if you are the person sitting in the White House making life and death decisions, not just about the armed forces but about the country itself, you really need to understand the complexities of this region. And you especially need to know the history of American involvement there. In these days of battling pro- and anti-Syrian demonstrations in Beirut, it is not at all clear how things are going to develop in Lebanon. (That "Confessional" system is still basically in place.) But one thing is certain: America cannot be seen as favoring one side or the other. However strong the Lebanese desire for genuine democracy, right now any group deemed to be pro-American and therefore sympathetic to Israel is doomed to fail. And as much as the United States opposes Hezbollah, it must recognize that as in Iraq, the Shiites have become major players in Lebanon too, and cannot be simply dismissed as terrorists. At this very critical time, we need leadership that can deal with such nuances. If you need brain surgery, you want a skilled neurosurgeon to do the job, not a plumber (nor a journalist), no matter how good their intentions.

July 27, 2008
Obama: Anything But Naïve

Somewhere in the lead paragraph of virtually every report in the "liberal" media on Senator Barack Obama's Middle East and European visit last week was some version of the phrase, "on a trip to burnish his foreign policy credentials." It reminded me of how President Richard Nixon's Middle East trip in the summer of 1974 was described by every White House reporter as Nixon's attempt to escape from the impending doom of Watergate. In both cases the way the news media framed these high-level trips was not incorrect. But such framing misses the significance of these visits to the countries involved and ignores their broader foreign policy implications.

Back in 1974 when I covered Nixon's visit to Egypt, I had spent nearly a decade reporting from the Middle East. I therefore saw Nixon's trip as evidence of a major shift in the strategic balance of the region. Egyptian President Anwar Sadat had essentially severed Egypt's ties with the Soviet Union, while America was about to reopen embassies in Cairo and Damascus that had been closed since the 1967 war. I tried to make these points on the air but my editors remained so obsessed with the Watergate connection that on one broadcast I drew a cheeky analogy between the news coverage of the trip and a notable lecture by Sigmund Freud. I recounted how Freud pulled a cigar from his vest and said, "Those of you who are my students know that this is a phallic symbol. But do not forget, it is also a cigar."

Watergate, of course, was of great importance and only a few weeks after the trip Nixon was forced to resign because of it. But Nixon's Middle East visit did serve to underscore to all the countries of the region that America was seriously back in the game. Five years later it was acceptance of America as an honest broker that led to the Israeli-Egyptian Peace Agreement which effectively meant that the Middle East conflict was no longer likely to ignite World War III, as it very nearly did during the October 1973 war.

No one would dispute that the Obama trip was designed in part as a way of trying to show the American people that he is presidential timber who not only would be a confident president but also a competent commander-in-chief. But there has been much more to it than that.

Obama's was not a "presidential" trip per se, although it had many of those trappings. One of the significant features of such high-level travel is that the very fact of it causes things to happen—sluggish bureaucracies move, policy options are honed, pending decisions get made.

This trip would have forced Obama himself to go far beyond his simple campaign rhetoric and to intensely focus on how America should be conducting itself in the world. By going first to Afghanistan and calling for a much larger American effort there because it was what he called "the central front in the war against terrorism," he appears to have shifted the national security debate away from Iraq. In this he was greatly assisted by the Iraqis themselves.

The Obama visit obliged the leaders of the host countries to give serious consideration to what they wanted to say and do with the man who may very well be the next president of the United States. They didn't want to hurt or embarrass him—and there might even have been a temptation to help him. That is doubtless part of the reason Iraqi Prime Minister Nouri al-Maliki and his government went out of their way to embrace the concept, if not the specific details, of Obama's plan to withdraw America's combat forces in Iraq within sixteen months after his inauguration. Maliki, of course, had his own political reasons for doing this. He is greatly concerned about provincial elections in October when his main opponents will be fellow Shiites who want the American "occupation" to end immediately. He is also currently negotiating with the Bush administration over the terms of the continued presence of American troops in Iraq after the United Nations mandate runs out at the end of the year. By seeming to agree with Obama on a withdrawal timetable, Maliki has even forced the Bush administration to consider such a thing—even though the Bushies had to dig deep into the diplomatic bag of meaningless phrases by calling it a "time horizon."

The Obama trip also forced Senator John McCain into a defensive and increasingly strident mode, when every day for nearly a week he charged that Obama was totally wrong in opposing the decision last year to increase American troops in Iraq by 30,000, the shorthand for which is "the surge." McCain is adamant that the surge, which he had strongly endorsed, is responsible for the major improvement in security in Iraq. And he is openly contemptuous of Obama for supposedly refusing to admit this reality.

Full disclosure: at its inception, I opposed the surge. But as early as last fall it was evident that things were improving in Iraq, and I happily conceded that in this space. But then, as now, it's a fact that Iraqi security improved for three significant reasons beyond the increase in American troops.

1. Gen. David Petraeus, the new U.S. commander in Iraq, began to employ a completely different strategy based on his expertise in counter-insurgency. Among other things, that involved moving American forces out of large isolated bases and into small units, integrated with Iraqi troops and deployed in volatile Iraqi neighborhoods in Baghdad and elsewhere.
2. Iraqi Sunnis, who previously had made up the bulk of the anti-American insurgency, turned against Al Qaeda in Iraq because of its outrages against Sunnis. Some time before the surge was fully underway, Sunni sheiks in Anbar province contacted American commanders to discuss joining forces against Al Qaeda. Eventually deals were made and Sunni fighters actually started receiving modest, regular paychecks from Uncle Sam for their cooperation in the fight against the terrorists. This effort has significantly diminished the power of Al Qaeda in Iraq.
3. The main Shiite militia leader, the cleric Muqtada al-Sadr, for reasons mainly having to do with internal Shiite power struggles, declared a six-month ceasefire a year ago and extended it again last winter. His militia had been involved in much of the killing of Americans using improvised explosive devices—not to mention the Shiite's internecine war against Iraqi Sunnis.

So with a new American military strategy, with the Sunnis now U.S. allies in the fight against Al Qaeda, and the Shiites no longer waging war against both Americans and Sunnis, it seems highly probable that even with the 140,000 American troops in Iraq before the surge, those factors alone would have led to important changes for the better in Iraq. The surge helped, but it was not the principal difference maker. I understand why McCain wants political credit for his early campaign to send in more American troops. However, I do not believe this justifies his challenge to Obama's integrity and patriotism with his repeated insistence last week that Obama "would rather lose a war in order to win an election campaign."

Initially, I thought Obama's stop in Israel might be a place he could get into hot water. Many Israelis and American Jews are nervous about Obama's firm commitment to Israel's security—particularly in view of his emphasis on diplomacy as a way to deal with Iran's nuclear threat. He may not have eliminated these concerns but otherwise he evidently touched the right bases and said most of the right things. He even scored some points with the Palestinians by going to see their leaders in the West Bank—something McCain neglected to do on a similar visit a few months ago.

As I write, Obama has not yet concluded all of his stops. But the admiring crowds in Berlin are a good indication of how well he is thought of in Europe. That may actually cost him some votes in this country among those who are always suspicious of those foreigners in Europe. But it nevertheless bodes well for major improvement between this country and its allies, should Obama be elected.

To sum up, on the question of style—how he looked and sounded and avoided any embarrassing gaffes—for most Americans Obama will have passed the test of looking credible as both president and commander-in-chief. That is important politically, but frankly I am more interested in the week's substance. Republicans would have us believe Obama is a naïve liberal who thinks he can charm America's enemies. His critics said that his first trip abroad since becoming the presumptive Democratic presidential candidate would expose his fundamental flaws. That did not happen. In fact, he proved to be what one of the best foreign policy analysts in journalism, Fareed Zakaria of *Newsweek* and CNN, wrote about him on the eve of the trip: Obama's "world view is far from that of a typical liberal [and] much closer to that of a traditional realist." It is ironic that the most recent presidency that could be accurately described as traditional realist was that of George H.W. Bush. He was not perfect, but we could (as shown by the past eight years) do a lot worse.

December 14, 2003

Peacemakers

Blessed are the peacemakers. Regardless of one's faith, it's a universal sentiment.

The most prestigious of the Nobel Committee's awards is its Peace Prize. History's statesmen and tyrants almost always claim to be motivated by their desire for peace. Go to the Middle East and chances are the first word you will hear is "Shalom" in Israel or "Salaam" in the Arab world. Both mean peace.

Reporting on the search for peace in the Middle East was a major part of my professional career. A look at the current situation in the area could lead you to conclude that the search has been for naught. But there actually have been some significant changes.

Forty years ago both the Arabs and the Israelis were in total denial. Israeli Prime Minister Golda Meir said to me numerous times, "There is no such thing as a Palestinian." Now even Israeli hardliners accept that the Palestinians need some kind of state of their own.

For decades, all Arab states refused to accept Israel's right to exist. That is no longer the issue.

With the United States and the Soviet Union continuing to back opposite sides, there was always the danger that the Middle East conflict could set off World War III. That came dangerously close to happening during the October '73 Middle East War. But those days are over.

In my view, the man who proved that one person can make a difference was Egyptian President Anwar Sadat. Twenty-six years ago last month, Sadat shattered all the Middle East preconceived notions with his dramatic trip to Jerusalem. It was something that no other leader on either side had the courage to do.

But peace didn't come easily. This Christmas will be the 26th anniversary of the first trip to Egypt by an Israeli prime minister. Menachem Begin was making a reciprocal visit about a month after Sadat's Jerusalem trip. I remember being in the town of Ismailia for that meeting. The world's media were present and there were huge expectations that peace was at hand.

At one point, Sadat suddenly appeared and got behind the wheel of his Cadillac with Prime Minister Begin in front and Israeli Foreign and Defense ministers Moshe Dayan and Ezer Weizman in the rear. Off they went on a totally unplanned tour of the Suez Canal while the security men on both sides went apoplectic. This was typical Sadat, and for those of us on the outside, it seemed to suggest things were going well inside. They were not. Ismailia ended in failure.

It would take another sixteen months of American coaxing, cajoling, and actual bribery to achieve the peace treaty between Egypt and Israel signed in Washington in March of 1979. Sadat and Begin got the Nobel Peace Prize. President Jimmy Carter did not, though he should have, because the agreement would never have been reached without him.

Sadat was assassinated two and a half years after making peace with Israel. And in 1995 Israeli Prime Minister Yitzhak Rabin was gunned down for signing an agreement with the Palestinians.

Making peace in the Middle East is dangerous. It requires leaders of great personal and political courage, especially the one in the White House.

2

Israel & Palestine

August 21, 2005

Peter Jennings' Middle East

"Peter Jennings is an enemy of the Jewish people." This was a phrase that Peter knew was being said behind his back throughout much of his career. It is not a view shared by most American Jews. But there were enough people who felt that way that hints of a pro-Arab bias were a feature of some of his obituaries. As someone who knew Peter well and who worked with him for more than forty years, a good deal of the time in the Middle East, I think I understand how this whisper campaign came to be. I also know it is dead wrong.

Peter first came to the Middle East as a reporter at the time of the June 1967 War. The young journalists who covered that war were not Middle East specialists. Most of us, including Peter, came to the region with a view very much shaped by the Bible and by such popular books of the day as *Exodus* by Leon Uris and James Michener's *The Source*. These are good books, but they tell the story and the history of the region largely from the Israeli perspective. Add to that our knowledge of recent Jewish history and it could be said our starting point was decidedly pro-Israel.

The reporting of the 1967 War in which the Israelis crushed the combined Arab armies in just six days became a celebration of Israel's overwhelming military superiority over its Arab foes. This was a clear sign that Israel's existence, which had often been on shaky ground since its creation twenty years earlier, was now firmly established. The likelihood that the Jews would ever be "driven into the sea"—the empty slogan of the Arab propagandists of the day—was now extremely remote. By capturing Arab territory on all its fronts and unifying the city of Jerusalem, the Israelis appeared to have achieved their dream: a viable state with defensible borders. At the time, it was generally assumed by all, including the Israeli government of the day, that with some adjustments the territories taken would be used as bargaining chips to establish an Israeli-Arab peace agreement. But that was not to be.

Peter Jennings' first extended overseas assignment began in Rome in 1969 where I was ABC's Mediterranean bureau chief. For a while, we shared a lovely old apartment on one of the city's oldest squares with the best Italian restaurant ever at our doorstep. However, most of the time we were in the Middle East. By '69 it was clear to the new generation of reporters who worked in the region that however sympathetic one might be to the idea of the state of Israel, there was another side of the story that basically had been untold. At the same time network TV news in America was expanding, and we foreign correspondents were being regularly assigned to report on events and political developments in the Arab countries as well as in Israel. Eventually, ABC would decide to have Peter open up a full-time news bureau in Beirut. (It's worth noting that in these years, the CEO and principal shareholder of ABC was Jewish—as were several senior producers in the news division—and not once did this have even the slightest influence on our news coverage.)

This was also a time when a new Palestinian nationalism was beginning to emerge. The Six Day War had been a disaster from their perspective. Palestinians living as refugees throughout the Middle East, as well as under Israeli military occupation in the territories captured in '67, were increasingly coming to the conclusion that they could no longer expect Arab armies to "liberate" their homeland. They were going to have to do it themselves.

This phenomenon of Palestinian nationalism was a major new factor in the Middle East equation. While many Palestinians lived in abject poverty in refugee camps, that was only a part of their profile. Palestinians were actually among the best-educated of all the Arabs. They had developed their own diaspora in the Arab world, and like the Jewish diaspora, they were discriminated against in their host countries. Palestinians made up most of the civil service of the Arab states of the Persian Gulf but were barred from real political power. They moved into areas open to them—banking, engineering, and education—but remained second-class citizens. This was the context for their decision to undertake what they called an "armed struggle" against Israeli occupation—what the rest of the world would define as Palestinian terrorism.

Early in 1970 Peter and I persuaded our bosses that this new development deserved more than short spots on the evening news. Our proposal for a prime time documentary was accepted and we spent the spring and early summer putting it together. One of our interpreters was a young student from the American University of Beirut named Hanan Mikael. She would eventually become the longtime spokesperson for the Palestinians under her married name, Ashrawi. One of the men featured in the program was Nabil Shaath, a professor at AUB with a doctorate from the University of Pennsylvania. Years later he would become the foreign minister of the Palestinian Authority.

The program, "Palestine—New State of Mind" was broadcast in June of 1970. Within a few weeks, the first major Palestinian hijackings took place and three international airliners and their passengers were taken to a desert airstrip in Jordan. The passengers were eventually freed and the planes were blown up. A month after that, a civil war erupted in Jordan between King Hussein and the various Palestinian resistance movements. It ended with the Palestinian leadership being driven out of Jordan into Lebanon—an event Palestinians would call "Black September," the name adopted by one of the terrorist factions involved in Munich.

The tragedy of Munich would happen two years later. Peter had been assigned to be at the Munich Olympics to do news stories. When the terrorists struck against Israel's athletes, he was the only journalist present who knew pretty much exactly what was taking place. As ABC had the television rights to the Olympics, his reports were given the highest prominence and the event became a watershed in his career. It also was the beginning of the suspicion among some Jewish Americans that Peter Jennings was their enemy. They took his knowledge of the Palestinians—who they were and what their motives might be—to be sympathy for their cause.

It is not uncommon for people to take the position "if you are not for us then you are against us." George W. Bush comes to mind. Those who feel that Peter Jennings was their enemy fit into that category. But an extraordinary reporter such as Jennings could never be trapped by such logic. He wasn't "for" one nation or one religion against another. He was a genuine internationalist and humanist who truly believed that some of the world's ills could be mitigated if we really tried to understand the other person's point of view. That did not mean you had to agree with your enemies, but at least you should recognize their humanity.

In the early 1970s, Jennings came to believe in the "radical" idea that for true peace in the Middle East there would have to be two states: one for Israelis and one for Palestinians. It took more than another twenty years, but the two-state formula now forms the basis for American policy in the region and has even been embraced (selectively) by Israeli Prime Minister Ariel Sharon. Peace is still not at hand, but it's closer than it once was. The goal of genuine peace for Israelis and Arabs was one thing Peter Jennings was most fervently for. It was what inspired his distinguished reporting on the region for nearly four decades.

November 14, 2004

Arafat's Checkered Legacy

Osama bin Laden said so. But so, too, did President George W. Bush's most significant ally, British Prime Minister Tony Blair: that the Israeli–Palestinian dispute is the issue in world affairs that cries out loudest for resolution.

This problem got little of President Bush's attention in his first term. But as fate would have it, his re-election has occurred almost at the same moment that Yasser Arafat, chairman of the Palestine Liberation Organization, has departed the scene. For now, the Palestinians plan to operate with a collective, interim leadership. So, in all probability, there will soon be an opportunity for the Bush administration to go back to mediating this dispute—something the last six U.S. presidents have all tried to do.

As long as Arafat was in the picture, Bush and Israeli Prime Minister Ariel Sharon had the perfect excuse not to negotiate with the Palestinians. Arafat had proven to be a feckless negotiating partner. In 2000, he had turned down the best deal for peace the Israelis were ever likely to offer. But with a new Palestinian leadership, the equation is changed.

The president says the ultimate purpose of the invasion of Iraq was to shake up the Middle East, get rid of a dangerous despot, and show the people of the region what freedom and democracy can achieve. Given the present turmoil in Iraq, it remains to be seen how long it will take to see that happen. But if it does, according to the Bush scenario, other Arab states would be inspired to reform themselves and eventually everyone in the region would be free. However, for much of the Muslim world, America's crusade for freedom in the Middle East doesn't square with its implicit support for Israel's treatment of the Palestinians. Extremist groups like Al Qaeda exploit this contradiction as proof of America's prejudice against Islam.

For many Americans, Israel is the unique example of freedom and democracy in the region and therefore worthy of America's political, economic, and military support. On one level, I agree with that. I have spent significant periods of my life working in Israel starting in the mid-sixties through the mid-nineties. I have enormous admiration and affection for the Israeli people, deep sympathy for their suffering, and great respect for their religion. But one cannot be blind to the darker side of the situation there.

Since the 1967 Middle East war, Israel has been the military occupier of the West Bank and the Gaza Strip. In '67, these territories were home to about 1.3 million Palestinians. That number is now more than 3.5 million. In the first few years the occupation was fairly benevolent, though it would become increasingly repressive. But either way, millions of people were trapped in what they consider their homeland—without virtually any rights or freedoms or political recourse, such as voting, to change their plight. (Municipal elections were last held there in 1976.)

It was that situation that led most Palestinians to conclude that as Arab governments and their armies were incapable of ever liberating their land, they must do it themselves. With no armed forces of their own, they could not expect to defeat Israel in traditional warfare. So they chose the PLO and Yasser Arafat, and in so doing, opted to use terrorism as the means of their liberation. It would have been infinitely better for everyone had they chosen the non-violent methods of Mahatma Gandhi or Martin Luther King, Jr. Such tactics might well have been effective, especially with the Israeli people. But in a seething cauldron like the Middle East, genuine peacemakers are an endangered species and certainly Arafat was no Gandhi or King.

He wasn't even a romantic revolutionary like Che Guevara. Rotund and rumpled, Arafat was hardly an imposing figure. He never even seemed to be able to grow that mandatory revolutionary staple: a proper beard. Instead he always looked like he simply needed a shave. Arafat's skills existed mainly in dealing with the politics of revolution, which is to say he knew how to play his enemies against each other. Much of the corruption of which he is justifiably accused has to do with how he used the PLO's money to buy off his political opponents and his enemies, both among Palestinians and throughout the Arab world.

Arafat had two major accomplishments. He brought the attention of the world to the cause of the Palestinian people and became their symbol. And by accepting a two-state solution, he tacitly gave the Palestinian blessing to the existence of Israel. This had great meaning in the region. But for his many detractors in Israel and elsewhere, Arafat was simply a terrorist, although two other men who later achieved international respectability, Eamon De Valera of Ireland and Menachem Begin of Israel, at one time used similar tactics. I don't say this to justify Arafat's use of terror, just to put it into historical perspective. And I believe that if Arafat had really and truly given up terrorism in favor of diplomacy when peace was at hand in 1993 and then had had the courage to actually say yes to peace in 2000, he would eventually have been lauded by the world as the legitimate father of his country—his terrorist background notwithstanding.

But Arafat will not be judged kindly by history because he couldn't bring himself to take the final step for peace. His most glaring weakness was that he never prepared his people to be willing to accept less than 100 percent of their demands. Perhaps he had never prepared himself, and that was why he would never quite give up using terror or acquiescing in its use by various Palestinian factions. It remained an option even after Israeli Prime Minister Yitzhak Rabin, reluctantly but publicly, shook Arafat's hand at a White House ceremony in 1993 ratifying the Oslo Agreement. That was the blueprint for peace between Israel and the Palestinians that satisfied most of both sides' bottom-line demands.

Had Rabin not been assassinated by an Israeli fundamentalist, it is possible that a final agreement might have been achieved by now. That we'll never know. We do know that in the last days of his presidency, Bill Clinton put forward a proposal based on the Oslo formula that came closer than ever to addressing the outstanding roadblocks to peace. Then Israeli Prime Minister Ehud Barak and his cabinet said yes. Yasser Arafat said no.

I believe he did so because he was incapable of letting go of his revolutionary persona. Arafat's greatest skill was that in a very tough neighborhood, where he had many more enemies than friends, he was a survivor. And he wasn't sure he would survive a peace agreement, no matter how good it was. But survive for what purpose? In the end, he will be remembered for having failed to achieve his people's ultimate goal: the creation of a viable and independent state of Palestine.

After nearly four decades of endless cycles of terror, reprisal, revenge, and repression, there are still no winners. So perhaps the elusive goal of peace may yet be desired by majorities on both sides. Clinton's proposals, once accepted by Israel and almost embraced by the Palestinians, remain a creative basis for breaking the current impasse.

With Arafat no longer in the picture, the question now is whether President Bush is willing to spend some of that "political capital" he was talking about the other day. He needs to be prepared to take an even-handed approach to the problem, which will not sit well with

Christian fundamentalists. Nor will it please Israeli Prime Minister Sharon and his supporters—including those in high places in both the White House and the Pentagon. It will take both political capital and political courage to shift U.S. policy back to evenhandedness. But in my view, the stakes could not be higher. A peace agreement between Israel and the Palestinians brokered by the United States would be the most important battle we could win in the War on Terror.

July 30, 2006

Middle East Peacemaking: Real and Imaginary

DEFCON III is Pentagonese for defense condition three, the state of full U.S. military alert. It is only two steps removed from DEFCON I, which during the Cold War meant nuclear war. Only once during all those years was the state of alert for the U.S. Armed Forces raised as high as DEFCON II—that was during the 1962 Cuban missile crisis.

It was extremely rare for all American commands to go to DEFCON III. The most significant time was near the end of the 1973 Middle East War. Historians would later conclude that in the four decades of the Cold War, only the Cuban missile crisis had brought us closer to World War III.

The U.S. military went to DEFCON III on October 25, 1973 in response to a Soviet threat to send troops and equipment into Egypt to help the Egyptians lift the siege of their Third Army. That army had been trapped by Israeli forces on the eastern side of the Suez Canal, after a cease-fire arranged by the United States and the Soviet Union. Both Egypt and Israel claimed the other had violated the cease-fire. (At the time, I was with an Israeli artillery battery a few miles east of Suez City. All I could tell for certain was that the Israelis resumed firing after the first cease-fire was announced—and very little was coming back from the Egyptians.)

The crisis was resolved when Egyptian President Anwar Sadat withdrew his request to have both American and Russian troops come to Egypt to intervene, allowing the Soviets to back off. Sadat also agreed to direct military talks with the Israelis—a historical first.

In his memoirs, then–Secretary of State Henry Kissinger wrote: "We had supported Israel throughout this war for many historical, moral and strategic reasons. And we had just run the risk of a war with the Soviet Union, amidst the domestic crisis of Watergate. But American and Israeli shared interests did not embrace the elimination of the Third Army. The issue of the Third Army was quite simply that Israel had completed its entrapment well after a cease-fire that we had negotiated."

Kissinger went on to make the point that while he understood Israeli anger at Sadat for having started the fighting on October 6, and their desire to end the war with his destruction, such an outcome would not have been in Israel's long-term interests. "Our exchanges with Cairo had convinced us that Anwar Sadat represented the best chance for peace in the Middle East." As indeed he was.

Things did not immediately go smoothly. Having achieved a cease-fire, Kissinger would spend much of the next year shuttling around the region, first between Israel and Egypt, and then between Israel and Syria. In doing so, he laid the groundwork for the peace between Israel and Egypt that came a few years later. And he cemented a border understanding between Israel and Syria that has never been violated by either side.

This example of skillful and nuanced management of a major crisis stands in stark contrast to the mystifying strategic thinking now being shown by the Bush administration amid a new Middle East war. This is not to imply that World War III is imminent, but if it continues unchecked, the current fighting could spread to directly involve Iran and Syria with catastrophic consequences for the region and for this country.

From the outset of this new crisis, the Bush administration has continued to cling to the delusional belief that it can transform the Middle East. It has evidently learned nothing from its experiences in Iraq—not to mention the recent electoral results in Palestine and Lebanon—which gave new power to Islamic fundamentalist extremists. Both the president and the alleged pragmatist among his foreign policy advisers, Secretary of State Condoleezza Rice, remain determined to reject the proven tactics of those godless realists like Kissinger. As Rice says repeatedly, "It is time for a new Middle East."

In pursuit of the mirage of a new, democratic Middle East magically cleansed of historical hatreds, these are some of the astonishing things this administration has said and done—or not done—since the crisis began:

- As hundreds of Lebanese and dozens of Israeli civilians have been killed in the bloody exchanges between Hezbollah and Israel, Rice went to the region, not to try to arrange a cease-fire, but to lecture those who wanted one on the reasons why trying to stop the killing now was a bad idea. When Lebanese Prime Minister Fuad Siniora pleaded for an end to Israeli bombing, Rice responded by telling him that any cease-fire has to be "sustainable" and has to result in a "durable solution." In Israel she added, "If we have learned anything, it is that any peace is going to have to be based on enduring principles and not on temporary solutions." In fact, if we have "learned anything" in the region, it is that military actions do not lead to "durable solutions." The best example of that is the Israeli invasion of Lebanon in 1982 that was supposed to destroy the Palestine Liberation Organization. Instead it led to eighteen years of Israeli occupation and the emergence of the extremist Shiite movement Hezbollah, now the most powerful force in Lebanon and Israel's new worst enemy.

- During her Middle East visit, Rice set her terms for a cease-fire. Hezbollah, which ignited the crisis by capturing two Israeli soldiers, must do the following: stop firing rockets at Israel, withdraw from Southern Lebanon, disband its militia, and return the soldiers. Certainly these are issues to be dealt with. But just as surely they are not going to be achieved as a pre-condition for a cease-fire. This package is going to require long and difficult negotiations for which Rice has shown little inclination or aptitude. An emergency meeting of interested Arab and European countries had to be held in Rome because no Arab "friend" of the United States would host it for fear of being associated with current American policy. As for the Europeans, there is great reluctance to provide troops for the "robust" multinational force Rice wants to have patrolling the Israeli-Lebanese border. That's because they realize they would be seen as occupiers and eventually would become Hezbollah targets (as did American and French troops trying to restore order in Lebanon after the Israeli invasion of '82.)

- There are seven key players in the current crisis: Israel, Lebanon, the PLO, Hezbollah, Hamas (the elected government of the Palestinians), Syria, and Iran. On her trip Rice saw only the Israelis, the Lebanese, and the PLO. Her administration refuses to engage Hezbollah and Hamas—or their patrons Iran and Syria—on the grounds that they are terrorist organizations and states.

This policy is based on the fallible notion that if you negotiate with such a party, you are somehow rewarding its bad behavior. That ignores a much older reality that you negotiate peace not with your friends or like-minded people, but with your enemies.

Of course, the Bush administration rejects such old realities. It wants to purge itself of such Kissingerian realism as it seeks to create that new Middle East.

Obviously, all the region's problems have not been solved by diplomacy. But for over thirty years, significant contributions to a more peaceful Middle East and safer world were made by a series of Republican and Democratic presidents and their secretaries of state.

As one who was often with them on the ground and on the shuttles, I certainly believe that without that cease-fire in October 1973— and without the intense American diplomatic effort that followed—a major Middle East war involving both the United States and the Soviet Union was highly probable. Then, as today, a cease-fire is where you have to start. And then you have to negotiate—with all the parties.

March 8, 2009

To Talk—Or Not to Talk

Throughout history the question of whether to negotiate with your enemies has been a contentious one. In this country, those who argue that it's a sign of weakness have often prevailed. President John Kennedy's oft-quoted advice in his inaugural address, "We must never negotiate out of fear, but we must never fear to negotiate," has been honored in the breach perhaps as much as in the observance.

Over four decades the epitome of America's hardliners has been Richard Perle, known not so affectionately as the "prince of darkness." Perle recently denied being a neo-conservative or that the neocons had played a definitive role in the decision to invade Iraq—two assertions that speak loudly to the issue of his credibility. As a young staffer working for the late Democratic Senator Henry "Scoop" Jackson, Perle manipulated Jackson's instinctive anti-Soviet attitudes which led to a fierce debate in the mid-seventies and a setback for the Nixon-Kissinger-Ford policy of "détente." During the Reagan administration Perle was one of the super-hawks in Cap Weinberger's Pentagon. As chairman of the Pentagon's Advisory Board during the Bush II administration he advocated for the invasion of Iraq—and was against talking to Iran. Considering the track record of Perle and his ilk, one wonders how their policies can still be taken seriously. But the debate goes on.

President Barack Obama has pledged to use diplomacy as a major instrument in his foreign policy—and diplomacy usually means talking to your adversaries as well as your friends. In these early days it is not clear just how far the new administration is prepared to go on in terms of talks with Iran. Secretary of State Hillary Clinton seemed lukewarm to negotiations when she said privately this past week that she didn't think Iran would respond positively to Obama's suggestions for diplomatic engagement. On the other hand, Clinton has decided to start talking again to the Syrians and has sent two ranking diplomats to Damascus this weekend. This overture could ultimately have implications for American discussions with Iran and for the Israeli Palestinian peace process which is near death. As for this latter problem, I would argue another dialogue needs to be opened up fairly soon with Hamas, the Palestinian movement that controls Gaza and has ever-growing support in the West Bank.

First a little history. In 1975 when he was negotiating a second disengagement agreement between Israel and Egypt, then-Secretary of State Henry Kissinger made a secret pact with the Israelis that the United States would have no diplomatic contacts with the Palestine Liberation Organization until the PLO changed its charter and recognized Israel's right to exist. At the time Kissinger believed he could do an end run on riff-raff like Yasser Arafat by dealing with Arab kings and non-elected presidents. That may have been true in 1975, but the ban on substantive contact between American diplomats and the PLO lasted for twelve years. By the time the PLO changed its charter in 1987 and America began to talk to Arafat, the situation in the Middle East had changed dramatically, for the worse. There had been an Israeli-Egyptian peace but Egyptian President Anwar Sadat was then assassinated by Islamic militants. Lebanon had been bogged down by more than a decade of civil war which involved the PLO, Iran, and Syria. Ultimately the Israelis invaded Lebanon in a failed effort to crush the PLO that instead created a new nemesis for them—the Shiite militant movement Hezbollah. Throughout this period the anger of the Palestinians in the territories occupied by Israel became more intense even as Israeli settlements in those territories continued to grow. If America had been a genuinely even-handed mediator during those twelve years, would it have been able to prevent the situation from becoming so intractable? There is no way to know. But historically when the United States was actively engaged as an honest broker trusted by all, it gave the region hope. When it is not so engaged, hope becomes despair.

Which brings us to Hamas. Like the PLO before it, Hamas doesn't recognize Israel's right to exist and uses terror as a weapon. But Hamas is not just a terrorist organization. It's a political movement that was, after all, elected by a majority of the Palestinians in the West Bank and Gaza. That happened in February 2006, in large measure because Palestinians were fed up with the corruption of the PLO and its inability to reduce the oppressive nature of the Israeli military occupation or to stop the encroachment of Israeli settlements. But Israel, the United States, and most of the European Union refused to deal with a Hamas government, calculating Hamas could be coerced into political concessions. In this atmosphere open warfare broke out in Gaza in June 2007 between Hamas and Arafat's Al Fatah Party. Hamas won that battle and Israel responded by setting up a blockade to restrict or eliminate access to or from Gaza. Egypt closed its side of the border too. So in effect Gaza was a prison with no trade, no jobs, and no hope. After an uneasy six month truce ended last December, Israel's three week assault on Gaza brought more destruction and misery but did not fundamentally change the struggle with Hamas, which continues its rocket attacks on civilian centers in southern Israel.

To break this impasse, America must start dealing with Hamas leaders. Yes, Hamas uses terror and refuses to recognize Israel. But how does that differ from an Israeli government made up of at least some members (in the next government, perhaps many) who do not recognize the right of a state of Palestine to exist—and a government willing to level Gaza to force Hamas to capitulate, even if hundreds of civilians are killed in the process. On the morality scale, I do not see a huge difference. More importantly, as a practical matter, there is no way to achieve peace between Israel and the Palestinians unless Hamas is included in the discussions.

February 22, 2009

Lost Hopes for the Middle East

When I first set foot in the Middle East in 1966, I blush to admit my knowledge of the history of the region was based largely upon the stories of the Bible. Growing up during World War II and its aftermath, I was keenly aware of the Holocaust and the struggle of the Jewish people to find a homeland, and to at last find peace. Needless to say, I was pro-Israel. When the Six Day War broke out in June 1967, I followed Israeli forces as they chased the Egyptians through the Sinai desert and celebrated with them when they reached the Suez Canal. At the time neither I nor any Israeli could have imagined just how much blood would be shed over the Arab territory they had just captured in six short days; or that forty-two years later they would be further than ever away from their goal of lasting peace.

After the war, as did most young reporters who worked in the region at that time, I discovered that the story of the Middle East was not simply a question of good-guy Israelis versus bad-guy Arabs. To be sure, for us Westerners with our shared Judeo-Christian values and history, Israel's existence and survival was a moral imperative. But it was also true that through no fault of their own, several million Palestinians had become homeless refugees or were living under often harsh Israeli military occupation with little in their futures but more suffering.

Throughout my career, I have tried to balance those two competing narratives. I have never condoned the Palestinian use of terrorism. I think it is morally wrong and the damage it has done to their image and cause far exceeds any possible tactical benefits. But given their impotence in the face of Israel's overwhelming military superiority, I understand why Palestinians might use such tactics. Likewise, I do not condone actions such as Israel's recent massive assault on Gaza, which left 1,300 Palestinians dead and caused a huge humanitarian crisis. I think it was excessive and greatly hurt Israel's moral standing in the world. But I do understand why Israel would find the repeated Hamas rocket attacks against its civilians to be intolerable.

The fact is that in the forty-odd years I've been watching, neither side in this dispute is blameless. It serves no purpose to recite all the atrocities, but it's fair to say both sides have committed them. And each side remembers in excruciating detail every act of violence committed by the other—making forgiveness virtually impossible. Yet unless this cycle of revenge and retaliation can be broken, each side is condemning itself to a future of never-ending death and destruction. After eight years of the Bush administration's openly pro-Israel policies, I hoped that President Barack Obama would have the courage to reassert the United States as a genuinely even-handed mediator, and that if he did so, a peace agreement might again become possible. But I have to confess I have recently come to believe that whatever Obama does, there is very little hope for Middle East peace in the foreseeable future. The long dream of a two-state solution—Israel and Palestine living side by side in peace—is now being declared effectively dead by pundits, academics, and political leaders on both sides. But of greater significance, while this solution was once supported by substantial majorities among both Israelis and Palestinians, that is evidently no longer the case.

In Israel's election earlier this month, a total of 65 of the Knesset's 120 seats went to parties of the right, the ultra right, and the religious right. All of these groups are opposed to almost any Israeli withdrawal from the West Bank, much less dismantling Jewish settlements and giving up enough occupied territory to make a viable, contiguous Palestinian state possible. And it says something about where "moderates" are on the current Israeli political spectrum that it was the former so-called center-left coalition government that planned and executed the recent war on Gaza.

Tzipi Livni of the Kadima party or Benjamin Netanyahu of Likud will be designated to form a coalition government. That means a real power in that next government is likely to be Avigdor Lieberman, whose Yisrael Beiteinu party of Russian immigrants won fifteen seats, making it the third largest in the Knesset. Both Livni and Netanyahu have indicated they would accept Lieberman as a coalition partner—a man Martin Peretz of the *New Republic*, who passionately supports Israel, has called "a neo-fascist...a certified gangster."

In the latest edition of *Newsweek*, the respected international columnist Fareed Zakaria devoted his column to Lieberman, noting that "His No. 1 target is Israel's Arab minority, which he has called a worse threat than Hamas. He has proposed the effective expulsion of several hundred thousand Arab citizens by unilaterally redesignating some northern Israeli towns as parts of the Palestinian West Bank. Another group of several hundred thousand could expect to be stripped of citizenship for failing to meet loyalty oaths."

Israel's Arabs are the descendents of the Arabs who stayed on their lands when Israel became a state in 1948. They now number 1.3 million, or about 20 percent of Israel's population, and in the view of a growing number of Israeli right-wingers, they represent a growing threat to Israel's very existence. Zakaria cites an influential Israeli who shares Lieberman's radical views on the Arab minority. Benny Morris, the once dovish historian who chronicled the forced expulsion of most Palestinians from the Jewish state in 1948, has turned to arguing that Israel needs to protect itself from the Arabs now living within its borders. "They are a potential fifth column. In both demographic and security terms they are liable to undermine the state. If the threat to Israel is existential, expulsion will be justified."

If there is no longer a two-state solution on the table, short of accepting a single democratic state that is home to both Israelis and Palestinians (a total non-starter because that would be the end of the Jewish state), there really are few options for Israel. If Lieberman has his way, Israel could expel all of its Arabs into the West Bank and perhaps gain itself a respite from the perceived Arab minority problem. But that would still leave more than three million Palestinians penned up in the West Bank and Gaza, more determined than ever to achieve freedom from more than four decades of military occupation. Or, Israel could more or less maintain the status quo in which Gaza is kept isolated and the West Bank is further carved up into smaller Palestinian enclaves, which would ultimately become the political equivalents of the Bantustans of apartheid-era South Africa. In either case, Israel would face an enormous loss of international respect while gaining only marginal, short-term security benefits.

But what matters most is that if there is absolutely no hope for peace, the level of violence and bloodshed will inevitably spike. Hamas in Gaza and the disillusioned remnants of Yasser Arafat's PLO in the West Bank will not sit quietly for long. And a new wave of Palestinian terror attacks followed by heavy Israeli reprisals could ultimately ignite a Middle East War like no other—involving numerous Arabs states and perhaps even Iran and other Muslim countries. As it has before, Israel might still lick them all. But at what price? Given the inordinate quantities of hugely destructive firepower that now exist throughout that region (dare I mention that includes nuclear weapons), I truly shudder to think of the toll such a war would take.

November 28, 2009

Dr. Ralph Bunche and the 1949 Armistice Agreements

He was an African American, raised by a feisty grandmother. He supported himself in college with an athletic scholarship and worked as a janitor to pay his personal expenses. He played basketball on his college's championship teams, wrote for the campus newspaper, was valedictorian of his class and graduated summa cum laude. These accomplishments led to a scholarship to Harvard where he would obtain two advanced degrees. He became a college professor and was eventually attracted to government service. As a still relatively young man he would be awarded the Nobel Peace Prize.

Anyone you know? While the above personal history may roughly match the current resident of the White House, it is actually a biographical sketch of Dr. Ralph Bunche, who played an important role in the founding and early years of the United Nations. He was the first modern Middle East peacemaker, who in 1950 would also become the first "member of the colored race" to receive Alfred Nobel's most prestigious award. I have returned to the story of Ralph Bunche because several credible Middle East specialists have now declared the two-state solution to the Israeli–Palestinian conflict officially dead. They say the best that can be hoped for in the foreseeable future is something like the 1949 armistice agreements that formally ended the fighting that broke out after the creation of the state of Israel in 1948. As a senior United Nations diplomat, Ralph Bunche negotiated those agreements.

From June of 1947 to August of 1949, Bunche had the assignment of a lifetime. He was principal secretary of the UN commission responsible for carrying out the partition of Palestine between Jews and Arabs that had been approved by the UN General Assembly. This plan died in 1948 after the Arabs rejected it and Israel declared its independence, setting off the first of many Arab-Israeli wars. The UN then appointed the Swedish diplomat Count Folke Bernadotte as mediator and Bunche as his chief aide. That September, Bernadotte was assassinated in Jerusalem by Jewish terrorists and Bunche replaced him.

After eleven months of virtually nonstop negotiations on the island of Rhodes, Bunche obtained signatures on armistice agreements between Israel and each of Egypt, Jordan, Syria, and Lebanon. The Arabs insisted these were not peace treaties. Still the armistice was seen by much of the world as a huge accomplishment, and Bunche came home to a hero's welcome. New York gave him a ticker-tape parade up Broadway. Los Angeles declared a "Ralph Bunche Day." The Nobel Prize came the following year and thirty universities eventually gave him honorary degrees.

Unfortunately the armistice of 1949 left much business unfinished. The United Nations Truce Supervision Organization, which was charged with trying to enforce the armistice, could do nothing to stop the full scale Middle East wars of 1956, 1967, and 1973. Nor could it or any other UN body do much to halt the lesser wars and the endless cycle of revenge and reprisals that have so dominated life in the region in the decades since.

There were some diplomatic successes from the 1970s through the 1990s, but during the past decade the "peace process" that was supposed to lead to a two-state solution has been a sham. Meanwhile, in response to Arab suicide bombers, Israel built a 250-mile separation wall that snakes around the West Bank, effectively annexing another 12 percent of Arab land. And Israel's blockade of Gaza to stop Hamas terrorists from shelling Israeli towns has turned Gaza into a virtual prison for a million and a half Palestinians.

Recently, there has been much criticism of President Barack Obama for initially demanding that Israel completely freeze the building of new settlements on occupied Palestinian territory, including East Jerusalem—and then acquiescing as the Israelis have rejected those demands. There is now a broad consensus among commentators of almost all persuasions that the American wobble has driven the final nail into the coffin of the two-state solution. That has prompted analysts such as Roger Cohen of the *New York Times* to write, "Stop talking about peace. Banish the word. Start talking about détente." What Cohen suggests is that a truce is the only straw left to grasp at. He quotes Shlomo Avenieri, an Israeli political scientist as saying, "A non-violent status quo is far from satisfactory, but it's not bad."

The idea of a long-term truce is also at the center of a lengthy analysis in the December issue of the *New York Review of Books,* written by Robert Malley, a member of President Bill Clinton's Mideast negotiating team and Hussein Agha, who has served as a Palestinian negotiator. The essence of their 5,000-word essay is contained in the following two paragraphs:

"Ending Israel's occupation of Palestinian territories is essential and the conflict will persist until this is addressed. But its roots are far deeper: for Israelis, Palestinian denial of the Jewish state's legitimacy; for Palestinians, Israel's responsibility for their large-scale dispossession and dispersal that came with the state's birth. If the objective is to end the conflict and settle all claims, these matters will need to be dealt with. They reach back to the two peoples' most visceral and deep-seated emotions, their longings and anger. For years, the focus has been on fine-tuning percentages of territorial withdrawals, ratios of territorial swaps, and definitions of Jerusalem's borders. The devil, it turns out, is not in the details. It is in the broader picture." In other words, truce now, peace later—perhaps much later.

After he gets his new Afghanistan strategy launched, perhaps Barack Obama, who is an appropriate figurative successor to Ralph Bunche, could start completely fresh and try to negotiate a long term interim arrangement. In 1949 Bunche offered the philosophy behind his efforts. "I have a bias in favor of both Arabs and Jews, in the sense that both are good and honorable and essentially peace-loving peoples, and are therefore as capable of making peace as waging war." But sixty years later even a truce, much less a peace, may be beyond the reach of such noble sentiments.

May 29, 2011

Status Quo Not Acceptable to Obama

I remember having dinner one night at the home of a Jewish American journalist friend in Tel Aviv. It would have been in the 1970s. He
was a New Yorker who had gone to Israel to cover the Adolf Eichmann trial in 1961 and decided to stay. I often visited with him when
I was in Israel but this particular conversation has stuck with me. That
night my friend was grumpy. His children were getting older and
his apartment, while pleasant, was quite tiny. But rents were high,
he was a freelancer, and he couldn't afford a larger place, which was
the source of his unhappiness that night. At one point he announced,
"I'm thinking of becoming a settler." He added that he could then get
a great new apartment on the West Bank near Jerusalem for significantly less than what he was paying in Tel Aviv. That's because then,
as now, the government was substantially subsidizing settlements to
create, as officials openly admitted at the time, "facts on the ground."
In other words, there has long been a deliberate effort to colonize
parts of the occupied Arab territories, which would ultimately make
returning the land very difficult if not impossible.

My friend actually never had any intention of becoming a settler
because he really didn't approve of them. And I specifically recall how
he went on that night to explain Israel's settlement policy. As he told
it, the Israelis were taking a page from America's nineteenth century
history: Washington would encourage settlers or pioneers to go out
West. The Indians would then attack the settlers. And the government would respond by sending in the U.S. cavalry to kill the Indians.
"That's how the West was won," he said with an ironic chuckle. Well,
that wasn't exactly what happened in this country nor is it exactly
what Israel has been doing. But there are certainly similarities in the
questionable morality of the expansionist policies of both—albeit a
century apart, which is an important distinction.

In Israel's case, I got the feeling the settlements issue had come full
circle when I heard Prime Minister Netanyahu vehemently oppose
President Obama's suggestion that the pre-June 1967 War boundaries
be a starting point for border negotiations between Israel and Palestine. Deliberately ignoring Obama's key qualifier that there should
also be "mutually agreed swaps" of land—a formula accepted by both
parties for at least a decade—Netanyahu claimed that Israel couldn't
possibly return to the '67 borders, which were "indefensible." The

real issue of course is that there are now nearly half a million Israeli "settlers" living on substantial pieces of occupied Palestinian territory, and the land swaps required to include most of them as part of Israel may now be unacceptable to both sides. So just as every American president since Jimmy Carter warned—and successive Israeli governments actually planned—the settlements are indeed "obstacles to peace." In fact, they are now a greater impediment than ever.

I couldn't write this column without noting the unseemly behavior of the United States Congress in its sycophantic response to Prime Minister Netanyahu and his speech last Tuesday. It is one thing to give a warm welcome to the leader of a close and important ally. It is quite another to jump to your feet twenty-nine times to cheer a speech that was a provocative reiteration of every hard-line position of the current Israeli government—a speech that did not contain one ray of hope for the future or a single crumb for the Palestinians.

President Obama ought not to be the only American leader who recognizes that the failure to resolve the Israeli-Palestinian conflict represents a threat to American troops in the Middle East region and to a range of American interests. Obama did not, as would-be Republican presidential nominee Mitt Romney put it, "throw Israel under the bus." (His comment demonstrates once again that Romney will say anything to get elected, without regard to the facts or his previous positions.) Obama is concerned, as are many of Israel's true friends, that the status quo, based on the military occupation of Palestine, is not sustainable and thus not in Israel's long term interests. I leave you with the thoughts of some important Israelis, who very much share that concern. Prior to Obama's controversial Middle East speech and Netanyahu's visit to Washington, a group that includes eighteen retired generals and twenty-seven winners of the prestigious Israel Prize purchased this ad (in Hebrew or English) in major Israeli newspapers:

RECOGNIZING A PALESTINIAN STATE
BASED ON THE 1967 BORDERS
IS VITAL FOR ISRAEL'S EXISTENCE

(The same ad was placed last week in the *New York Times* by J Street, the liberal Jewish-American, pro-Israel, pro-peace group that claims about 200,000 members.)

Perhaps even more significant was this development noted by J. J. Goldberg in a recent column in the *Jewish Daily Forward*. Since Israel's inception in 1948, only eighteen men now living have headed the main security services: the Israeli Defense Forces, the Mossad intelligence agency, and the Shin Bet internal security service. Four are old and inactive. But in recent weeks twelve of the remaining fourteen have challenged Netanyahu's policies as a threat to Israel's future. This vigorous new policy debate, apparently inspired by the historic political changes now underway in the Arab world, is led by those who feel Netanyahu is seriously miscalculating both the meaning of these changes and what Israel should do about them.

Once again, I regret that the healthy discussion that takes place among Israelis critical of the policies of their government is rarely noted or joined in on here in this country. If it were, we might see fewer sorry spectacles in the Congress as occurred this past week. We may also see that uninformed political pressure would have less power to reduce the options of the president of the United States as he pursues Middle East policies that are in America's best interests, and, I would argue, in Israel's as well.

Iraq & Afghanistan

May 3, 2011
The Death of Osama Bin Laden

For very many people in this country and abroad, every day Osama bin Laden was alive he was a symbol of American impotence. For nearly ten years, the world's greatest superpower with its all-powerful military and sprawling intelligence operations aided by the very highest of high technology could not capture its number one enemy, a supposedly ailing man believed to be living in a cave somewhere on the Afghanistan-Pakistan border. (It turned out he had been residing in comparative luxury in a million dollar mansion in a garrison town, forty minutes from Islamabad, Pakistan's capital city. But that's another story.)

Even though he seemed to have become mostly a figurehead for terrorist ideology as opposed to its operational leader, Bin Laden's continued prominence on the international scene became a malignancy on the American psyche. This accounts, at least in part, for the majority of Americans continuing to feel that their country is going in the wrong direction—and of course for the great sense of relief as well as jubilation that has greeted the Al Qaeda leader's death.

The joy being shown by young people is also informative. My youngest daughter Campbell, who is a student at New York University, was the first to call (actually text) me Sunday night with the news. She then joined the many at Ground Zero for a night of demonstrations of celebratory patriotism. Monday morning she told me that she and her friends wanted to be there to be part of what they felt was a historic occasion. Certainly, for her generation it was. For much of their lives Bin Laden was evil incarnate and a realistic threat to the American way of life. As one who lived through World War II and the Cold War, I have never been able to equate Bin Laden with Hitler or Stalin, who had been genuine threats to my generation's very existence. But I certainly understand why younger generations would feel as they do.

As to the meaning of Bin Laden's death, I believe his would-be successors will almost certainly want to show their ideological fervor. In the short term, we can expect various off-shoots of Al Qaeda in Afghanistan, Pakistan, and Yemen to try to mount major revenge attacks. So it would be wrong to assume that the fight against Al Qaeda and Islamic extremists generally is over.

Yet there are other signs that this ideology has already lost its grip on a younger generation of Muslims. The best evidence for that is the Middle East, where the Arab world is experiencing a historic political shift. The mainly peaceful demonstrations that overturned governments in Tunisia and Egypt—and the government-directed violence being used against protestors in Libya, Yemen, and Syria—are in the process of completely changing the political landscape in the region. While much remains to be settled, one thing is certain. No protestors in any of these countries were carrying the portrait, or chanting slogans in praise of Osama bin Laden and Al Qaeda. About half of the current population of the Arab world is under the age of twenty-five and for these people, Al Qaeda is very much old news. For all of his bluster, Bin Laden has never overthrown nor taken over a government. These Arab youngsters have already changed two and there may be more to come.

Finally, it's a statement of the obvious that President Barack Obama will benefit politically from this event. There has been praise, even from some of his critics, for his handling of this matter. Zbigniew Brzezinski, President Carter's National Security Advisor, has recently been denigrating Obama's leadership. On Monday morning he was lauding it. Also Obama will now be more difficult to diminish with superfluous issues about where he was born and his early college grades—although these were largely race-driven and are not going to go away completely. So how long the present feel-good period will last is questionable, especially with a tough presidential election fight now underway.

There is, however, one tangible way in which Obama has been helped longer term, and that is in Afghanistan. With a drawdown of U.S. troops scheduled to begin in July, Bin Laden's elimination is going to give Obama much more flexibility to accomplish this. Therefore we might expect the American "footprint" in Afghanistan to be substantially reduced and perhaps faster than it might otherwise have been. That will be good for Obama—and for the country.

October 17, 2004

Even the World's Only Superpower Needs Friends

Back in the days before Trivial Pursuit, there was a board game called Diplomacy. It was designed for adults and could take many hours to play. The board was the map of pre–World War I Europe—for many centuries a continent more often than not at war. After drawing lots to see what country you would represent, the object of the game was to protect your country. You did this by making alliances and/or invading your neighbors.

I've long forgotten most of the rules, but there are two things that I do remember about the game. One: no matter how many armies and navies you had, you could not win unless you had allies, which you had to coax, cajole, bribe, or even lie to, to get them on your side for the next military offensive. Two: I never, ever saw Germany win. Because of its position in Europe, it was vulnerable on all sides and could never make enough alliances. I seem to recall that Germany was even given larger armed forces to compensate for this fact, but they were never enough to prevail.

I occasionally think of this game when I hear the debate over what to do in Iraq and how to fight the War on Terror. President Bush implies that it doesn't matter that America has become estranged from key allies such as Canada, Germany, and France because the U.S. must never be beholden to any international organization or any other country. He repeatedly declares that he will not give a country like France a veto over American foreign policy. It's a guaranteed rousing applause line at political rallies, but it's based on a false premise, the premise that the U.S. compromises its security when it gives weight to the views of its allies.

In political campaigns, candidates say lots of things to stir up the crowd, things that may not be exactly true but are politically effective. My concern is not what the President says on this subject in his stump speech. It's what he has done since he took office and what we have to assume he would continue to do; namely, through a combination of ignorance and arrogance, he has alienated this country not only from its natural friends and allies but from much of the rest of the world as well.

President Bush took office with a thin resume when it came to knowledge of history and the world, despite the fact that his father had been a devoted student of foreign affairs. Before becoming president,

Bush senior had been head of the CIA, Ambassador to the United Nations, and first American Ambassador to Communist China. But his son showed no interest in such matters. It is striking that as the son of a wealthy and prominent American, George W. Bush basically chose to take no advantage of this to travel abroad. (I believe he had made one or two short trips to Europe and one to the Middle East prior to becoming president.) This is not to suggest that going abroad makes you smart or wise. But when someone has the economic means and the political connections to go virtually anywhere and consciously decides not to, it suggests to me an extraordinary lack of intellectual curiosity about our planet, its history, and its people.

In a world that through instant communications has become ever so much smaller and interdependent, lack of knowledge about that world really matters, especially when you are the leader of its only superpower. Without some firsthand knowledge, you can't develop a feel for other peoples and cultures. And perhaps inevitably, without that feel, you end up showing them a lack of respect. In that mindset, it's easy to dismiss the need for traditional allies when you go off to war and to grossly miscalculate the reaction you're going to get from the people of the country you've just invaded. It leads to the failure to make adequate contingency plans, to the incompetent management of the occupation, and to under-sizing the military force required to do the job.

But in my view, the go-it-alone mindset is even more likely destined to fail when applied to the War on Terror. To begin with, that war is misnamed. As defined by the 9/11 Commission's report, we are in an ideological struggle with Islamic extremists who use terror as their principal weapon. Thus we are not fighting a single state or organization but a radical idea shared by Islamic militants in countries spread around the globe. Their ideology is that fundamental Islamic values, culture, and power have been polluted and usurped by the Judeo-Christian western world and must be restored by whatever means. The idea has supporters in every Arab country as well as Turkey, Pakistan, Iran, the Philippines, Indonesia, and Nigeria to name the larger Islamic states. The former White House terror expert Richard Clarke said recently that of the world's 1.3 billion Muslims perhaps only 40,000 are hardcore Al Qaeda types. But he claims many millions more are sympathetic to their cause.

The United States can hardly go into any or all of those Muslim countries with guns blazing to root out the extremists. It will need the cooperation of each country's government in areas like intelligence gathering, police work, and banking, among many other things. But getting that assistance is not going to be easy because helping the United States is becoming increasingly unpopular.

A recent poll of international attitudes by the respected public opinion expert Daniel Yankelovich contains some sobering numbers. Only 12 percent of Muslims believe the United States respects Islam. Only 11 percent of them approve of President Bush. And huge majorities—74 percent in Indonesia, 72 percent in Pakistan and Nigeria, and 71 percent in Turkey—are worried about a military threat from the United States.

Meanwhile among our erstwhile allies in Europe the numbers are equally troubling. In Germany, France, Britain, and Italy an average of more than 75 percent of those polled said the United States is acting solely in its own interests without regard for the interests of its allies.

These numbers illustrate the enormity of the problem the United States faces as it struggles against this new Islamic ideology. For most of its existence, this country has had the protection of two oceans. For the nearly five decades of the Cold War it enjoyed the mostly solid support of like-minded democratic states in Europe and elsewhere. But today, the U.S. reminds me of that Germany of pre-World War I—a country that could never ultimately prevail in spite of its military power, because it had too many enemies and too few friends.

September 4, 2005

Confessions of a Wavering Pundit

I supported the invasion of Iraq. I did so publicly in a TV commentary in late February 2003. Previously, I had had grave misgivings about such a policy. Much of my professional career had been spent in the Middle East. I had covered the first Gulf War. I had seen (although never spoken to) Saddam Hussein in action several times while on assignments in Iraq and had absolutely no illusions about him. I had gone into Northern Iraq via Turkey in 1988 at the time of Hussein's poison gas massacre of thousands of Kurds. I spent time in the refugee camps that sprang up on the Turkish border and talked to survivors, who were sometimes hopelessly disfigured, about this cruel attack. So I did not need to be persuaded that Saddam Hussein was a very bad man.

Yet as 2003 began, I felt strongly that invading Iraq was not the appropriate way to fight the War on Terror because there was no credible link between Hussein and Al Qaeda and certainly no proven connection between Hussein and September 11. As such, an invasion would just make things in the region worse.

But in February 2003, I flip-flopped. After hearing former Secretary of State Colin Powell's presentation to the UN Security Council, I was persuaded that Iraq did indeed have weapons of mass destruction. I concluded, reluctantly, that given the huge buildup to war it probably made sense to go in now and eliminate that problem. I believed Powell because he had actually been to war and led men in combat. He was known to have tried for many months to stop the rush to war. And because I had had personal dealings with him, I felt he could be trusted. At that point I and numerous people like me who had previously opposed a preemptive war publicly changed our positions.

After the invasion, it of course did not take long to discover there were no weapons of mass destruction. It also became evident almost immediately that the Bushies had made virtually no plans to win the peace once Hussein had been deposed and the country thrown into chaos. Who can forget, as Iraqi mobs rampaged through the shops and museums of Baghdad, Defense Secretary Donald Rumsfeld's fatuous remark, "freedom is messy"? That should have been a clue that this enterprise could end badly.

Still, I took what seemed the sensible view—that America could not instantly pack up and leave after the invasion. However ill-conceived the war may have been or how badly the post-war had been planned, the United States had a responsibility to the people of the country it had shattered to help them pick up the pieces. American credibility in the world, and especially in the Middle East, was at stake. I have stayed with that position, with varying degrees of conviction, until fairly recently. But with the tempestuous creation of a new Iraqi constitution, I can no longer see any good that can come from the continued military occupation of Iraq.

Iraq's new constitution was drawn up under enormous U.S. pressure to fulfill an arbitrary deadline set by the Bushies (in the faint hope of removing Iraq as a factor in the 2006 American elections). While some issues remain unresolved, the new draft does give us a pretty good indication of what kind of Iraq may ultimately emerge in the coming months and years. It will be an Islamic, federal state with strong autonomous regions located in the north and south where all the oil is. The Kurds will remain independent in the north and conservative Shiite clerics, with strong ties to Iran, will control the south. There will be a weak central government in Baghdad with limited oil revenues. There are some human rights protections for women and other religions, but with Muslim clerics to be part of the judiciary, those freedoms could be undermined. And especially in the religious southern region, the situation for women and minorities could become much like it was for freed slaves in this country after the Civil War. According to federal statutes, African Americans were equal and free. But for another century in the South, Jim Crow laws made them anything but, as they were barred from any form of integration with whites and mostly from voting, too.

The Sunnis, who live mainly in the central region, have ruled Iraq since its creation in the 1920s. But with only 20 percent of the population, in any kind of a democracy they are a minority—subject to the desires of the majority—and they are not content with that. As disgruntled Sunnis make up most of the current insurgency, some analysts are predicting a new wave of violence in response to the new constitution. A full-scale civil war remains an ever-present possibility.

In the meantime there are some events of importance on Iraq's political calendar that still need to play out. The new constitution will be voted on in a national referendum on October 15. It could be defeated if two-thirds of the voters in three of Iraq's eighteen provinces vote against it. That would then require a December election for a new National Assembly to start writing another constitution from scratch. The Sunnis probably have the votes in two provinces and with some help from Shiites in the slums of Baghdad, they might succeed in a veto. But right now, given the confusion and fear among Sunni leaders it looks as though the constitution will probably pass, and the elections on December 15 will be for a full-fledged National Assembly that would then begin the process of actually governing.

But whatever the outcome of these political events, there is nothing to suggest that this process is going to turn Iraq into an American-style democracy at peace with itself any time in the foreseeable future. Since the first National Assembly and government were formed in April following the January elections, more than 4,000 Iraqis have been killed in various kinds of political violence. Most of Baghdad's six million people are without electricity for days on end. Children are kept at home for fear of kidnapping. Barbershops have stopped shaving men after months of barbers being killed by religious extremists. In the south, religious militias are already enforcing strict Islamic law. And 50-60 percent of Iraqis are unemployed. It is this situation that evidently prompted a burst of candor from a senior Bush official involved in Iraq policy. This unnamed official told the Washington Post two weeks ago, "What we expected to achieve was never realistic...we're in the process of shedding the unreality that dominated the beginning." Great. But having expended more than $200 billion and more than 1,800 American lives, how can one believe that more of the same is going to make things substantially better?

Perhaps if there were a strategy beyond the president's mantra that we will "stay the course," there might be some point in keeping large numbers of combat forces in Iraq. But it is clear to me that "the course" we are now following is doomed to fail. That being said, we can prolong the agony, as in Vietnam and as the Soviets did in Afghanistan. Or we can cut our losses—sooner, I would hope, rather than later.

October 16, 2005
Iraq: A Case for Withdrawal

As I write, the results of yesterday's vote on the new Iraqi constitution are not yet known, but the preponderance of informed opinion is that it will be ratified. That being the case, there is one more election to go. On December 15, Iraqis will go to the polls for the third time this year, this time to elect members of a National Assembly to actually govern their country under the terms of their new constitution. At that point, I believe the United States should, in the prophetic words of the late Vermont Senator George Aiken, "Declare victory—and get out." If President Lyndon Johnson had heeded that advice on Vietnam, many lives—American and Vietnamese—would have been saved and both countries would have been spared the misery of eight more years of war.

I went public in this space last month about the fact that I no longer see any benefits to the continuing American military presence in Iraq. (I was hardly the first to come to that conclusion. In fact, it could be argued I came to it quite belatedly.) In the time since I made that statement, President George W. Bush has made a major speech in defense of the war. Nevertheless, polls show a continuing decline in support with only four out of ten Americans still believing that the invasion of Iraq was the right thing to do. And significantly, some of the voices now speaking out against the war are not the usual (dovish-leftist) suspects.

One such voice is that of retired U.S. Army Lieutenant General William Odom. During the second term of the Reagan administration, Odom was the director of the National Security Agency. In the first term, he had been assistant chief of staff for intelligence, meaning he was the Army's senior intelligence officer. In my years covering national security matters, Odom had a reputation for being a competent, conservative hawk.

I was therefore quite taken by a speech Odom gave to the Nieman Foundation for Journalism at Harvard a couple of months ago. (I am indebted to Haviland Smith—a retired senior CIA official and operative, now fellow Vermont resident—for bringing it to my attention.)

Odom began his remarks, "If I were a journalist, I would list all the arguments that you hear against pulling U.S. troops out of Iraq, the horrible things that people say would happen, and then ask, Aren't they happening already?"

Odom then went on to list those arguments against pulling out (many of which were made by President Bush in his recent speech) and then offered the counter argument. Here's a summary of his main points.

1. We would leave behind a civil war.
   Iraqis are already fighting Iraqis. Insurgents have killed far more Iraqis than Americans. That's civil war. We created the civil war when we invaded. We can't prevent a civil war by staying.
2. We would lose our credibility on the world stage.
   If the United States were some other insecure nation that might be true. But this country is a superpower, which gives it the luxury to admit a strategic mistake and reverse it. This enhances our credibility. Staying is more damaging than leaving.
3. It would cripple the move toward democracy.
   The United States will not leave behind a liberal, constitutional democracy no matter how long it stays. Holding elections is easy. Imposing such a democracy cannot be done in a hurry, in part because the Arab-Muslim culture is one of the most resistant to change of any in the world.
4. Iraq would become a haven for terrorists
   Iraq is already a training ground for many terrorists. The CIA has told the White House and Congress that so many terrorists have been spawned in Iraq that they are now returning to their homes in many other countries to practice what they have learned.
5. Iranian influence in Iraq would increase.
   The United States' invasion has vastly increased Iran's influence in Iraq, not sealed it out. The U.S.-sponsored elections have allowed the Iranian-supported Shiites to take power legally.
6. We haven't fully trained the Iraqi military and police forces yet.
   The issue is not military training. The insurgents are fighting effectively without outside help. But soldiers and police of the present Iraqi regime are ineffective because they are afraid to take a political stand and to risk their lives for what they see as American-created institutions.
7. Debating a pullout shows lack of support for American troops.
   Actually what many U.S. officers in Iraq are angry about are the deficiencies in their material support from the Pentagon and about the "irresponsibly long deployments they must endure" because the secretary of defense refuses to enlarge the Army's

ground forces to provide shorter tours. Of even greater significance, "the repressive and vindictive behavior of Rumsfeld toward the senior military, especially the Army leadership" has made it impossible for field commanders to make political leaders see the facts as they truly are.

While this is indeed a stinging indictment of the Bush administration, Odom was only slightly less scathing in his criticism of the Democratic leadership. He wonders "why leading Democrats have failed so miserably to challenge the United States' occupation of Iraq." The answer, he says, is that most "voted for the war and let that vote shackle them later on. Now they are scared to death that the White House will smear them with lack of patriotism if they suggest pulling out."

One retired army general does not have all the wisdom of the world. But Odom's are certainly informed opinions, and they ought to be part of the debate about where we go from here in Iraq. Unfortunately, for the moment there really isn't much of a debate. And there probably won't be until prominent Democrats have the courage to force the issue. In that context, it's worth remembering that four decades after Senator Aiken's sound advice on Vietnam, another Vermonter ran for president by campaigning against the war in Iraq. For this, Howard Dean was soundly trashed by the Democratic Party establishment and by most pundits. I did not trash Dean, but at the time I also did not think his positions on Iraq were good politics, either for him or for his party. That may have been true then, but no longer. Based on what we have seen in the past year, a rousing debate on Iraq policy with a view to fundamental changes is desperately needed, not for the sake of any political party but for the good of the country.

June 18, 2006
Ugly Portrait Emerges Dot By Dot

In the aftermath of 9/11 it became a favorite expression among politicians and pundits that American intelligence agencies had failed to "connect the dots." It was considered a useful metaphor to explain that if the information that the CIA, the NSA, and the FBI actually had in their files about the 9/11 hijackers had been properly processed and analyzed, then a picture of what the terrorists were planning to do would have emerged—just the way an image is created by connecting the numbered dots in a children's coloring book.

Now however, there are some other, very significant dots that need to be connected not by U.S. intelligence agencies, but by the American people. For as the following stories are connected, they present a picture that is not a pretty one.

- February 2002. The White House announced that while the United States would adhere to the Geneva Conventions in the war in Afghanistan, Taliban fighters would not be designated prisoners of war. Also under the new presidential directive, neither would Al Qaeda fighters nor other suspected terrorists be designated as POWs, meaning they would not have the protections of the Geneva Conventions.
- April 2004. CBS News and the *New Yorker* magazine revealed the torture and prisoner abuse scandal in the Abu Ghraib prison in Baghdad. The photos showing naked prisoners being humiliated and threatened by vicious guard dogs became an international scandal. The president and the secretary of defense were said to be sickened by the pictures and there was much talk about bad apples in the barrel. There have been trials and convictions of low-level soldiers, but so far no senior military or civilian official has been held accountable.
- May 2004. *Newsweek* magazine obtained internal memos of the administration's debate over the classification of Al Qaeda and other terrorist detainees. It seems the White House top lawyer at the time, (now the Attorney General) Alberto Gonzales, urged President Bush to declare the war in Afghanistan, including the detention of Taliban and Al Qaeda fighters, exempt from the Geneva Conventions. In his January 2002 memo, Gonzales wrote that making this declaration "substantially reduces the threat of domestic criminal prosecution under the War Crimes Act."

- June 2004. The *Washington Post* published the infamous "torture memo." This was the 2002 document from the Justice Department advising the White House that torturing Al Qaeda terrorists in captivity abroad "may be justified" and that international laws against torture "may be unconstitutional" if applied to interrogations conducted in President Bush's War on Terror. According to the fifty-page document, inflicting moderate or fleeting pain does not necessarily constitute torture. Torture, the memo says, "must be equivalent in intensity to the pain accompanying serious physical injury, such as organ failure, impairment of bodily function or even death."

- June 2004. The *Wall Street Journal* reported on a Defense Department review on the limits that govern torture. In their review, Pentagon lawyers agreed with the conclusions of the Justice Department that domestic and international laws prohibiting torture could be trumped by the president's wartime authority. In reference to a U.S. law enacted in 1994 which barred torture by U.S. military personnel anywhere in the world, the Pentagon report said, "in order to respect the President's inherent constitutional authority to manage a military campaign, ...[the prohibition against torture] must be construed as inapplicable to interrogations undertaken pursuant to his commander-in-chief authority." After the major public furor provoked by publication of these Department of Justice and Department of Defense documents, the torture memo was disavowed by the White House. However, as follow-up stories later revealed, Vice President Cheney and his current Chief of Staff David Addington (who is largely responsible for both of the offending documents) never gave up the fight to preserve president's "inherent authority" prerogatives.

- November 2005. The *Washington Post* reported that the CIA has been hiding and interrogating some of its most important Al Qaeda captives in Soviet-era compounds in Eastern Europe and other sites in eight different countries. These so-called "black sites" appear to be linked to another CIA program called "rendition," which involves sending detainees to countries known to use torture in their interrogations.

- December 2005. Congress passed the Detainee Treatment Act which prohibits cruel, inhuman, and degrading treatment of detainees. But there are questions about its effectiveness. First, the act included an amendment that would prohibit detainees in Guantanamo from invoking the law to challenge their detention. And perhaps even more significantly, President Bush attached one of his "signing statements" to the bill that states that under his "inherent authority" as commander-in-chief he is not bound by this law as he prosecutes the War on Terror.

• May 2006. A United Nations Committee on Torture called on the United States to close its detention center at Guantanamo Bay and to "permit access to the detainees to a judicial process or release them as soon as possible." It also said the United States should clearly ban interrogation techniques such as holding inmates under water to create the fear of drowning, sexual humiliation, and the use of dogs to induce fear. It said detainees had died during interrogation involving improper techniques.

• June 2006. Three inmates in Guantanamo prison committed suicide by hanging themselves with their bed sheets. They were among the roughly 465 men being held there, some for more than four years. Neither the American public nor the inmates themselves have been told precisely why they are being held and so far only ten have been charged with any crimes. The camp commander called the suicides "an act of warfare, waged against us."

As a former senior Pentagon official, Alberto J. Mora was present when a number of these dots were in the making. Until February 2006, Mora was the general counsel of the U.S. Navy, a civilian position equal in rank to a four-star general. He is a conservative Republican who continues to support the war in Iraq. However, for three years he waged a campaign inside the Bush administration against policies that sanctioned mistreatment of detainees. Late last month, Mora received the John F. Kennedy Profile in Courage Award "for his moral courage and his commitment to upholding American values."

Here are a few sentences from his acceptance speech.

"Our government issued legal and policy documents providing, in effect, that for some detainees labeled as 'unlawful combatants', interrogation methods constituting cruel, inhuman and degrading treatment could be applied....

The fact that we adopted this policy demonstrates that this war has tested more than our Nation's ability to defend ourselves. It has tested our response to our fears, and the measure of our courage. It has tested the depth of our commitment to those certain truths that our forefathers held to be self-evident....

It is astonishing to me, still, that I should be here today addressing the issue of American cruelty—or that anyone would ever have to....

We need to be clear. Cruelty disfigures our national character. It is incompatible with our constitutional order, with our laws, and with our most prized values... In this war we have come to a crossroads. Will we continue to regard the protection and promotion of human dignity as the essence of our national character and purpose, or will we bargain away human and national dignity in return for an additional possible measure of physical security?"

I can add nothing to that, except that I was surprised and disappointed with how little attention this important speech received, even from major news organizations.

September 6, 2009
History's Conflicting Lessons

Historical analogies are a powerful part of the human thought process. So much of what we learn is from what has gone on before us. The philosopher George Santayana's famous quote, "Those who cannot remember the past are condemned to repeat it," is often the operative philosophy of those responsible for the security of their nations. But the great difficulty comes in deciding *which* lessons from history are relevant to contemporary security challenges. In recent days there has been a growing chorus in the news media that Afghanistan is becoming President Barack Obama's Vietnam. Is that a fair analogy? In some respects it is not. That war was rooted in the Cold War. It lasted some fourteen years and took the lives of close to 60,000 American troops. Very few people are predicting a war in Afghanistan to be anything like that magnitude. Where I do see similarities is how perceived historical lessons played an important role in shaping policymakers' decisions to become more deeply involved.

As they considered an escalation of the Vietnam War, President Lyndon Johnson and his advisers were always mindful of the failure of Britain and France to challenge Adolf Hitler in the 1930s—a failure that ultimately led to World War II. By the mid-sixties, communism in Asia had already triumphed in China, caused a stalemated war over Korea, and was threatening all of Indochina. Thus it was decided that America must draw the line in Vietnam to prevent further communist expansion. As things turned out, local conditions—not lessons of the 1930s—would dictate the outcome in Vietnam.

As the country in which Al Qaeda trained and planned terrorist actions (culminating in the catastrophe of 9/11), Afghanistan has become the place where America is drawing another line, this time against radical Islamic terrorism. President Obama has said that America's goal in the region is to "disrupt, dismantle, and defeat Al Qaeda in Pakistan and Afghanistan and to prevent their return to either country in the future." That means the Taliban too must be defeated because "if the Afghan government falls to the Taliban...that country will again be a base for terrorists who want to kill as many of our people as they possibly can." The president then dramatically upped the ante by saying there must also be a "comprehensive approach" in Afghanistan that, in effect, involves a fundamental remaking of Afghan society and its institutions. The initial down payment on that new strategy was an additional 21,000 American troops. Now there are news reports that General Stanley McChrystal, the commander of U.S. and NATO forces in Afghanistan, just sent the Pentagon his latest classified analysis on the deteriorating situation there. While not specifically asking for more troops, Pentagon sources suggest his report lays the groundwork for such a request in the near future

And so it would seem President Obama is soon going to be faced with a decision similar to President Johnson's in 1965, when Johnson ordered a major escalation of the war in Vietnam. For Obama, apparently, the historical parallel to Afghanistan's situation today is what happened there after the Soviets gave up their occupation and went home in the late 1980s. At that time the United States decided not to become further involved in Afghanistan's internal affairs, and that led to a Taliban takeover which in turn opened up the country to becoming Al Qaeda's main base. But there is another possible lesson from Afghanistan's past Obama may be ignoring. In its history, not the British or the Soviet Union or other invaders before them, ever managed to significantly change the nature of Afghanistan. Among other things, it remains as it has always been, implacably resistant to foreign intervention—and to central governments—because it is essentially tribal at its core. At least one genuine expert considers this bit of history particularly relevant today.

Rory Stewart is a former British diplomat and army officer who served during both the Iraq and Afghanistan wars. In 2001 and 2002, Stewart walked alone across Afghanistan and wrote a highly acclaimed book about his journey. Recently he has been an unofficial advisor to Ambassador Richard Holbrooke, Obama's diplomatic designated hitter for that region. In a lengthy article in the *London Review of Books*, Stewart has laid out a very compelling case against further military escalation in Afghanistan by the United States. He does not call for total withdrawal, but for a major reduction in the size of the U.S./NATO military footprint from more than 100,000 down to 20,000. In his words, "In that case two distinct objectives would remain for the international community: development and counter terrorism. Neither would amount to the building of a [new] Afghan state." To support that conclusion he makes the following points:

- The Taliban are very unlikely to take over Afghanistan as a whole. They are no longer seen, as they were by some in 1994, as young student angels saving the country from corruption.
- Millions of Afghans came to dislike the Taliban's brutality,

incompetence, and primitive attitudes and don't want them back.

• The Afghan national army is now reasonably effective in fighting Taliban insurgents.

• Pakistan is no longer able to provide the substantial support for the Taliban it once did.

But even if the Taliban were to retake Kabul, Stewart questions how much of a threat this would actually pose to American and European national security. As he writes, "They could give Al Qaeda land for a camp, but how would they defend it against American Predators (pilotless drones) or U.S. Special Forces? And does Al Qaeda still require large terrorist training camps to organize attacks? Could they not meet in Hamburg and train at flight schools in Florida?"

I confess that for some time I have wavered over future American policy in Afghanistan. But given all the unfavorable conditions facing the United States there today, plus Afghanistan's history—not to mention the evident dwindling support among the American people for what is now an eight-year war—I now believe that a policy of continuing military escalation is probably doomed to fail.

November 15, 2009

Afghanistan and Vietnam's Legacy

As President Barack Obama left for Asia last Thursday, the process of deciding on a new strategy for Afghanistan received a jolt with a leaked report that the current U.S. ambassador in Kabul recently sent two classified cables to the president expressing strong reservations against sending in any more troops. The fact that Ambassador Karl Eikenberry is a retired three-star general, who from 2005 to 2007 commanded U.S. and NATO troops in Afghanistan, gives great weight and credibility to his arguments. His concern is that corruption and its ties to the opium trade make the government of President Hamid Karzai an unreliable partner—and this is not likely to change. The fact that Eikenberry's advice is directly contrary to the recommendations of the current commander, General Stanley McChrystal, who has fiercely lobbied for as many as 40,000 additional troops, makes it political dynamite. The White House added to the drama by revealing that the president has rejected all four of the options the military presented to him last Wednesday and wants to see new thinking with more emphasis on an exit strategy.

Whatever happens now, his critics will inevitably accuse Obama of playing politics with this issue and of making the decision in terms of what is best for his party's re-election. This ignores the historic role of public opinion in shaping war policies.

Time and again at some of the most crucial points in the history of the United States, presidents have had to make wartime decisions based on essentially political considerations. Abraham Lincoln repeatedly faced that issue during the Civil War. His decision on when or even if the Emancipation Proclamation should be issued was carefully calibrated for how its influence on public opinion would affect the war effort. Franklin Delano Roosevelt knew that a total Nazi victory in Europe would pose a huge threat to this country. Yet while he helped the British with things like Lend-Lease, he stayed out of World War II for more than two years because of the strong current of American public opinion against getting involved. That only shifted after the Japanese attack on Pearl Harbor. Of course, during the Vietnam War the actions of both Lyndon Johnson and Richard Nixon were shaped first by a growing disillusionment with and later a violent opposition to that war.

With his decision pending, President Obama remains under

enormous pressure. For some time, those who opposed escalation have used the debacle of Vietnam as a compelling argument. But this past week's *Newsweek* has a cover story on "How We (could have) Won in Vietnam." It's based on a 1999 book titled *A Better War* by Lewis Sorley, a retired Army lieutenant colonel. His premise is that America could have won in Vietnam if the U.S. Congress hadn't cut off military aid to South Vietnam. *Newsweek* reports that General McChrystal has been impressed by Sorley's argument that if it hadn't been for feckless American politicians, the military could have won that war.

I believe Sorley's premise is wrong. It is true that following the Paris Accords that ended the war for the United States in 1973, Congress started cutting military aid to South Vietnam and planned to end it entirely by 1976. But I witnessed the final six weeks of the Vietnam War, which left me with some vivid impressions. When the final North Vietnamese offensive began in March of 1975, the problem for the South Vietnamese was not a shortage of military equipment. They had three times as much artillery and twice the number of tanks and armored cars as the North. They also had 1,400 aircraft and a two-to-one numerical superiority in combat troops over their communist enemies. But South Vietnam's leaders felt abandoned by the peace agreement that Nixon had forced upon them and by 1975 they and much of their military had lost the will to fight. By the time the communists reached the outskirts of Da Nang, once the site of huge American military installations, I saw hundreds of South Vietnamese soldiers throw down their rifles and begin to run from the city. That Easter Sunday, Da Nang fell after a few rockets were fired at the airbase. There was total chaos as tens of thousands of soldiers and civilians were desperate to escape. Thanks to my friend Tony Hiroshiki, a veteran ABC News cameraman, I got a seat on one of the last flights out. We saw men and women literally trying to jump onto the wings of the aircraft as it taxied for takeoff. From bumps we could feel it seemed likely that some of them were run over. And as we learned on landing in Saigon, several people had even tried to crawl into the wheel-wells of the aircraft only to be crushed when the plane took off and the wheels came up. Such was the level of the panic in those final days.

However, by that time South Vietnam's fate had already been sealed. That occurred when after a decade of war, the loss of nearly 60,000 troops and the repeated lies and broken promises of presidents and generals, the majority of the American people emphatically demanded that the war must end and the troops brought home. In 1973 Nixon and Congress finally yielded to that demand. Revisionist history cannot change those facts.

I have written previously that I do believe America has strategic interests in Afghanistan and Pakistan, and especially for the sake of stability in Pakistan where nuclear weapons are in play, the United States cannot simply walk away from the region. But I am concerned, based on the views of experts I respect, that to win a war against insurgents like the Taliban in Afghanistan could require ten times the 40,000 troops General McChrystal supposedly wants—and could take five or even ten years to accomplish. If true, this latest request for more troops will not be the last.

So, whatever President Obama decides to do in the coming days, I want to be assured that it doesn't take us irrevocably down the road of repeated escalation. If it appears that's where things are headed, I trust that the American people will ultimately again decide they want no part in continuing such a journey. That is the true legacy of Vietnam.

Iran & North Korea

October 7, 2007

Iran: Here's a Crazy Idea

I just heard an item on the BBC that the University of Tehran was going to invite President George W. Bush to address its student body and answer their questions. By the time you read this column, the story may have been gobbled up by half the pundits in the country—or at least seized upon by the TV talk show comedians. In the wake of the notorious appearance of Iranian President Mahmoud Ahmadinejad at Columbia University, the irony is just too perfect to ignore. One can just imagine the image of G.W.B, smiling nervously while the president of Tehran U. spends ten minutes trashing him for his performance as leader of the free world these past seven years. However, given Middle Eastern traditions regarding the treatment of guests, I suspect Mr. Bush would receive a far more polite reception than was given Mr. Ahmadinejad in New York.

As I write this, there has been no White House reaction to the Tehran invitation. If there is any reaction at all, I would be shocked if it is not dismissed as Iranian propaganda. And of course, that's probably what it is. But what if Bush were to demonstrate the kind of profile in courage he so much admires in the great men of history to whom he so desperately wants to be compared? What if he took the Iranians up on the invitation, went to Tehran, said his piece, and honestly answered their hard questions? And then, while there, what if he spoke to the Iranian Majlis (parliament) and met with some of Iran's genuine powerbrokers, if not with the hapless Ahmadinejad? And what if he told them of his concerns about their country's policies while also expressing at least some degree of understanding of their concerns about his? Sounds crazy, and it will, of course, never happen.

But thirty years ago in November 1977, that is almost exactly what Egyptian President Anwar Sadat did. After decades of war and the Arab world's adamant refusal to accept Israel's right to exist, Sadat went to Jerusalem. He spoke to the Israeli Knesset (parliament) and he met with Israeli leaders and answered their questions. He didn't give away the store. He didn't offer huge political concessions. He explained his hopes and fears, but most significantly by his very presence he recognized theirs. In his presidential memoirs, *Keeping Faith,* former President Jimmy Carter wrote, "President Sadat's visit to Jerusalem on November 19-21 and his speech to the Knesset were among the most dramatic moments of modern history.... Sadat made a great speech, spelling out in very blunt terms the Arab requirements for any peace settlement. The meaning of the words themselves was muted by the fact that he was standing there alone, before his ancient enemies, holding out an olive branch. The Israeli welcome to him was truly remarkable. The Israelis were also facing their ancient enemy."

This didn't immediately bring peace between Egypt and Israel. It would take another sixteen months of tortuous negotiations and an enormous effort by Carter and his foreign policy team. But on March 26, 1979, the Israeli-Egyptian Peace Agreement was officially signed in ceremonies at the White House. This treaty was hugely important because it took Egypt, by far the largest Arab state, out of the military equation. And without Egypt, the Arabs would not be able to threaten Israel's very existence. The agreement also meant that World War III was no longer likely to be fought over the Middle East—an epic disaster that had loomed very close only a few years earlier. (During the October 1973 War, the United States went to DEFCON III two steps short of all-out war to prevent the Soviet Union from intervening on the side of the Egyptians. After the 1962 Cuban missile crisis, that is the closest the Cold War ever came to becoming a hot one.)

Sadat's trip to Jerusalem took extraordinary political and personal courage. I covered the event and particularly recall how we reporters held our collective breaths when he returned to Egypt, as he drove in an open convertible in a slow moving motorcade from the airport to his presidential residence in the center of Cairo. That day, his reception by the Egyptian people was remarkably enthusiastic. However, a little more than three years later he would be assassinated by Islamic fundamentalists in his own Presidential Guard, in part for recognizing Israel. Fifteen years after that, Israeli Prime Minister Yitzhak Rabin would be gunned down by a fundamentalist Jew, in part for trying to make peace with the Palestinians. While Middle East peacemakers may be blessed, they are also extremely rare and exceptionally vulnerable.

As I said, I do not expect George W. Bush to accept the invitation to go to Tehran. But just as Sadat's trip to Jerusalem broke the long destructive stalemate in Arab-Israeli relations, there are significant things America could still do short of a Bush visit, which could reverse the current momentum toward a major American-Iranian confrontation. As I have written on several occasions, if the United States wants to see a change of behavior by Iran, it must engage in serious negotiations at a high level for an extended period of time.

These talks cannot have preconditions. If the United States wants Iran to stop developing nuclear weapons it cannot expect Iran to freeze that program before negotiations to freeze the program actually take place. That defies any kind of logic or reason.

That does not mean that Iran should be absolved of its many hostile acts against the United States. This country and many others are justifiably concerned about Iran's nuclear ambitions, about its support for terrorism, and its current spoiler role in Iraq. But one of the principal lessons of the Iraq debacle is that war must be the last option—not the first. Serious diplomacy and severe economic sanctions have yet to be tried and the success so far in the talks with North Korea would seem to provide at least a rough model for how that might be done.

Iran is not a Jeffersonian democracy but it is not a total dictatorship, either, and Iranian public opinion is important to the theocrats who run the country. These days, with the drumbeat of war-like signals coming from Washington, it is very easy for the clerics to persuade the Iranian people that the United States is implacably hostile toward them. In addition to the shabby treatment of their president in New York, there is much more substantial proof of such hostility—both historical and contemporary. In the 1950s the CIA overthrew the elected Iranian government and returned the Shah to power—evidently to protect the Iranian oil industry from being nationalized. In the 1980s the United States gave arms and satellite intelligence to Saddam Hussein in his eight-year war with Iran—a war that cost hundreds of thousands of Iranian and Iraqi lives. Recently, there is the Bush "axis of evil" designation that can't help but be interpreted by the mullahs as a vital threat to their regime. I know that if I were now living in Tehran, I would be checking out the location of the nearest bomb shelter.

November 4, 2007

Some Unpleasant Truths about Terrorism

The decision to designate a part of the Iranian Revolutionary Guard as a terrorist group was announced by the Bush administration last month. It is said this will make it possible to broaden some of the American economic sanctions now in place against Iran.

The idea of labeling part of another country's armed forces "terrorist" is unprecedented and the practical effect remains to be seen. But in my view, this War on Terror that America is presently fighting is in need of a serious reality check.

For many critics, the notion of a War on Terror is simply silly—because terrorism is a tactic, not an ideology. But for me it goes far beyond being just a semantic argument. In a lifetime of dealing with this issue on numerous fronts, I have found that there is a profound lack of understanding of what constitutes terrorism, and no shortage of hypocrisy when it comes to calling the other guy a terrorist.

Let's begin with some definitions:

Terrorism (Webster): "use of terror and violence to intimidate, subjugate, etc., especially as a political weapon or policy."

Terrorist (Oxford): "a person who uses or favors violent and intimidating methods of coercing or intimidating a government or community."

Although not specifically included in those dictionary definitions, military actions directed against non-combatant civilians are also commonly thought of as terrorism.

But, while it is very politically incorrect to say so, terrorism is also in the eye of the beholder. As the saying goes, "One man's terrorist is another man's freedom fighter." Any time I use that line it drives many people up the wall because it appears I am condoning the use of terrorism. I am not. But I would argue that if one examines the issue dispassionately and historically, there's a lot of truth in the concept.

We all know the terrorists on the other side. But numerous twentieth century leaders in countries supported by this one, at one time in their lives, have been called terrorists by their opponents. These are just two examples:

• Eamon De Valera, long time Prime Minister and President of Ireland and one of the leaders of Irish independence from Britain.

In 1916 he was second in command of the Dublin Brigade during the famous Easter Rising rebellion. He and several others were sentenced to death for that action but he escaped execution, in part because he was an American citizen. For the next decade he was in and out of British prisons for his support for and involvement with operations by the Irish Republican Army, which the British Government condemned as a terrorist organization.

• Menachem Begin, Prime Minister of Israel.

In the early 1940s Begin assumed leadership of the militant Zionist underground army known as the Irgun. Its many attacks on the British included the bombing of the King David Hotel, which killed ninety-one people, including British officers and soldiers, and also Jewish and Arab civilians. The British called him a terrorist. And even his political rival and the first Israeli Prime Minister David Ben-Gurion denounced Begin's Irgun as "an enemy of the Jewish people."

Given their contexts, the actions of these men may be understandable. Most Western historians have forgiven them. However, I cite these examples to make the point that in time of war, what on the receiving end is unquestionably a blatant act of terrorism is often defended by those responsible for such actions as justified in their struggle for freedom and independence.

But I would like to expand this discussion of terrorism to include not just individuals, but to look at some recent history of countries closer to home. For many, World War II has come to be thought of as the "Good War." It was good, goes the argument, because the fight was clearly drawn between good and evil. And if that evil side had prevailed, those of us in the free world would all now be living under totalitarianism and speaking German or Japanese. That's true, though I have always been uneasy with the notion of a good war. However, the recent PBS Ken Burns documentary on World War II provided me with a much better phrase. It wasn't a good war, according to one of the veterans interviewed, "It was a necessary war." Amen. One could say even absolutely necessary. But as time goes on, I believe we must also not forget that while it was a necessary war, some things that our side did during the fighting were neither good nor necessary.

In 1984–85 I was assigned to write and produce several extended reports on the key events in the final year of the war in Europe for a series ABC News broadcast during the 40th anniversary of World

War II. I spent several months on this project, reading the history, visiting the sites, and interviewing many of those who had been directly involved on all sides. One of the events I reported on was the bombing of the German city of Dresden—known as the jewel of Germany for its architecture, music, and art. Its renaissance city center had no military significance, which is why it had escaped unscathed.

In the days leading up to the Yalta Conference of February 1945, where the allies wanted to make sure the Russians would continue the fight against Germany and would ultimately join in the war against Japan, British Prime Minister Winston Churchill instructed British Bomber Command to come up with a plan that would impress the Russians and assist them as they pressed on Germany's eastern front. The plan was code-named Operation Thunderclap—designed to cause so much death and destruction in one area that it would shatter German civilian morale everywhere. Ironically, bad weather prevented that bombing campaign from taking place before or even during the Yalta Conference. As Stalin agreed at Yalta to stay in the war in Europe and to join the fight with Japan, Operation Thunderclap became unnecessary. But Sir Arthur "Bomber" Harris, head of the RAF Bomber Command, went ahead with it anyway.

On the night of Feb. 13, 1945, the bombing began. Over the next twenty-four hours some 1,300 British and American planes, most carrying incendiary bombs and facing virtually no opposition, totally obliterated the city of Dresden. The death toll was originally estimated at 35,000. But as Dresden's population had grown to half a million because of huge numbers of refugees fleeing the Soviet advance, by 1985 credible British estimates put the death toll at 135,000. If true, that would make it greater than Hiroshima's.

At the end of my report from Dresden I said, "The arguments about the efficiency versus the morality of the bombing of population centers remain unresolved. However it can be said of the British and American destruction of this city forty years ago—it was not their finest hour." Nothing I have ever said on the air in five decades of broadcasting has ever provoked as much anger, protest, and hate mail as that closing comment. "What about London!" "What about the tens of thousands of British civilians killed by the Germans by the blitz, the buzz-bombs, and the V-2 rockets!" my critics howled. I was sympathetic then, as I am now, to the fact that Britain suffered grievously because of Hilter's evil intentions. The scope of his malevolence also cost the lives of millions of other Europeans, including twenty million Russians and six million Jews.

As an act of revenge or retribution Dresden is quite understandable. But it cannot be defended as an act of military necessity because it was not. And, as the goal of much of the RAF's bombing of German cities strategy was to create terror among civilians and so encourage them to stop fighting or to cease assisting their Nazi leaders, it could be argued that this was a clear case where terror was being used on civilians to achieve a political goal—which meets most definitions of terrorism.

There are at least two lessons in this history that need to be remembered.

First: bad things can happen even in necessary wars, much less unnecessary ones, such as the war in Iraq or a future one in Iran.

Second: terrorism is not solely something engaged in by your enemies. Former Defense Secretary Robert McNamara dramatically made that point in a 2002 interview that touched on his work during World War II as a planner of the firebombing of Tokyo—a series of devastating air raids by American B-29 bomber planes under the command of General Curtis LeMay. "If we had lost World War II," McNamara told his video-biographer, "LeMay and I would probably have been tried as war criminals."

October 17, 2006

North Korea and the Nuclear Club

Let us begin with the not unreasonable question: who is responsible for the crisis ignited by North Korea's entry into the nuclear club? Inevitably, such a question sets off a partisan debate. With the mid-term elections now just two weeks away, the political implications of that question are not insignificant. But it seems to me the more important question is, what do we do now? To answer that question, looking at past policies has merit, not for the purpose of assessing blame, but in figuring out what might work in the future.

Of course, North Korea is first and foremost responsible for this problem. It is a cruel and repressive regime that for decades has sought nuclear weapons. It is also quite capable of selling nuclear components such as plutonium or even an actual bomb to a terrorist group such as Al Qaeda. But saying North Korea is evil doesn't get us anywhere. Yes, China, South Korea, Japan, and Russia have a stake in this issue, so the so-called six party talks (these four plus the United States and North Korea) can play a role in pressuring the North Koreans. And yes, the United Nations Security Council sanctions might help if they were tough enough, although at first glance they don't appear to be. But for President George W. Bush and his national security team, North Korea needs to be treated as a threat to America and its interests that is urgent and that some other country simply cannot be expected to resolve.

From the Korean War in the 1950s to the present, North Korea has seen the United States as the most serious threat to its existence. Now that America is the world's only superpower (and has demonstrated, as in Iraq, a willingness to use military force to change a regime it didn't like) it can hardly be surprising that North Korea's leader Kim Jong Il wants to deal directly with Washington. Former President Bill Clinton decided to engage in direct negotiations with the North Koreans. The Bush administration rejects such talks. Referring to the Clinton policy, President Bush says "the strategy did not work." Others, such as Republican Senator John McCain have taken that much further by claiming that the policy of engagement is actually the reason North Korea is now a nuclear power. But let's look at the facts.

In the early 1990s, North Korea was building facilities to reprocess spent fuel from its nuclear reactor in order to produce plutonium—a key ingredient of one type of nuclear weapon. It also announced its intention to withdraw from the Nuclear Non-Proliferation Treaty because the treaty prohibited such reprocessing. Under a Clinton threat of military action if they began making plutonium, the North Koreans entered into talks with the United States that led to something called the Agreed Framework which was signed in October 1994.

These were its main elements:
- North Korea would freeze operation and construction of those facilities suspected of being part of a nuclear weapons program.
- North Korea would remain a member of the Non-Proliferation Treaty and its nuclear facilities would be put under International Atomic Energy Agency (IAEA) safeguards, including the presence of on-site inspectors.
- The United States and an international consortium would help North Korea develop a peaceful nuclear energy program, and while that was being constructed, would provide 500,000 metric tons of heavy fuel oil annually to meet its existing energy needs.
- The United States and North Korea were committed to moving toward normalizing economic and political relations and ultimately exchanging ambassadors.

That was the deal. And under the watch of the IAEA inspectors, this North Korean program was indeed frozen and no plutonium for nuclear weapons was produced for eight years.

However, in 2002 the Bush administration received credible evidence that the North Koreans were cheating. In the late 1990s, the father of Pakistan's nuclear bomb, the infamous A.Q. Khan, sold Pyongyang the components and materials for developing a nuclear weapon using uranium. This could have led to a bomb, though not as rapidly as their plutonium program would have produced had it not been suspended. Nevertheless, they had clearly circumvented the Agreed Framework.

After confronting the North Koreans with the evidence of their perfidy, the Bush administration stopped its own compliance with the Agreed Framework and cut off the oil shipments. It also refused any further high level talks on the subject. North Korea responded by unfreezing its plutonium reprocessing facilities, withdrawing from the NPT, and kicking the IAEA inspectors out. This past week, an American intelligence analysis of the North Korean nuclear test concluded that the explosion was powered by plutonium. That means it was made from materials that came from the program that was restarted in 2002, after being frozen since 1994.

So given the fact that the North Koreans were caught cheating, was the United States justified in breaking off talks and nullifying the Agreed Framework? If this were just a matter of a business deal, then the answer is yes. If you can't trust your business partner then you don't want to deal with that person any longer. But in the real world of nuclear politics, the United States doesn't have the luxury of being shocked by the questionable ethics or treacherous policies of its enemies.

In 2002, when the United States learned for certain from the Pakistanis that North Korea had a covert uranium enrichment program, North Korea's plutonium program was still frozen and under IAEA inspections. Wouldn't it have better served America's security interests to keep those restrictions in place while firmly negotiating terms for dealing with the new threat raised by the secret uranium facility? If a dangerous felon is making trouble in prison, you don't solve the problem by setting him free.

The reason the Bush administration decided against further direct negotiations with the North Koreans goes back to the Cold War period of the 1970s, when influential hard-line conservatives consistently argued that negotiating with your enemies simply rewards them for their bad behavior. In other words, it's a form of appeasement. Some of the people who opposed negotiations with the Soviet Union back then are the very same people who are dead set against high level, one-on-one talks between this country and North Korea or Iran. And despite being discredited, their argument remains a powerful one within the Bush administration.

It was therefore very refreshing to hear a prominent Republican and former Secretary of State James Baker declare on national television a couple of weeks ago, "I believe in talking to your enemies. It's got to be hardnosed. It's got to be determined. You don't give away anything, but in my view it's not appeasement to talk to your enemies." Baker has since rolled that back a bit, saying in later interviews that his statement was "generic" and not meant to apply to North Korea. But why not? And why not Iran, too?

These days, what passes for American diplomacy is Secretary of State Condoleezza Rice prattling on with lines such as: the North Koreans/Iranians/Syrians know what they're supposed to do. This hectoring, schoolmarm approach to international relations doesn't cut it in the real world, where crisis management requires long, intensive discussions to allow mutual enemies to find out what their adversary really thinks, fears, wants, and might be willing to compromise.

The art of diplomacy rarely results in long-term solutions to major complex problems. Rather, it usually tries to resolve acute issues and puts off the really hard ones until conditions change or improve, all the while trying to prevent disputes from escalating to the point of war. And as history has amply demonstrated, refusing to engage in this kind of diplomacy with your enemies is not a demonstration of strength—it is a sign of weakness.

March 7, 2010

A Short History of the Nuclear Club

The United States of America was the first member of the nuclear club. It lost its nuclear monopoly on August 29th, 1949, when the Soviet Union successfully tested its first atomic bomb. While he got the news a day or two later, President Harry Truman waited almost a month before making it public.

This delay was not at all surprising. This was an event of monumental military and political importance. From the time atomic weapons were first used against Japan in 1945, it had been assumed that the Russians would try to build their own bomb. But American intelligence estimates, even in 1949, assumed that the Soviets were still years away from doing so. Then suddenly, the United States was faced with a nuclear threat. Before going public, Truman had to decide how best to respond.

What he told the American people and the world on September 23, 1949 was that the United States would immediately begin a crash program to develop a far more powerful weapon. That would be the hydrogen thermonuclear device which would make the bombs dropped on Hiroshima and Nagasaki seem like firecrackers by comparison. And so, the nuclear arms race was duly underway.

But what is most notable is that for the remainder of his term, Truman did not succumb to growing pressure to use American nuclear weapons to wipe out the Soviet's incipient capabilities before they could be expanded. There was no shortage of such pressure. Five months before the Soviet test, General Curtis LeMay, the head of the U.S. Strategic Air Command (SAC), had drawn up plans to attack seventy Soviet cities with 133 atomic bombs. By February of 1950, a Joint Intelligence Committee predicted a rapid buildup of the Soviet nuclear arsenal and an attack against the United States "at the earliest possible moment." By April the president's own National Security Council was warning against a surprise Soviet attack "once it has sufficient atomic capability." Yet Truman held firm against a pre-emptive nuclear attack against Russia, and in his final State of the Union address he declared that nuclear war was "impossible" for "rational men."

Britain joined the nuclear club in 1952. France in 1960. China in 1964. India in 1974. Pakistan in 1998. North Korea in 2006. Israel does not admit to having nuclear weapons and has never signed the

Nuclear Non-Proliferation Treaty. However, it is widely known that Israel received crucial nuclear assistance from France in the 1960s that led to a significant Israeli nuclear program. American intelligence agencies estimate that Israel now has about 200 warheads.

The point of this history lesson is to set the context for renewed attention on Iran's apparent attempt to join the nuclear club. In the next few weeks we'll be hearing a lot about that—and about the Obama administration's efforts to get the United Nations Security Council to impose punishing economic sanctions on Iran to dissuade it from pursuing its nuclear goals. But amid much pessimism that sanctions will work, we are already hearing in this country—and we can expect these cries to get much louder—that the United States cannot tolerate the possibility of Iran having nuclear weapons and that America must be prepared to go to war to prevent that from happening.

I have repeatedly written about the likely consequences of war with Iran, from the closing of the Persian Gulf and the spiking of oil prices, to Iranian military proxies going against American interests in Iraq, Afghanistan, and Lebanon—just for starters. But today I'd like to pose this question: would a nuclear Iran constitute the kind of threat that Soviet Russia posed to this country and its allies in 1949? Surely not. Yet Truman opted for containment and deterrence over pre-emption. Likewise, in 1964 a nuclear China posed a genuine threat to this country—yet eight years later there was President Richard Nixon swapping toasts with Chairman Mao in the Great Hall of the People. And in 2006 when North Korea joined the club, President George W. Bush didn't see that as cause for going to war.

So is Iran really worse than all of the above? Iran's theocratic leadership has a hideous record, but compared to Stalin or Mao, two of history's greatest mass murderers? No contest.

What Iran does have is President Ahmedinejad, who has repeatedly threatened to wipe Israel off the map while regularly denying the reality of the Holocaust. Given the history of the Jewish people, it is understandable they would take these threats seriously and worry that a nuclear armed Iran was a threat to Israel's very existence. This is the position taken by Prime Minister Benjamin Netanyahu and most of his cabinet—and is the basis for Israel's threat over the past year to attack Iran's nuclear facilities, with or without American assistance. But one current cabinet minister has a very different view. Defense Minister Ehud Barak, Israel's most decorated soldier and a former Israeli Prime Minister, does not believe that Iran's leaders are religious zealots who cannot be deterred by the threat of nuclear extinction. In a recent speech in Israel, Barak said the following.

"I don't think that the Iranians, even if they got the bomb, are going to drop it immediately on some neighbor." In an obvious reference to Israel's own nuclear deterrent, Barak went on, "They fully understand what might follow. They're radical but not total *mishuginas*." (Rough translation: stupid or crazy people.) "They have quite a sophisticated decision-making process and they understand realities."

Barak does believe Iran is developing the bomb, that it wants to dominate the region, and that this could set off a nuclear arms race in the Middle East which might someday lead to terrorists getting their hands on a nuclear device. These are completely rational anxieties that need to be addressed. But in my view, and in the opinion of people like Defense Secretary Robert Gates, such concerns would not justify the disastrous consequences to American—and Israeli—interests that would certainly follow an American/Israeli military strike against Iran, now or in the foreseeable future.

December 16, 2007
What a Difference a Letter Could Make

In the past two weeks, the sixteen American intelligence agencies reached a consensus in a National Intelligence Estimate that Iran had frozen its program to develop nuclear weapons four years ago, and as far as they knew, it had not been restarted. This was a total reversal of the NIE of 2005.

Then, in an equally major about-face, President George W. Bush wrote a "Dear Chairman" letter to North Korean leader Kim Jong Il—a man he had once described as a "tyrant" and a "pygmy." The letter urged the North Korean leader to make good on his pledge to reveal all of his nuclear programs by the end of this year and raised the possibility of normal U.S.-North Korean relations in return.

The charter members of the 2002 Bush "axis of evil" were Iraq, North Korea, and Iran. Changing the regime in Baghdad has turned out to be extraordinarily more difficult than the president and his neo-conss calculated. However, setting aside the policy of regime change is apparently having results in North Korea—as American inspectors are currently supervising the dismantling of North Korea's large plutonium facility. If Kim makes good on his promise to disclose all of his other nuclear programs and weapons (I suspect there will still be some stalling) the world will be a safer place.

So what about Iran? It was fascinating to see that Iran's English language newspaper, the *Tehran Times*, ran a story about the Bush letter to Kim with the headline "U.S. President's Letter To Boost Kim's Prestige." This immediately set me thinking about the contents of a letter the president could send to Iran's Supreme Leader, the Ayatollah Ali Khamenei, that might also change the world.

Dear Supreme Leader,

You have no doubt heard the report that my intelligence agencies have determined that you froze your effort to built a nuclear weapon four years ago. I am still worried about your uranium enrichment program but you and I both know that this latest intelligence assessment makes it virtually impossible that I could get the American people to support an attack on your nuclear facilities. So that's off the table. Actually, I was never going to do that anyway, as Condi (my secretary of state) and Gatesie (my secretary of defense)—not to mention most of my Pentagon generals—were strongly opposed to the idea. Like you, I have my lunatic fringe—your President Ahmadinejad keeps going around saying he's going to wipe Israel off the map, and my Vice President Cheney wants to do the same to you. Fortunately, those two are not in charge.

What I would like to do is clear the air (as we say in Texas, where the air isn't so clear these days). I'd like to be perfectly frank about the things your country has done that make Americans very hostile toward Iran and highly suspicious of your intentions. Then with Condi's help, I'll acknowledge some of what my country has done over the years that might make you feel the same way about us.

These are my major worries:

1. You are continuing to reprocess uranium as fast as you can. As this produces the critical ingredient to making a nuclear bomb I have to assume that's what you're doing. You once had a secret nuclear weapons program (which you have always denied). For all I know, you have secretly restarted the one my spies told me you had shut down. Right now this is the key stumbling block to improving our relationship.

2. It seems you may have backed off a bit in sending those highly lethal roadside bombs to the Shiite militias in Iraq that they've been using to kill Americans. But we know you are still training many of these people and that you maintain significant influence with the key Shiite militia leaders—not to mention with the Iraqi government itself. The Shia refusal to reconcile with the Sunnis makes it very difficult for us to stabilize the country, which at this point is all we want to do—so that we can leave gracefully and not look as though you and Al Qaeda in Iraq have driven us out.

3. Your use of proxies—Hezbollah in Lebanon and Hamas in the Palestinian territories—has made life miserable in those countries and constantly threatens civil war. We can understand you wanting to have political influence in the region. It is, after all, your neighborhood. But your use of terrorism is unacceptable. I believe that the whole Middle East would benefit greatly if the Israelis and the Palestinians could reach a true peace. But your policies—like supporting Hamas and opposing any peace agreement—have made achieving that settlement more difficult, if not impossible.

4. On the subject of terrorism, we still hold Iran responsible for the U.S. Marine barracks bombing in Beirut in 1983 that killed 241

Americans. We know your Revolutionary Guards stationed in Lebanon's Bekaa Valley were working directly with the group Islamic Jihad, which claimed responsibility. A lot of people in my country will never forgive you for this—as they won't for you holding those fifty-two American diplomats hostage for more than a year back in 1979.

These are previous American actions or policies I concede could bother you:

1. My country did interfere in Iran's internal affairs by helping engineer the coup that overthrew your elected Prime Minister Mohammed Mossedegh in 1953. It wasn't all about oil, although his nationalizing the Anglo-Iranian Oil Company was a factor. But we were also worried about Mossedegh's links to the pro-Soviet Tudeh party and fears that he might make Iran part of the Russian sphere of influence in the region. We continued to prop up the Shah from that point until your revolution in 1979 for the same reason—to keep the Soviets out of the Gulf.

2. The United States did tilt toward Saddam Hussein during the 1980–88 Iran-Iraq War. It provided weapons and even chemicals that were used (illegally) against Iranian forces, and later against Kurdish civilians. It also provided battlefield intelligence to Iraq, including satellite photos. As you know, my old friend Rummy (my former defense secretary) helped to shape those policies at the time on the grounds that, as a Shiite theocracy, Iran was a threat to the Sunni Muslims of the Persian Gulf and therefore to our oil supply.

3. In Afhganistan in 2001–02, you did try to help us with the overthrow of the Taliban and the containment of Al Qaeda. However, once again Rummy scuttled any chance for improving our relations, as he convinced me you couldn't be trusted.

4. In July of 1988, the U.S.S. Vincennes did shoot down one of your civilian airliners, killing 290 people, including 66 children. The captain said it was an accident—that he thought it was one of your F-14 fighter planes. But our own investigations later found our ship should have been able to determine your plane was a civilian one and that our captain was a little trigger happy. My own father refused to apologize for the incident at the time, but I think most Americans, including their president, would say today that they were sorry this happened.

There you have it. I have my reasons to mistrust you and your country—and I appreciate that you could be skeptical of our ambitions. It is clear to me that we have good reasons to talk seriously to each other and that we both would benefit from ending this nearly thirty-year feud we've been having. I understand that you want to be a big power in your region. But you don't need nuclear weapons to do that. If we thought for a second you or one of your proxies was behind any nuclear attack on us or our allies, we would bomb you back to the Stone Age. And if you don't believe that threat, do you really expect the Israelis would not use their formidable nuclear arsenal against you if they were hit by any kind of nuclear device?

I'm not promising anything. But if I can write a letter to that pygmy—oops—*Chairman* of North Korea suggesting we could have normal relations if he'd give up his nuclear ambitions, I see no reason that I couldn't promise you the same. As they might say at the Pentagon, regime change in Tehran is no longer operative.

Yours sincerely,
George W. Bush

Author's note: The specifics concerning each country's grievances in the history of the U.S.-Iran relationship are accurate. The rest is fiction, based on fact or wishful thinking.

June 28, 2009

Obama's Iran Options

When there is a major news story such as Iran, by its very nature 24/7 cable news magnifies the event. And as is so often the case, with magnification comes distortion—from the endless repetition of the crowds and bloody images to the less than brilliant commentary of breathless anchors, most of whom have likely never heard a shot fired in anger. There are very few advantages to being old, but if there is one, it is to be able to see contemporary events with a lifetime's perspective.

That said, I do not wish to minimize the courage of the Iranians who have challenged their leaders on the streets of Tehran, nor the loss of life and serious injuries they have suffered. But for at least the first week and a half of this crisis, the actions taken by the Iranian authorities against protesters were not dramatically different from what I saw in Paris in May of 1968 when then French President Charles de Gaulle's gendarmes were trying to suppress a major student uprising that had spread to general strikes involving millions of workers; or in 1984–85 when then British Prime Minister Margaret Thatcher's police regularly battled with tens of thousands of coal miners protesting her decision to shut down much of Britain's coal industry.

I'm not equating the way Iran violates the human rights of its citizens with French or British social problems. The comparison is solely with security force tactics, which in the above cases were harsh. In France there were hundreds of serious injuries with at least one death. In Britain there were 7,000 injured and ten deaths. (In this country one might recall the way the Chicago police violently attacked protesters at the 1968 Democratic Convention—or that in 1970, National Guardsmen opened fire on an anti-war demonstration at Kent State University, killing four students.) This is not to give a pass to the Iranian mullahs. Rather, it is to highlight the reality that when governments feel threatened by major political or social unrest (even governments of historical democracies)—their reactions can be violent. And as tempting as it may be to deliver threats or ultimatums to the offending governments—or to urge the demonstrators on—that usually doesn't help. In fact, if the protesters are given a false sense of hope, it could make their situation worse, perhaps much worse.

A classic example of the sad consequences of creating false hopes took place during the 1956 Hungarian Revolution. In his first election campaign Dwight Eisenhower adopted the Republican theme that President Harry Truman's "containment policy" in dealing with the Soviet Union wasn't working. When referring to Eastern Europe, Eisenhower and his people began talking about the "liberation of captive nations." After his election, the idea of "liberation" became a staple of broadcasts then being transmitted into the Soviet bloc by the Voice of America and the CIA-backed Radio Free Europe. Then-Secretary of State John Foster Dulles was frequently heard on these broadcasts talking about "rolling back the Iron Curtain." So when Soviet troops and tanks rolled into Budapest to put down the revolt, Hungarians had certain expectations. But as author Michael Korda wrote in *Ike*, his recent Eisenhower biography, "The Hungarians might expect arms, support, supplies and even intervention from America, and feel they had been promised all that and more by Radio Free Europe; but Ike needed no threatening message (from the Soviets) to know that all this was out of the question and would very likely trigger a nuclear war." Stephen Ambrose, another of Ike's biographers, put it more bluntly. "Liberation was a sham. Eisenhower had always known it. The Hungarians had yet to learn it." Learn it they did, the hard way. Forty thousand Hungarian freedom fighters died in the rebellion. When it ended, 1,200 people, including virtually all of Hungary's anti-Soviet political leaders, were executed. (I was intrigued to hear Senator John McCain, who has been one of the strongest proponents of a much more bellicose American response to the Iranian crisis, concede in his recent appearance on CBS News *Face the Nation*, "We may have made a mistake when we gave too much encouragement during the Hungarian Revolution.")

Again I must stress that I am no apologist for any government that systematically brutalizes its own people. Most certainly that applies to the aging Chinese communists who sent troops and tanks against mostly young protesters in Tiananmen Square twenty years ago, killing many hundreds, perhaps even thousands. But the first responsibility of any president of the United States is to pursue policies for the greater good and protection of the American people. When you sit in the Oval Office, you cannot be guided by the passions provoked by television images, no matter how compelling. Criticism by political opponents and pundits is to be expected. As President Obama noted in his news conference last week, politicians have the freedom to say pretty much what they please—the president can do no such thing. In his responses, he continues to weigh both the last sixty turbulent years in American–Iranian relations and the likely effect of his words or actions on America's long-term interests. Over the past week, the president has escalated his rhetoric in condemning the violence used against the protesters, although he has notably refused to threaten specific consequences for the regime's actions.

After numerous crises over many decades, the Cold War ended peacefully because with each crisis, the policy of talking instead of fighting ultimately prevailed. Today the United States has significant political and economic (although not exactly warm) relations with both Russia and China, formerly its two greatest enemies. Likewise, regardless of what happens in Iran in the coming weeks and months, the United States is going to eventually want to deal with whatever powers-that-be in Tehran on issues that are of great importance to this and many other countries, including Iran's spoiler role in the Middle East and its potential threat to the region if it becomes a nuclear power. America's ability to directly influence current events inside Iran is slim to none. Keeping the diplomatic option open may not feel satisfying, but it remains the best policy.

Soviet Union/Russia

November 1, 2009

Twenty Years After the Fall of the Wall

On the night of November 9, 1989, I stood on a camera platform at the Brandenburg Gate. The Berlin Wall, which for twenty-seven years had separated West from East and cut an ugly scar across the city, loomed directly behind me. On most nights this west side of the Wall would be shrouded in darkness, hiding behind it the "death strip" of mines and booby traps where border guards constantly patrolled with orders to shoot to kill. Over the years, as many as 192 people were indeed killed trying to escape over the Wall. (About a thousand died fleeing across the full 300-mile East German border.)

But on that particular night, the Wall was bright with television lights as I and other correspondents did live reports describing the truly unbelievable scenes before us to viewers in the United States and throughout the world. On top of the Wall, thousands of East Berliners were singing, dancing and drinking—euphorically celebrating their newfound freedom. Some with sledge hammers, axes, ice picks, and even fingernails were trying to deface the dreaded Wall. Young and old, men and women, could not stop embracing one another. It was as though a giant love-in had swept over an entire nation whose people had been imprisoned for all or most of their lives. They had suddenly stormed through and over their prison wall, and the only shooting done by their notorious guards was with water cannons—in an apparent attempt to dampen the crowds' enthusiasm that failed miserably.

With the perspective of time it is now easy to say that this was the most momentous night in the history of the second half of the twentieth century. The night the Berlin Wall came down effectively ended the Cold War—the war that had threatened the entire world with nuclear annihilation for some four decades. But as the theme music for ABC News *Nightline* came into my earpiece, and I awaited the first question from Ted Koppel, the moment was not as crystal clear as all that.

Over the previous three years, reporting on the changes taking place in what was then the Soviet bloc was my main assignment. I had seen Soviet leader Mikhail Gorbachev transform the politics of his country; heard him signal he would not intervene in the affairs of other countries of the bloc; and watched him establish an amicable and productive relationship with President Ronald Reagan, the man who once labeled the Soviet Union the "Evil Empire." Already in 1989, I'd covered the Communist Party losing its stranglehold on power in Poland and Hungary. Since early September I had been reporting mainly in East Germany as tens of thousands of its citizens fled to the West, many through a new hole in the Iron Curtain opened up by the Hungarians. In October, the long-time East German communist strongman Erich Honecker had been deposed by his own politburo, and massive protests, once unheard of in this most repressive of police states, were now occurring almost daily.

Extraordinary change was palpable. But still there was a burning question of doubt in the minds of top Eastern European reformers with whom I spoke regularly throughout 1989; namely, at what point might the Soviet Union suddenly decide to intervene militarily to save its crumbling empire? Even in November 1989 there were still many skeptics about Gorbachev's true intentions, including in the White House of President George H.W. Bush. Others worried that Gorbachev could be overthrown by Soviet hardliners who would again crack down on reform movements in Poland, Hungary, and East Germany as they had so brutally done in the past.

One other reason for the element of uncertainty that night was that no one seemed to know exactly what had happened. At a news briefing in East Berlin that evening, televised live in both Germanys, Gunter Shabowski, the new politburo's official spokesman casually mentioned that for the first time, every East German would have the right to a passport and exit visa. When a chorus of reporters began shouting, "When? When?" Shabowski didn't seem to know. He looked back at his papers and finally responded, "Immediately."

Given that freedom to travel outside of the Iron Curtain was the most critical issue of the day, this was momentous news. But did this announcement, so off-handedly presented, really mean what it appeared to say? First dozens, eventually thousands decided to find out for themselves by gathering at the various checkpoints to West Berlin. It turned out the border guards had no new instructions regarding passports or visas and refused to let anyone pass. A crisis began building. Guards were seen trying repeatedly to call for new guidance, but apparently were unable to reach anyone in high authority. Meantime, the mood at places like Checkpoint Charlie was shifting from joyful to ugly as once-docile East Germans began shouting at the guards and pressing hard against the barricades. Finally, after more than four hours, each nervous border commander on his own simply gave up and threw open the gates. With that, what seemed like much of the population of East Berlin began flooding into West Berlin through the checkpoints and over the Wall (as at the Brandenburg Gate). The Berlin Wall, at least for that night, was no more.

We learned much later that spokesman Shabowski had made a mistake of literally historic proportions. The new regime had decided to grant passports for all and to issue new travel regulations to government ministries, passport officials, and border guards. But on the night of November 9, none of that had yet happened, because the new policy was not to begin until November 10. What was actually envisaged was a slow, orderly process that could take weeks or more. The calculation was that the promise of passports for all would take the steam out of the pent up demand for freedom to travel. But when Shabowski mistakenly said the new policy was to begin immediately, instead of a controlled departure of East Berliners over days and weeks, the entire city of more than a million seemed to virtually empty that night. Most people returned, but with that massive breach of the once-invulnerable Berlin Wall, history had been made and forever changed.

It's satisfying to report that when Ted asked me on the air that night if we were being carried away with that euphoria of the moment I said no, adding that he and I would have other stories to cover but this one (the Cold War, which the two of us had reported on for twenty-five years) was basically over. In my closing thoughts, I mused that the gods sometimes punish us by giving us what we ask for. I wasn't predicting anything, just expressing an anxious feeling I had that night. As I look at the world twenty years later, it appears my anxiety was not entirely misguided.

It must be said that Bush-the-father's administration deserves high marks for smoothly persuading Europe and Russia to accept German unification; for quietly getting perhaps half a million Russian troops and their weapons out of Eastern Europe; and especially for helping to secure the former Soviet Union's nuclear arsenal. Nevertheless, the voices of American triumphalism—the boasts that "We won the Cold War" and "We are now the only superpower" (and therefore we can do what we please) were soon to be heard, and by the turn of the century they would once again dominate U.S. foreign policy. The lesson that the Cold War was not "won," but "ended"—in part because Reagan reversed course from confronting Gorbachev to seriously engaging him and supporting his reforms—remains totally lost on those who falsely claim victory for the policies of confrontation. No matter how many times these people are proven wrong, they keep coming back to haunt us.

June 10, 2004

Reagan's Role in the Soviet Union's Demise

With all due respect for the important contributions made by the fortieth president, to say Ronald Reagan was the man responsible for bringing down the Berlin Wall and ending the Cold War gives him more credit than he deserves.

To suggest that when Mr. Reagan said, "Tear down this wall, Mr. Gorbachev," that the Berlin Wall began to crumble, is like the rooster thinking it's his crowing that makes the sun come up. The Wall eventually came down for many reasons. Mr. Reagan's policies were a factor, but the five-decade long Cold War was won by the efforts of all American presidents going back to Harry Truman. And the Wall also came down because of the reform policies of then Soviet President Mikhail Gorbachev.

The conventional wisdom now seems to be that it was Reagan's hard line toward the Soviet Union, labeling it the "evil empire" and significantly increasing American defense spending, that ultimately brought about its collapse. Perhaps it's not so much conventional wisdom as the liberality of hindsight. In any case, I believe there were forces that were more important.

Among these forces was the fact that by the 1980s the Soviet Union was already on the verge of collapse after seven decades of political repression and economic stagnation.

Also, Mikhail Gorbachev was a Soviet leader like no other. As one who spent a good deal of time in Moscow in the eighties, I watched Gorbachev struggle to change his country by owning up to its repressive past while trying to create a democratic future.

But there was another, rarely noted force: what might be called the Nancy factor.

I was very interested to read in Gorbachev's tribute to Reagan his description of Nancy Reagan as "… wife and friend, whose role will, I am sure, be duly appreciated."

It isn't yet. But I have long held the view that it was Nancy Reagan who brought her husband around to making the arms control deal that made it possible for Gorbachev to expand the domestic reforms that ended Soviet Communist rule.

Her motives were not necessarily strategic. I heard from White House insiders at the time that Nancy was furious that Gorbachev was becoming the darling of the international news media as a man of peace, while Reagan was portrayed as a cold warrior. Nancy was smart enough to realize that this impression could shape her husband's place in history. That much is fact. We can only speculate on what transpired in private conversations between the Reagans. But we do know that the United States eventually eased its conditions for a new treaty limiting mid-range nuclear weapons. With that treaty, U.S.-Soviet relations became better than they had ever been. Mr. Reagan even went to Moscow and declared that he did not see Gorbachev's Soviet Union as an evil empire. And the rest, as they say, is history.

July 1, 2004
A Triumph of Realism

After all the fulsome eulogies upon his death in early June, it would be easy to conclude that Ronald Reagan won the Cold War. Although Reagan himself never made such a claim, his Vice President and successor did. "We won the Cold War," boasted President George H.W. Bush, while campaigning for a second term. But as Jack F. Matlock Jr. points out in his new book, *Reagan and Gorbachev: How the Cold War Ended,* "In fact, the Cold War had ended in spirit before he [Bush] took office as President. All he had to do was set the terms of settlement."

Matlock is uniquely qualified to make the judgment that the Cold War "ended" and was not won—at least not by any one person or side. A career diplomat and Russian scholar, he had three assignments to Moscow starting in 1961. Two decades later, while running the U.S. Embassy there as charge d'affaires, he was named ambassador to Czechoslovakia. In 1983 Matlock was brought back to Washington to be the Soviet specialist on the National Security Council (NSC). He thus became a key participant in developing U.S. policy and was at Reagan's side during the Geneva, Reykjavik, and Washington summits. In 1987 he was made ambassador to the USSR and had unprecedented access to President Mikhail Gorbachev and his reform team. His peers whom I have spoken to praise him for the balance of his skepticism and pragmatism.

Since the end of the Cold War, two schools of thought have developed about how this menace that dominated international affairs for nearly half a century was defused. One school, popular among Republicans, attributes the turn of events to Ronald Reagan's hard line. His denouncing the USSR as "the evil empire," his dramatically increasing American defense spending, and his doggedly pursuing the Strategic Defense Initiative (SDI) is said to have forced the Soviets to capitulate. The other school, favored by Democrats and by many Western Europeans, thinks it was Gorbachev's courageous efforts to restructure his country—which did indeed end the power of the Communist Party and ultimately cause the breakup of the Soviet Union—that finally changed the world.

As the diplomatic correspondent for ABC News during Reagan's first four years and the senior foreign correspondent working in Europe and the Soviet Union during the next four, I tended to lean toward that second school. In my view, Gorbachev was unique among

Soviet leaders in his desire to reform his country and any American President would have recognized that and tried to help him.

But Matlock belongs to neither school. Instead he gives us a sophisticated insider's look at the people and happenings of the 1980s, one of the more tumultuous periods in the history of the Cold War. The potential nuclear Armageddon was always present to focus the mind, but for all the verbal fireworks of those years, there were actually no major military crises along the lines of the 1962 Cuban missile crisis or the 1973 Middle East War when the United States moved to stop Russian arms shipments to Egypt. Still, when Reagan took office a lot of the world, especially Europe, held its breath.

Matlock was not involved in fashioning the hard-line approach of Reagan's first term, but given the Soviet invasion of Afghanistan and the rapid turnover of aging leaders in the Kremlin, he supports it. Similarly, he applauds Reagan's setting firm, realistic goals for the U.S.-Soviet relationship that proved helpful to both sides.

After Gorbachev came on the scene, Reagan was energized and engaged. By June 1985 he was eager for his first summit. But National Security Adviser Bud McFarlane was "struck by the President's spotty command of historical facts," so he encouraged Matlock to create a program that would provide Reagan with some knowledge and understanding of the Soviet Union before he faced its new leader. The result was what became known among the NSC staff as "Soviet Union 101." Matlock got the top analysts in the government to prepare twenty-four papers, each eight to ten single-spaced pages long and organized to present a rounded picture of the Soviet Union and its people and of Gorbachev, the man. "To his credit" Matlock says, "the President was acutely aware that there were serious gaps in his knowledge," and made a real effort to cooperate in this cram course.

By October Reagan was ready to discuss concrete issues and to work on talking points for his meetings. The day before the Geneva summit, with Matlock "playing" Gorbachev, he went through a full rehearsal using his ever-present three-by-five cue cards.

Of his adversary Matlock writes: "When he came to power Gorbachev still believed in the Soviet system as it had evolved. He knew it had its flaws, and serious ones. But he thought that a little tinkering with the mechanism was all that was needed...It is an irony that Gorbachev's policies eventually turned out to be not only more radical, but truly revolutionary, for they ended by destroying the system they were intended to save."

Matlock faults Gorbachev for obsessing about SDI, a weapons system that would never have been a threat to the Russians because it wasn't ever likely to work. But his nuanced portrait shows Gorbachev to be a man of substance, "the only Soviet or Russian leader in history to use force last, not first, to solve political problems...the only Soviet leader to place principle above personal rule."

There is a strong cast of supporting players here too, beginning with Secretary of State George P. Shultz and Soviet Foreign Minister Eduard A. Shevardnadze. "They were far more than lieutenants carrying out their superiors' orders," Matlock stresses. "Without their efforts neither the American President nor the Soviet General Secretary would have gotten his priorities right and neither would have been able to implement what he wanted to do."

Then there are some unusual cameo roles. In 1984, we learn, Dr. Lawrence Horowitz gave the White House details of important contacts he had with a senior Soviet official in Moscow. Interestingly, Horowitz was an administrative assistant to Senator Edward M. Kennedy (D-Mass.), who signaled to Reagan's people that he considered certain foreign policy matters above partisan politics and said he was happy to cooperate—and keep quiet about it. Matlock writes, "At a time when other Democrats were telling [Soviet] Ambassador [Anatoly F.] Dobrynin that Reagan was dangerous, Senator Kennedy's quiet coordination with the White House helped convince the Soviets eventually that Reagan was serious about negotiations."

In the summer of 1986 French President Francois Mitterrand visited Moscow just after a meeting with his American counterpart. Mitterrand told Gorbachev that he would get nowhere with Reagan if he insisted the United States give up SDI before there could be an agreement to reduce nuclear weapons. He continued, "Notwithstanding his political past, Reagan has the intuition that the tension must be ended. He is not a machine. He likes to laugh and more than others is influenced by the language of peace." Gorbachev later told one of his aides, "This is extremely important and I am taking special note of it." (Ultimately, he would sign the agreement to eliminate intermediate range nuclear weapons without resolving the SDI issue.)

Of course there were also those, on both sides, who devoted themselves to blocking any improvement in U.S.-Soviet relations. On the American side, Defense Secretary Caspar W. Weinberger was almost constantly at odds over Soviet policy with the Joint Chiefs of Staff, the NSC, the State Department, and—hardly least—the president. In

Matlock's words, "Whereas most departments would obey a decision by the president, one could never be sure that Weinberger would... Weinberger was utterly convinced that there was no potential benefit in negotiating anything with Soviet leaders and that most negotiations were dangerous traps."

In those days Weinberger was the embodiment of the hard-line, conservative wing of the Republican Party and he had important allies, extending to the White House Office of Communications. At the close of the Geneva summit, the speechwriters put together several addresses on the summit's results for Reagan to deliver to NATO, the Congress, and the American people. "All of the initial speech drafts were larded with disparaging statements about the Soviet Union and communism," Matlock says, "and even contained slighting references to Gorbachev."

He and others on the NSC tried to explain to the writers that to use Reagan's report to attack Gorbachev and the Soviet Union "would strike the public as proof that he had no intention of trying to improve relations." Yet such explanations were usually met with charges that Matlock was being "soft," "defeatist," and "somewhat pro-Soviet." After hours of laborious editing there remained three passages in one of the speeches that Matlock was certain Gorbachev would take as a direct personal insult. "I knew that was not what the President wanted, but Peggy Noonan, who had written them, and Pat Buchanan, who supervised the preparation of the speeches, were adamant. They refused to take them out."

By 4:30 a.m. an exasperated Matlock gave in. "Send in your draft without any indication that the NSC objects and we'll see what happens."

A few hours later Reagan came into breakfast carrying the speech draft with the three offending paragraphs marked out. Turning to Buchanan, Reagan said, "Pat, this has been a good meeting. I think I can work with this guy. I can't just keep poking him in the eye!"

Reagan's willingness to let realism trump ideology is a theme that runs through Matlock's important book. It is the author's view that this was a crucial factor in bringing the Cold War to a happy end. And he has persuaded me.

June 29, 2008

Real Lessons from the Cuban Missile Crisis

"Imagine a President McCain or a President Obama receiving the following top-secret briefing from his national security adviser. 'Iran has successfully developed a nuclear warhead and may have already mated it with a medium-range Shahab-3 missile targeted at Israel. A preemptive strike could trigger a nuclear exchange. What do we do, Mr. President?'"

That scenario was posed last week by *Washington Post* reporter Michael Dobbs, author of the chilling new book, *One Minute To Midnight: Kennedy, Khrushchev and Castro on the Brink of Nuclear War.* This book is not simply a regurgitation of the old tales of the Cuban missile crisis. Dobbs adds many new and sobering facts to the now well-tread story line of those thirteen terrifying days in October 1962 when history's only superpower nuclear confrontation very nearly became World War III. But perhaps of greater significance, he strips away much of the mythology of the crisis that he shows is "riddled with basic errors of fact." He attributes many of these errors to Kennedy hagiographers.

Dobbs' account is so unsettling because it illustrates that even though Kennedy and Khrushchev ultimately both decided during the crucial final hours of the crisis that they wanted to avoid a catastrophic war, many of their advisers did not share that view and such a multitude of things could and did go wrong that the fact we escaped a nuclear holocaust is nothing short of miraculous.

Dobbs writes, "Much of what Kennedy thought he knew about Soviet actions and motivations during the crisis rested on flawed intelligence reports and assumptions. Far from being an example of 'matchlessly calibrated' diplomacy, the Cuban missile crisis is better understood as a prime illustration of the limits of crisis management—and the importance of the ever-present screw-up factor in world affairs."

If Dobbs' perfectly plausible Iran scenario ever materializes, it is well and good that either a President Obama or McCain should consider how Kennedy dealt with this ultimate crisis. But in doing so they must go far beyond their present sound bites—that America needs to be tough with its enemies, or that it must not fear to negotiate. To that end, Dobbs has offered some useful suggestions "for any future president struggling with an Iranian missile crisis" by pointing

out what he believes are the real lessons of 1962. What follows is a
summary of some of his book's central findings and Dobbs' analysis.

1. The view from the Oval Office can be very limited.
   As much as the president may be the best-informed person in
   the world, there is much he does not know and the beginning
   of wisdom for any president is realizing that he is often groping
   about in the dark. For example:

   • Kennedy did not know the Soviets had deployed nuclear cruise
     missiles within fifteen miles of the U.S. naval base at Guan-
     tanamo Bay, Cuba. These missiles had Hiroshima-sized war-
     heads that would have destroyed that base in five minutes.
   • On October 27, the key day of the crisis, called Black Satur-
     day by White House aides, Kennedy did not know where the
     Soviet missiles capable of striking the American mainland were
     actually located on the island.
   • He was also woefully misinformed about the size of the Soviet
     troop presence. He'd been told there were some 6,000 to 8,000
     "technicians" on the island. In fact, there were 43,000 heavily
     armed Soviet troops, equipped with tactical nuclear weapons.
     Luckily Kennedy rejected the Joint Chiefs' calls to invade as
     too risky (without knowing just how risky it would actually
     have been).

2. Somebody always screws up.
   Also on Black Saturday, the most dangerous day of the Cold
   War, an American spy plane on a routine mission to monitor
   Soviet nuclear tests became disoriented at the North Pole and
   flew far into Soviet airspace. The Russians scrambled MiG
   fighters to shoot it down and the American Alaskan Command
   sent up nuclear armed interceptors in response. Again, miraculously, the Cold War did not become a hot one. When Kennedy
   was told belatedly about the incident his reaction was laconic:
   "There's always some sonofabitch who doesn't get the word."
      Calibrated crisis management is impossible. Kennedy under-
   stood that once the machinery of war is set in motion, the odds
   that dangerous and unpredictable events will occur dramatically
   increase. History is determined not just by rational actors but
   also by blinkered generals and excitable ideologues.
      In terms of potential screw-ups, Dobbs also adds some detail to
   one of my favorite factoids of the crisis. In those days there were

communications satellites. But when the Soviet ambassador to Washington wanted to communicate with Moscow, even with messages of great urgency during the height of the tension, the system was unbelievably primitive. The ambassador's message would be encrypted. The Soviet Embassy would then call the local Western Union office which would dispatch a courier—on a bicycle—to pick up the cable. Soviet diplomats would then watch the young black messenger cycle slowly down the street, and wonder if he would stop along the way to chat with his girlfriend (or my thought, be hit by a bus).

3. Personality matters.
Kennedy was the most dovish member of his thirteen-member executive committee on national security. Although both he and Khrushchev were bellicose in the early days, Kennedy later tried to look at the crisis from Khrushchev's perspective. When he decided to hold off an immediate invasion and to set up a naval blockade to stop further Soviet arms shipments into Cuba, he was bitterly opposed by some of his hard-line advisers. General Curtis LeMay, the Air Force chief of staff, speaking to the president as though he were a dim pupil, said a blockade would send a message of weakness. "It will lead right into war. This is almost as bad as the appeasement at Munich."

By Black Saturday, Kennedy understood better than any of his advisers that things were spiraling out of control. He moved to end the crisis by telling his brother Robert to summon Soviet Ambassador Anatoly Dobrynin to a meeting at the Attorney General's office in the Department of Justice. Dobrynin has written that he was previously unimpressed with Robert Kennedy, who Dobrynin claimed was often combative and rude. However, at this meeting, Kennedy was subdued, almost distraught, and addressed Dobrynin as a fellow human being trying to save the world from nuclear destruction.

Kennedy told the ambassador that time was fast running out. He said America would promise not to invade Cuba, and would remove its Jupiter missiles in Turkey in a few months if the Soviets immediately withdrew all their nuclear missiles from Cuba. (The Jupiter missile was obsolete. But the issue was politically sensitive for Kennedy so that detail was kept secret—for three decades.) The deal outlined to Dobrynin was also proposed in a separate letter from the president to Khrushchev and ultimately was the basis for the end of the crisis.

Earlier in 1962 Kennedy had read *The Guns of August*, Barbara Tuchman's then-new history of how Europe blundered into World War I. He was so impressed he had the book distributed to every U.S. military base worldwide. One passage in particular stuck with him. A German statesman asks why the war broke out and receives the reply, "If only one knew." Kennedy was determined no survivor of a nuclear war would ever ask, "How did it happen?" only to be told, "If only one knew." As Dobbs concludes, "Had someone else been president in October 1962, the outcome might have been very different."

If JFK thought that *The Guns of August* should be required reading at American military bases in 1962, I would suggest that *One Minute To Midnight* also be mandatory study for the 2008 presidential candidates and all of their senior advisers. The word nuance is almost always denigrated in political campaigns where bumper sticker slogans are substitutes for political thought. But such phrases as "Wanted Dead or Alive" and "Bring-em on"—two of GWB's more infamous utterances, the first in reference to Osama bin Laden, the second, regarding the Iraqi insurgency, represent precisely the kind of cowboy mentality that got this country into the huge international mess it is in today.

The United States needs a president who is not so overdosed on his own testosterone that he not only understands the meaning of nuance but is actually prepared to conduct his relations with the rest of the world in a balanced, thoughtful manner. That means deftly using all of the strengths of this country—economic, diplomatic and yes, moral—not just military. And ultimately it means showing the judgment of a John Kennedy rather than the jingoism of a General LeMay. The stakes may not be as high as they were in October 1962, but then again, they may well be.

June 1, 2008

What Appeasement Is and Isn't

I read commentaries written by well known right-wing ideologues. I even occasionally listen to the rants of Rush Limbaugh and Bill O'Reilly.

It's part of knowing your adversary, and because they are usually so far over the top, I actually can find them amusing. But every once in a while, I get blindsided with something that gets me so steamed up that I need reminding that spikes in blood pressure can be dangerous to a geezer's health.

So it was on the morning of May 22 when I saw the headline on a column on the op-ed page of the *New York Times*, "Kennedy Talked—Khrushchev Triumphed." It was written by two men—one a journalist, the other a Columbia University doctoral candidate— neither of whom has any standing in the field of diplomacy. But their supposed scholarly, historical analysis of the dangers of negotiating with your enemies was given credibility by being published in the great bastion of liberalism.

Timing, of course, is everything, and in the preceding days, President George W. Bush and his would-be successor Senator John McCain had been attacking Senator Barack Obama's willingness to meet with some of the world's bad guys without preconditions (not without preparations, which his critics erroneously use interchange-ably). Bush and McCain accused Obama of being "inexperienced and reckless" and of pursuing policies of "appeasement." A casual reader of the *Times* op-ed that morning could be forgiven for at least won-dering if Bush and McCain might have a point.

While not wanting to give it further prominence, if I am going to rail against it, at least I have to give you the gist of the offend-ing *New York Times* article. It begins by asserting that President John F. Kennedy was ill-prepared for a summit meeting in Vienna with Soviet Premier Nikita Khrushchev in June 1961; that he insisted on it against the advice of his top foreign policy advisers; that for two days Khrushchev had totally bested him in the debate. That's putting the worst-case spin on it, but that's still old news. However, it was the conclusions the column drew from this old news that are extremely bothersome. The authors claim that Khrushchev came away from Vienna thinking Kennedy was a lightweight, and therefore, two months later, this would lead to the building of the Berlin Wall. Even worse, they theorize that a year later, still thinking Kennedy was a pushover, Khrushchev decided to put nuclear missiles into Cuba, almost setting off a global nuclear war. The last line of the article is, "Sometimes there is good reason to fear to negotiate." That is what sent my blood pressure soaring.

On a purely factual level the article is a highly questionable read of the events that followed the Vienna Summit. The Berlin Wall was built because at that time East Germany, one of Russia's most important client states, couldn't stop the flood of East Germans who wanted to escape to the West. The border between the two German states had been sealed for several years, but in Berlin movement between East and West was still relatively easy. For East Germany and for the Soviets, this became increasingly intolerable and so the decision was made to put up a wall in Berlin. The calculation was that the western powers would see the wall as preferable to war, which indeed they did.

As for the Cuban missile crisis, Khrushchev was under pressure from Castro and from hardliners in the Kremlin to prevent the United States from making another attempt at regime change in Havana. The Soviets were also increasingly unhappy with their own encirclement by NATO. Evidently Khrushchev thought he could get away with putting missiles into Cuba. There is no hard evidence that the Vienna Summit was a factor in this decision, but one could speculate it might have been. However there is no question that Kennedy very skillfully negotiated with Khrushchev on this occasion. He left the Soviet premier a face-saving escape, which he took, and the Soviet missiles were indeed removed. Some respected historians even argue that it was the lessons Kennedy learned from his encounter with Khrushchev in Vienna that were crucial in defusing a crisis that brought human life on our planet dangerously close to extinction.

It is precisely because the stakes in American foreign policy are so incredibly high that my emotions can be aroused by this nonsensical debate over whether one should negotiate with one's enemies. Since the dangerous days of the Cold War, I have been listening to some of the same people making the same discredited arguments that negotiating with your adversaries is a form of appeasement. When GWB trotted out that old canard in a speech to the Israeli Knesset on the occasion of Israel's 60th anniversary, I once again sought comfort in the pages of *The Gathering Storm*, the first volume of Winston Churchill's World War II memoirs. Here is a man who knows all there is to know about appeasement—and it has absolutely nothing to do with negotiating with your enemy.

Throughout much of the 1930s, Churchill, who in those years was merely a member of Parliament with no official standing in the government, warned repeatedly against the British policy that in its day was unashamedly known as appeasement. It was built on a widely-held belief that countries such as Britain and France were still suffering from the aftershocks of World War I, and if they had to make some modest accommodations to Hitler's desire to re-unify the German speaking peoples, this was preferable to still another war.

Churchill's problem was not that the British government talked to Hitler. The issue was what it was telling or not telling him, especially in the wake of Hitler's ever greater provocations. On each occasion both Britain and France chose to ignore the threat and not to challenge it with military force (much to the consternation of German military commanders). Those provocations were:

- In 1935, Hitler announced national military service or conscription, in violation of two League of Nations treaties.
- In 1936, 35,000 German troops occupied the demilitarized Rhineland, a zone on either side of the Rhine that according to the Treaty of Versailles, German forces were explicitly forbidden from entering. Doing so, according to the treaty, would be "an unprovoked act of aggression."
- In March of 1938, Hitler invaded and absorbed Austria. ("The Rape of Austria" is Churchill's title for this chapter.)
- In September of 1938, at a summit meeting with British Prime Minister Neville Chamberlain in Munich, Hitler got Britain to agree to allow him to effectively dismember Czechoslovakia on the specious grounds that he was protecting the rights of German speakers in the area known as the Sudetenland. That was the meeting from which Chamberlain returned home to Britain declaring, "I believe it is peace in our time."

Throughout these years Germany was continuing to rearm at a rapid rate, eventually outstripping Britain and France in divisions of troops, tanks, artillery, U-boats, fighter planes, and bombers. By the time Hitler invaded Poland in 1939 and the British and French sheepishly honored their treaty obligations to Poland by declaring war on Germany, it was much too late. The French and British had missed four opportunities when they could have prevented World War II at relatively little cost. Now they had a war on their hands that would take the lives of some sixty to seventy million people worldwide.

Even so, as Churchill ends his chapter on "The Tragedy of Munich," he does not blame the war on the policy of talking with Hitler. These are some of his closing thoughts. "Those who are prone by temperament and character to seek sharp and clear-cut solutions to difficult and obscure problems, who are ready to fight whenever some challenge comes from a foreign power, have not always been right. On the other hand, those whose inclination is to bow their heads, to seek patiently and faithfully for peaceful compromise are not always wrong. On the contrary, in the majority of instances they may be right...How many wars have been averted by patience and persisting good will!...How many wars have been precipitated by firebrands!"

By citing those words I don't mean to imply that Churchill was a closet pacifist. He most surely was not. In summing up the policy of appeasement he wrote, "There is no merit in putting off a war for a year, if when it comes, it is a far worse war or one much harder to win. These are the tormenting dilemmas upon which mankind has throughout its history been so frequently impaled."

We've often been told how much President Bush and Vice President Cheney admire Winston Churchill. Nothing wrong with that. It's just unfortunate that so little of Churchill's courage, his eloquence, and especially his wisdom seems to have rubbed off on them. And even when they use him as an example, as in the recent Bush speech on appeasement, they evidently have learned the wrong lessons.

November 28, 2010

Dr. Strangelove and the Fate of the New START

The other night I discovered that Turner Classic Movies was about to show *Dr. Strangelove*, the chilling satire on nuclear war by director Stanley Kubrick. I hadn't seen it for decades, so I settled down for another look—but not just because the baseball season was over and I had time on my hands. Actually, the subject of nukes was on my mind because the fate of the most recent Strategic Arms Reduction Treaty (START) may be decided by the Senate in the coming days. More on this to come.

With Peter Sellers playing three roles including the U.S. president and a mad German scientist, the film is darkly funny. I do recall that when it came out less than two years after the 1962 Cuban missile crisis—when nuclear war had just barely been averted—I did not find the idea of nuclear Armageddon particularly amusing. The plot involves a rogue American Air Force General who bypasses all the failsafe measures and sends the nuclear-armed B-52 bombers under his command to attack the Soviet Union. Even as "President" Sellers and his national security team desperately try to stop them, a Pentagon general played by George C. Scott argues instead for a full-scale attack to "finish off those Ruskies, once and for all," adding that Soviet retaliation "would kill *only* ten million Americans."

Kubrick, of course, was mocking the politics of fear being used to sustain public support for the Cold War. A decade later when I chose to specialize in arms control reporting, the politics of fear was still the weapon of choice by those who opposed any agreements with the Soviet Union. Even at a time when both sides had thousands of warheads which could obliterate each country many times over—along with the entire planet—the American nuclear arsenal was never big enough for the hawks. Furthermore, anyone who advocated reciprocal arms reductions had their courage, their sanity, and their patriotism challenged by these same hardliners.

A notable example: when Paul Warnke was nominated in 1977 by President Carter to be chief negotiator at the Strategic Arms Limitation Talks (SALT II), Warnke was viciously attacked. In part this was because of his 1975 Foreign Affairs essay "Apes on a Treadmill," in which he ridiculed the conservative idea that the only way to counter the Soviet nuclear threat was to build ever more nuclear weapons. The famous cold warrior Paul Nitze called Warnke's ideas "demonstrably unsound...absolutely asinine...screwball." An anonymous congressman charged him with secretly working with both communists and terrorists. And the neo-conservative Committee on the Present Danger circulated a memo accusing Warnke of favoring "unilateral abandonment of every weapons system which is subject to negotiation at SALT."

At the time, *New York Times* columnist Anthony Lewis noted "a peculiar, almost venomous intensity in some of the opposition to Paul Warnke; it is as if the opponents want to destroy him...It signals the rise of a new militant coalition on national security issues." Lewis was prescient because the militant coalition of neo-cons, religious and economic conservatives, did become dominant in American foreign policy for much of the next three decades—in spite of its record of being consistently proven wrong.

The New START treaty was signed by President Obama and Russian President Medvedev in Prague in April 2010. It now requires a two-thirds vote in the Senate to become law. Much of START I was negotiated during President Reagan's second term (to the hard right's consternation—even though communism was collapsing) and concluded by George H.W. Bush in 1991. It made dramatic cuts in American and Russian nuclear arsenals and included on-site inspections for verification. It expired a year ago.

The New START treaty:
- Will further reduce each side's long-range nuclear missiles from about 2,200 to around 1,500.
- Calls for even more rigorous on-site inspections.
- Offers more help to keep Russia's "loose nukes" out of the hands of terrorists.
- Is an important element in improved American-Russian relations, which among other things have led to significant Russian cooperation with sanctions against Iran.

Among those who firmly support expeditious ratification are: The U.S. Joint Chiefs of Staff; the secretaries of defense and state; Senator Richard Lugar (R-Ind), who has worked tirelessly to make Russia's nuclear arsenal more secure; NATO, with its many once-captive Soviet states; former Republican Secretaries of State James Baker and Henry Kissinger; and Reagan/Bush START negotiator Richard Burt.

On the other side—those who wish to delay ratification in the hopes of killing the treaty—are the remnants of the discredited neo-cons who brought us the Iraq War. They include John Bolton, George W. Bush's United Nations ambassador who holds the UN in total contempt; and John Yoo, the Pentagon lawyer responsible for most of the memos justifying the use of torture of terrorist suspects. Then there is Sarah Palin with her nuclear expertise and coterie at FOX News.

Given all of the above, the treaty's ratification should be a slam dunk. But never underestimate the politics of fear.

Senator John Kyl (R-Ariz.), the Republican point-man on arms control, has put the brakes on ratification by claiming there wasn't enough time to consider it in the lame duck session—this despite the fact that to appease Kyl, Obama and the Democrats held eighteen hearings, answered 900 questions, and agreed to spend $85 billion over the next decade to modernize America's existing nuclear stockpile. Given Republican Senate Minority Leader Mitch McConnell's repeated assertion that his number-one priority is to make Obama a one-term president, we can only conclude that Kyl, along with all the other Senate Republicans except Lugar, are acquiescing in the political strategy to block everything that might benefit Obama politically—even if this damages America's national interests. Of course, they will never admit to such a thing, so don't be surprised if they try to concoct a threat which makes the new treaty itself something Americans should fear. Where is Stanley Kubrick now that we really need him?

December 26, 2010

Conservative Politics and Arms Control

Not long after President Ronald Reagan's first Inauguration in 1981, I received a somewhat unusual invitation to lunch. At the time I was covering the State Department for ABC News and was focused on U.S.-Soviet relations, particularly arms control. I say unusual because while reporters often take sources to lunch it was much less common for a reporter to be invited by a source, especially one who was a prominent member of the new administration. So I was pleased but curious to dine with Kenneth Adelman, the newly appointed director of the United States Arms Control and Disarmament Agency.

Adelman, whom I had never met, was intelligent, friendly, and engaging. I will not attempt to reconstruct our conversation with quotes (I have always been amazed when people do that, thirty years after the fact). But I do remember vividly what Adelman's message was. He told me that arms control was basically a sham being foisted upon naïve American liberals by a conniving Soviet Union that could never be trusted. I suggested that high-level meetings including summits, even ostensibly dealing with arms control, at least provided a vehicle for a continuing dialogue between the two nations with the power to blow up the planet. He dismissed that as fanciful, adding that virtually all U.S.-Soviet summits had been worthless and often only resulted in propaganda victories for the Russians.

Adelman wasn't giving me a bum steer. In its first term the Reagan administration pretty much followed that hard-line philosophy. Fortunately, in his second term, Reagan himself rejected that idea—much to the chagrin of neo-conservatives like Ken Adelman—and began a productive, multi-summit dialogue with Soviet leader Mikhail Gorbachev that brought about the end of the Cold War. (I should note that Adelman eventually had his own conversion. While he had strongly encouraged the invasion of Iraq, he became disillusioned with the conduct of that war and in 2008 publicly announced he was voting for Barack Obama.)

All of this came to mind as I watched the Senate debate the new Strategic Arms Reduction Treaty on C-SPAN—the treaty the Senate ratified this past week. It was almost amusing to hear certain Republican senators trot out so many of the thirty-year-old clichés of the Cold War: that this new arms control treaty heavily favored the Russians; that the American negotiators had been unduly sensitive to

Russian demands; that the inspection regimes were not nearly strong enough; that New START would preclude the United States from developing and deploying a new missile defense system.

The problem for these critics was that they had no facts or genuine experts to support their case. Robert Gates, the current secretary of defense (a Republican), the chairman of the Joint Chiefs, and the generals in charge of nuclear weapons all urged the Senate to ratify the new treaty. So did the six living former Republican secretaries of state going back to Henry Kissinger. And not insignificantly, so did former President George H.W. Bush, who had signed the first Strategic Arms Reduction Treaty, the negotiations for which had begun under President Reagan.

Two of the strongest arguments for the treaty are that it will help America help the Russians keep nuclear weapons out of the hands of terrorists. And it will improve Russian cooperation in stifling the Iranian and North Korean nuclear programs. Tough to vote against that. So the opponent's fallback argument became that there was not enough time to deal with such an important issue. Yet the modest seventeen-page START document had been public knowledge for seven months, and the Senate had held more than a dozen hearings on it, answering hundreds of Republican questions.

Then things became silly. A headline in the *Washington Post* referred to the final stages of the New START debate as "The Days of Whine and Poses." In that column, Dana Milbank wrote that Republicans against the treaty really had only one concern: "What they care about is preserving the sanctity of ...Christmas vacation? 'The fact that we're doing this under the cover of Christmas,' complained Sen. Jim DeMint (R-S.C.), 'is something to be outraged about.' Sen. Lindsey Graham (R-S.C.) was outraged. 'Here we are, the week of Christmas, about to pass potentially a treaty,' he protested. And the leader of the group, Sen. Jon Kyl (R-Ariz.) said the Democrat's legislative agenda amounts to 'disrespecting one of the two holiest of holidays for Christians.'"

Apparently missed by the whiners was the irony that even as American troops are slogging through their tenth Christmas fighting wars in Afghanistan and Iraq, Republican senators were complaining about having to work a few days before Christmas to prevent the spread of nuclear weapons to terrorists. Thus, playing the Christmas card was not endearing.

Of course, the real reason the treaty was being opposed was

political—as Senate Minority Leader Mitch McConnell (R-Ky.) made clear in a remarkably candid statement on the Senate floor. The man who had earlier admitted that his "number-one priority" was to see that Obama was not re-elected, declared he was not about to accommodate "some politician's desire to declare a political victory and host a press conference before the first of the year."

"Some politician" is McConnell's derisive description of President Obama—indicating that the mirage of bipartisanship that we witnessed during the surprisingly productive final session of the 111th Congress will likely vanish. When a new Congress convenes early next year it will have a Republican majority in the House beholden to Tea Party budget-slashers, and the Senate minority leader will have six more senators and the filibuster rule to work on his "number one priority" of getting rid of the president. However, given his performance in the weeks since his election defeat, Obama looks to have a new lease on his presidential life. So bearing in mind that the 2012 presidential campaign has already begun, we should brace ourselves for some great political battles. Happy New Year!

April 26, 2007

Remembering Yeltsin and Halberstam

The recent deaths of Boris Yeltsin and David Halberstam set off a stream of memories for me this week. When Halberstam arrived in Paris for the *New York Times* in 1967, he was as famous as any foreign correspondent could be. He had been among the first reporters to challenge the American government's rosy descriptions of the situation in Vietnam. This provoked the anger of the Kennedy White House, which tried unsuccessfully to have him fired. Ultimately, it also earned him a Pulitzer Prize.

In 1967, I was an eager young correspondent in Paris—very much in awe of the new *New York Times* man. On those occasions when we were both covering the same story, he was always amiable. I don't recall any memorable utterances on his part, and certainly not mine. But his very presence there in Paris was validation for me that I had chosen the right career and that France, then led by the haughty and often anti-American Charles de Gaulle, was a very good place for a reporter to be.

"In 1972 Halberstam published his best known book, *The Best and the Brightest*. This account of the folly and tragedy of the Vietnam War told of how the advisers of Presidents Kennedy and Johnson, ostensibly the ablest group ever to serve in the American government, led the country into what Halberstam called, "the greatest American tragedy since the Civil War." The book helped to crystallize the antiwar movement of the day. And in substance, I find its parallels to the current war in Iraq quite remarkable.

Two decades after Paris, I was working regularly in the Soviet Union. As Boris Yeltsin appeared likely to become the first democratically-elected president of Russia, I spent about three weeks in Yeltsin's home region in the Ural Mountains, trying to get a sense of the man. In his early years, Yeltsin had grown up dirt poor and barefoot in western Siberia. I found lots of friends who praised him and some enemies who didn't. And one day I even had tea with his mother. She was a woman in her eighties who lived alone in a small and very modest two room apartment. Her chipped tea cups were kept in a small china cabinet, which displayed a colored photo of her famous son. It was actually an unframed cover of *Newsweek* magazine. In a country where Communist leaders and their families inevitably lived like the Czars they had overthrown, this told me that Yeltsin was not your average communist. That would later be demonstrated as he presided over the dissolution of the Soviet Union and the demise of the Communist Party. Yeltsin was no saint, but without him and his former colleague and rival Mikhail Gorbachev, the Cold War might still be with us.

Yeltsin and Halberstam had little or nothing in common. Yet to me, they demonstrate that regardless of one's economic or political circumstances, strong individuals willing to break with the pack and challenge conventional wisdom can truly make a difference—even to the point of changing the world.

April 18, 2010

Life Under Totalitarian Rule

There was a time, not so long ago, when millions of people died and hundreds of millions lived under cruel, repressive regimes; where saying anything against the authorities, even in your own bedroom, could land you in prison or worse; where you could trust no one, as everyone around you was a potential informant; where even if you were completely apolitical you knew there was a good chance that every mundane detail of your life was being secretly recorded and meticulously inscribed in the infinite files of the secret police, likely to be used against you in some coercive way; where personal privacy was non-existent and freedom to travel to the next town, much less another state or country, was firmly controlled; and where everything from what you read to where you worked was dictated by the state. We forget, much too easily, that such was the way of life during much of the twentieth century for many of the people on this planet.

I have recently been absorbed by stories of life under totalitarianism, told by two friends of mine who have firsthand knowledge on the subject.

Middlebury College history professor Michael Kraus, who was born in then-Czechoslovakia, has been digging through the Cold War era archives of the Czech secret police to find his and his family's dossiers. There were no great surprises for him, but in a recent lecture Kraus detailed and analyzed the pervasive nature of the intrusion of state security organizations into the everyday lives of ordinary Czech citizens. In describing the activities of the secret police, Kraus used the phrase "banality of evil"—part of the title of a 1963 book on the Jerusalem trial of the infamous Nazi mass murderer Adolf Eichmann.

Kati Marton, who was born in Hungary and was once a correspondent for ABC News, has written a powerful new memoir about her parents titled *Enemies of the People*. Having survived the Nazi occupation of Hungary, Marton's father Endre was, by the 1950s, the Budapest correspondent for the Associated Press, and her mother Ilona wrote for United Press. For their knowledge and their courage, the Martons became famous for their unique perspective in reporting from behind the Iron Curtain. But of course, the Hungarian secret police would get their revenge. In 1955, both Endre and Ilona were arrested and imprisoned, leaving toddlers Kati and her sister Julia as virtual orphans for a time. The family was eventually reunited and ended up in Washington D.C., but it's a story with many unexpected twists and turns.

Kati was able to tell it in such detail because years after the fall of Communism, she finally persuaded the Hungarians to open their file on the Martons, which they told her was "one of our biggest." She describes the moment in the old secret police headquarters in Budapest: "I am terrified and eager to plunge into a growing mountain of manila files that clerks in white coats are wheeling in on shopping carts." With this trove she constructed a page-turning family history that has all the elements of a Cold War spy novel. But that's not its major significance. As she writes near the end of the book, "...this is not my story. A large segment of humanity lived...this way. It is important that we know this, before we move on, before it is forgotten."

Unfortunately, it can be argued that in this country today, the story of much of humanity's recent past has evidently been forgotten. In the incendiary rhetoric of the Tea Party, Republicans in Congress, FOX News, and talk radio, President Barack Obama is almost daily demonized. He is called a "radical," "socialist," and "totalitarian," by those who apparently know neither the meaning nor the history of those words. Former Republican House Leader Newt Gingrich, who, with a PhD in history should know better, recently called Obama "the most radical president in American history." Liz Cheney, the former vice-president's daughter and possible Virginia Senate candidate, caricatured Obama's foreign policy as "apologize for America, abandon our allies, and appease our enemies." In her critique of the latest arms control treaty that Obama signed with Russia, Sarah Palin (famous for her expertise on all things Russian because she can see it from Alaska) said, "No administration in American history would, I think, ever have considered such a step."

My thanks to Norman Ornstein, a noted congressional expert and respected scholar at the conservative American Enterprise Institute, for gathering the above paragraph's quotes—and then in a column this past week in the *Washington Post*, proceeding to shoot them down. Ornstein writes, "To one outside the partisan political wars, charges of radicalism, socialism, retreat and surrender are, frankly, bizarre." In examining the new health care legislation, Ornstein points out that it contains no public option; that the individual mandate (the obligation of everyone to buy health insurance) was an idea that came from the Heritage Foundation (another conservative think tank) which provided the basis for the Massachusetts health plan, signed into law and bragged about until recently by former Governor Mitt Romney. And Ornstein adds that many of the other elements of the new federal law were in a 1994 plan proposed by such "radical" Republicans as Charles Grassley and Bob Dole.

In foreign policy, Ornstein notes that the new nuclear treaty with the Russians has been endorsed by Indiana Senator Richard Lugar, the GOP's resident expert on arms control. And that Obama's larger foreign policy has the seal of approval of James Baker (Ronald Reagan's chief of staff and George Bush-the-father's secretary of state). Ornstein is not alone in his observations. The conservative *New York Times* columnist David Brooks has repeatedly written that while he often disagrees with Obama, he sees him as a pragmatist, not a socialist, and most certainly not a totalitarian.

Is it, therefore, too much to ask that at least a few leaders of the so-called loyal opposition party would desist from using pejorative adjectives about the president that have zero relationship to historical or any other kind of fact? Apparently so.

1974, Cairo, Egypt
Author with Peter Jennings, Egyptian President Anwar Sadat, and Elmer
Lower, then President of ABC News

1968, Tel Aviv
Interview with Golda Meir for ABC's Issues and Answers

1984, Washington D.C.
Waiting to board plane used to transport Secretaries of State

1984, Washington D.C.
Aboard plane with former Secretary of State George Shultz

1982, Washington D.C.
A holiday photo with the Reagans at the White House

1995, Washington D.C.
With former President Bill Clinton at a White House movie screening

1991, Gobi Desert, Outer Mongolia
With former Secretary of State James Baker

1990, London, England
Interview with Margaret Thatcher for ABC World News Tonight

1985, London, England
Reporting for ABC World News Tonight on the promenade across from the
Houses of Parliament and Westminster Abbey

1985, Dresden, Germany

1986, Cairo, Egypt
Visiting the pyramids

1986, Jerusalem
Reporting in front of the Israeli Knesset for ABC World News Tonight

1987, Jerusalem

1984, Washington D.C. State Department balcony
Site of stand-up reports from the State Department for ABC News

And Back

Part II

AND BACK: Commentary on the United States

I came back to America—once again to Washington as diplomatic correspondent—in 1992. But it was a different world from the one I had left eight years earlier. The Cold War was over. The Gulf War of 1990–91, on which I had reported from Saudi Arabia, had put major stresses on newsroom budgets. Most news organizations were starting to significantly reduce their foreign coverage. This was rationalized by the argument that Americans weren't really interested in international news. Maybe. Maybe not. But it was apparent that the future didn't look particularly promising for us old war horses. So early on I decided that when my contract was up in 1995, I would retire early and focus on my family and my health—parts of my life I had neglected for much of three decades.

As I said goodbye to ABC News in the spring of 1995, my good friend Marvin Kalb invited me to become a fellow at the Kennedy School of Government at Harvard where he had created the unique Joan Shorenstein Center on the Press, Politics and Public Policy. I enjoyed the academic atmosphere and in the spring of '96 Harvard published my study of the potential consequences of live television coverage of war. After that, we headed for the Green Mountains.

My first goals in Vermont were to unwind and to be a good stay-at-home husband/dad with plenty of time for reading, skiing, and tennis. I was grateful not to be constantly rushing to airports, but my intellectual curiosity hadn't diminished. I soon wanted to fill in the black holes in my knowledge of American history. In doing so, I was surprised to learn that for nearly a century the South essentially never came to terms with the actual outcome of the Civil War. I was also shocked to discover just how frequently throughout the country's history presidents, Congress, and the Supreme Court suppressed constitutionally guaranteed civil liberties in times of war.

Vermont is far enough away from the country's big power centers to escape their worst aspects, but close enough not to feel isolated. It provided the perfect perch for a slightly detached view of America. In much of my work since I came back, I've tried to apply history's lessons and my experience as a foreign correspondent to my analyses of the American scene. Politics and political leadership fascinate me and no country is more diverse in its range of characters than this one. The aftermath of the tragedy of 9/11 and the wars in Iraq and Afghanistan presented an excess of material. The 2008 presidential campaign and the election of the country's first African American president were historic. And when he was running for president, who could ignore former Vermont Governor Howard Dean?

But America is not all about politics. And as I did overseas, I sought to convey part of the texture of this country with commentary on elements of its culture: religious fundamentalism, the power of drug companies, professional sports, the social impact of the crash of '08, and the death of gun control. This section concludes with a speech I gave to the Vermont Human Rights Commission just a few weeks before the 2008 election on race in American politics and the on-going presidential campaign. It is still valid on the past and the then-present. My expressed hopes for the immediate future may have been overly optimistic.

6

Political Leaders & Politics

January 25, 2004

Howard Dean's Run for President

I confess. I am disappointed. I allowed myself to begin musing about how great it would be if Howard Dean were president. I was enjoying the phone calls and e-mail I was getting from friends around the country, wanting to talk about our former governor. It was refreshing to have Vermont be seen by the rest of the country as something more than skiing, cows, and fall foliage. We were suddenly on the cutting edge of twenty-first century politics, where for the first time in history the Internet was playing a major role in presidential campaigns and "our guy" made it so. Virtually everyone in the state seemed to be following the campaign during the last few months. As nearly as I could tell from countless conversations with friends and total strangers, most Vermonters hoped and recently expected that Dean would win. So I know I am not the only one who is disappointed.

If you're a political junkie as I am, you are probably sated with all the Iowa post-mortems as to why Dean came in a bad third where he once had a big lead, had the most money, supposedly the best organization, and where most of the voters are liberal and anti-war. So what next?

The New Hampshire primary is only two days away. It is of course possible that Dean will have a strong rebound there. New Hampshire victories after Iowa losses are fairly common. Again he has a strong organization and lots of money. But that scenery-chewing performance of his on Iowa's election night would have raised questions in some minds in New Hampshire and elsewhere about his suitability for the presidency. And that, in my view, is the most significant message out of Iowa. Namely, most Democratic voters do not believe Howard Dean can beat George W. Bush, and beating Bush is their number one priority.

As has been noted before, George W. Bush promised that he was going to change the political climate in Washington and that may be the only promise he has kept. As the most conservative president in recent memory, Bush is also the most polarizing and partisan, which has made the political climate worse than at any time in the forty-odd years that I have been covering politics in this country.

That's why Dean caught on in the first place. As a strong opponent of the war in Iraq and the budget-busting tax cuts, at one time he appeared to be the only Democrat who was prepared to confront

Bush head on. As one pundit put it, the Doctor gave the party a much needed "backbone transplant."

But the more successful he was, in the polls and in raising money, and the more likely it seemed that he could win the nomination, the more nervous traditional Democrats became. They may agree with Dean's policies and appreciate that he shook the party up. But after 9/11 and its aftermath, they want the man who goes up against Bush to have credible national security credentials. John Kerry and Wesley Clark have such credentials. John Edwards of North Carolina does not, but as a smooth-talking southerner, apparently without a bimbo problem, he still looked more electable to Iowans than our feisty former governor. All of which leads me to conclude, rather sadly, that whether this week in New Hampshire, or next month in South Carolina or some other place, the often quixotic Dean campaign will come to an unhappy end—for the candidate, and for those of us who, for a time at least, got caught up in the dream.

May 29, 2007

George W. Bush: A Legend in His Own Mind

President George W. Bush sees himself in the image of the great men of history who made decisions that went against the public opinion of their day, but were in the long-term best interests of their respective countries.

This is the thrust of a provocative commentary by Arnaud de Borchgrave, now a United Press International editor at large, who for many years was the chief foreign correspondent for *Newsweek* magazine. Among the sources he cites for his column, although he does not quote them directly, are Mike McConnell, the current director of national intelligence, and John Negroponte, who used to have the spymaster's job and is now deputy secretary of state.

De Borchgrave begins his column with an anecdote about a bet the president and his adviser Karl Rove made on who would read the most books in a year. Rove won—117 to 104—but Bush demanded a recount based on words and edged out Rove by less than 2 percent. Virtually all of the books they read were about history or biographies of famous American and world leaders. Bush apparently identifies with men such as Washington, Lincoln, Truman, Reagan, and Winston Churchill, writes de Borchgrave, "all men of courage who did what was right when it was most difficult."

According to de Borchgrave and his sources, "Mr. Bush sees his decision to invade Iraq in the same historical league" as Truman's decisions to use the atomic bomb to end the war with Japan, to recognize Israel in the face of strong opposition from the State Department and to go to war in Korea; and Ronald Reagan's defeat of the Soviet Union. As for the comparison with Lincoln, de Borchgrave writes that Bush showed a recent visitor a portrait of Lincoln as a way to talk about the extremely difficult decision to go to war to free the slaves, implying that he (Bush) "had done something comparable in his decision to free twenty-six million Iraqi slaves from Saddam Hussein's tyranny."

In the case of Churchill, whose warnings throughout the 1930s about the growing threat to Britain and Europe posed by Adolf Hitler and Nazi Germany were ignored, Bush sees a personal parallel. "In Bush's perspective," says de Borchgrave, "the mullah's Iran, the Iraq insurgency, Al Qaeda, transnational terrorism, all add up to a moral danger for Western civilization."

To those who would like to put Bush's vision of himself into historical perspective, I would recommend the new book, *Presidential Courage—Brave Leaders and How They Changed America 1789–1989* by Michael Beschloss, the respected presidential historian. Beschloss writes in his preface, "This book shows how American presidents have, at crucial moments, made courageous decisions for the national interest although they knew they might be jeopardizing their careers."

As one reads these fascinating stories, the fundamental flaw in Bush's comparisons of himself to some of history's great leaders soon becomes obvious. The courage each president was able to summon up was not so much to resist the pressures of public opinion. Rather it was more often to defeat the doubts and inner weaknesses each president had within himself.

These are some examples:
- Even as John F. Kennedy moved slowly toward proposing much-needed civil rights legislation, he often denigrated Martin Luther King, Jr. He initially shied away from school integration confrontations in Mississippi and Alabama. And with an eye to his re-election in 1964, he went out of his way to court political favor with southern white segregationists while doing and saying things that certainly could be considered racist. However, when it became evident that racial issues in both the South and the North could explode in the summer of 1963, JFK said to his brother Robert, "If we're going to go down, let's go down on a matter of principle." With that, Kennedy did finally propose major civil rights legislation—although his assassination would mean that southerner Lyndon Johnson, demonstrating his own courage, would ultimately have to pay the political price attached to getting the new Civil Rights and Voting Rights acts passed by Congress.
- Harry Truman agonized over whether to recognize Israel, swinging back and forth many times. It's true that Secretary of State George Marshall opposed giving America's blessing to the new Jewish state. But in finally deciding to make the United States the first country to grant Israel recognition, Truman mostly had to combat and suppress the lifelong anti-Semitic feelings he harbored within himself—not to mention the even stronger feelings held by his wife Bess. More than any other single person, a Jewish American named Eddie Jacobson, who had once been his business partner, made Truman's transformation possible.
- Abraham Lincoln had not always supported abolition. Initially, he had actually tried to entice Southern states back into the Union

by promising slavery could continue where it already existed. And even after he had issued the Emancipation Proclamation, he was greatly tempted by peace feelers from some Southerners during the last year of the Civil War, that they could accept a return to the Union—but not if that meant giving up slavery. Despite that, and in the face of a very possible electoral defeat in 1864, Lincoln ultimately decided that peace could be truly achieved only through a restoration of the Union—and the abolition of slavery throughout that Union.

- Ronald Reagan is now praised as a hero by the hard right for his challenging of the "evil" Soviet Empire. But as Beschloss tells us, much of Reagan's success with Mikhail Gorbachev came when he ignored the advice of those hardliners as he tried to forge a close personal relationship with the Soviet leader and to seek massive nuclear weapons reduction—something urged by his wife Nancy and then-Secretary of State George Shultz. Clearly the American people were not against better relations with Moscow. The strongest opponents to Reagan's efforts with Gorbachev were people in his own cabinet such as William Casey, his CIA director and Caspar Weinberger, his secretary of defense. As Beschloss puts it, "Like the most effective American presidents, Reagan ultimately proved he was not the captive of his political base, but its leader."
- With Churchill, no one would question his courage. But in the new book, *Those Troublesome Young Men* by Lynne Olson, we learn that Churchill too, could be torn between personal ambitions and loyalty to his country. While he had been a forceful government critic before the war, once World War II began and he was made first lord of the admiralty, he valued this post so greatly that he was unwilling to publicly criticize what continued to be the appeasement policies of Prime Minister Neville Chamberlain. It was, in fact, the political courage of a group of young, backbench conservative members of Parliament, prepared to risk their careers by ousting Chamberlain, who cleared the way for Churchill to brilliantly lead Britain through the darkest days of the war to victory five years later.

In none of these stories of the triumph of personal courage over character weaknesses and political ambitions do I see the likes of George W. Bush. Bush shows no evidence of self-doubt. And rather than paying a political price for launching an unnecessary and now unpopular war, Bush and his pal Rove continually sought to exploit that war for political gain as was evident in the three federal elections that followed 9/11. With no further elections to face himself, Bush is not agonizing over what he should now be doing in Iraq. Instead, he is deluding himself, and the country, with the notion that somehow a "victory" can still be achieved. What seems apparent is that "the decider," as he calls himself, has decided to simply run out the clock and leave the problem to his successor. That is not an act of political courage.

Through hundreds of history books, we now know much about men like Washington, Lincoln, Roosevelt, Truman, Kennedy, Reagan, and Churchill. They all had their flaws, to be sure. But "knowing" these men as we do now, it is my firm conviction that we can confidently say that George W. Bush is not one of them.

November 5, 2004

Moral Values of Kerry Supporters

If it is true that President Bush was re-elected on the strength of "moral values," what does that say about the moral values of the 48 percent of the people who voted for John Kerry?

My old friend, I'll call him John, is a Christian. He goes to church regularly, and contributes to the church and to a number of local, national, and international charities.

John is honest in all his dealings and he pays his taxes without complaining. He is moderate in his personal habits. He loves his family, is faithful to his wife, and strongly supportive of his children. He is kind to his relatives, cares about his community, and doesn't kick his dog.

John is strongly opposed to discrimination on the basis of race, religion, age, gender, or sexual orientation. John does not support gay marriage. But he believes that people who establish themselves as a couple should have equal protection under the law—that they should have things like hospital visiting rights and a claim to the partner's health insurance and pensions. That's why he supported Vermont's Civil Unions Bill.

John is uncomfortable with late-term abortions but thinks banning such procedures without regard to the woman's health is wrong. John thinks a woman and her doctor should be able to determine if a pregnancy should be terminated—not the state. John wonders about those who are so uncompromising in their desire to preserve life in the womb but have no apparent interest in what happens to the infant after it is born. He has what may be a different moral value from those who voted for "moral reasons" last Tuesday. John believes that a society as heavily laden with riches as this one ought to be willing to shoulder responsibilities to help those in need of help. He supports government programs that do this and thinks this country should be able to provide adequate health care for all of its citizens. And as someone in the upper-middle class, he is willing to pay the taxes to accomplish this.

John strongly believes that it is important for this country's political leaders, especially its president, to tell the truth. He was unhappy when former President Clinton lied about his relationship with a White House intern and would have supported a public censure of this behavior. But John also believes that President Bush seriously misled the country on the reasons for invading Iraq. And he considers the Bush deceit, because of its far-reaching consequences, of greater magnitude than Clinton's.

Finally, John believes in God—and in this country—and in what Abraham Lincoln said as the Civil War began: that we should not expect that God is on our side, but pray that we are on His. In the wake of the election, John wonders, as do I, why many of those who voted for George W. Bush seem to think that John, and millions like him, have no moral values.

May 15, 2005

Distorting Yalta, Demeaning Roosevelt

American presidential historians, almost without exception, rate Franklin Delano Roosevelt among the top three or four presidents in the history of the country.

But hard-line conservatives have always bristled at that. For them, Roosevelt was "a traitor to his class." This group, which historically opposed such things as income tax, child labor laws, and trade unions, considered the New Deal and Social Security to be borderline communism.

In their efforts to discredit his presidency, one of their customary points of attack has been the Yalta conference of 1945 when Roosevelt met with British Prime Minister Winston Churchill and Soviet leader Joseph Stalin to plan post-war strategy.

Hardliners have consistently accused Roosevelt of giving his blessings to Soviet domination of Eastern Europe during that conference. Eight days ago, President George W. Bush, in an extraordinary speech in Riga, Latvia, publicly joined the ranks of those who would demean the legacy of FDR.

In this speech Bush said, "The agreement at Yalta followed in the unjust tradition of Munich and the Molotov-Ribbentrop pact." Here Bush is linking the agreement at Yalta with Munich (where in 1938 Europe's leaders, including the British, caved in to Hitler's territorial demands) and the Molotov-Ribbentrop pact (the secret 1939 deal reached between Hitler and Stalin to divvy up Europe). That is an odious and totally inaccurate comparison. But Bush went on: "Yet this attempt to sacrifice freedom for the sake of stability left a continent divided and unstable. The captivity of millions in Central and Eastern Europe will be regarded as one of the greatest wrongs of history." He concluded, "We will not repeat the mistakes of other generations, appeasing or excusing tyranny and sacrificing freedom in the vain pursuit of stability."

Twenty years ago as the 40th anniversary of World War II was approaching, I was assigned to do a series of lengthy reports for ABC News on major events of the final days of the war. One such report was on Yalta.

I started my account from Yalta by noting, "There are almost as many myths about Yalta as there are realities." To sort out what was myth and what was reality, I read much of the available historical material. I then went to the Crimea to see the Czar's palaces where the meetings were held. And I interviewed people in Washington, London, and Moscow who had directly participated in the conference.

One of those I talked to at length was Lord Gladwyn, who had been one of Churchill's political aides at Yalta and in 1985 was a Liberal member of the British House of Lords. One of the first things he said to me was, "There's a great deal of nonsense about Yalta, to the effect that Europe was sold down the river and divided into two parts and all that. It was divided into two parts because Hitler declared war and the Russians defeated Hitler."

Although the Russians by no means defeated Hitler by themselves, in fact, by the time of the Yalta conference in February 1945, Soviet troops had pushed the Nazis back into Germany, occupying most of Eastern Europe in the process. Meanwhile the American and British forces had barely crossed the Rhine far to the west.

Going into the meeting, Roosevelt and Churchill had several objectives but two were of utmost importance. First: they needed a firm agreement from Stalin that the Soviet Union would remain at war with Germany until Hitler was completely defeated. Second: even after peace in Europe, the United States particularly wanted Stalin to continue fighting in the war against the Japanese. (At the time, the top-secret atom bomb had not been tested and a bloody battle to defeat Japan was anticipated.)

Kathleen Harriman, the daughter of Averell Harriman, American's wartime ambassador to Moscow, was at Yalta as a junior advisor to Roosevelt. She recalled how happy the American military members of the delegation were when Stalin promised to keep his country in both the European and Asian theaters of the war.

Harriman told me, "I remember Admiral King [Fleet Admiral Ernest J. King, the highest ranking American military officer at Yalta] came out of the military conference and he said, 'this is going to save two million Americans.'"

While there was a secret pact giving the Soviets control of some islands claimed by Japan, the only territorial deal concerning Europe was that Germany would be carved up between East and West. It was otherwise understood that the other countries would have free elections. The Soviets already occupied Poland and had installed a puppet regime in Warsaw. Stalin actually agreed to allow some members of the Polish government-in-exile into that government and to hold free elections. But he reneged on both those promises.

And if you still don't believe me that Yalta wasn't a giveaway, would you believe President Ronald Reagan? This is what he said about Yalta in 1984: "Let me state emphatically, we reject any inter-pretation of the Yalta agreement that suggests American consent for the division of Europe into spheres of influence. On the contrary, we see that agreement as a pledge by the three great powers to restore full independence, and to allow free and democratic elections in all countries liberated from the Nazis after World War II."

A final thought. The Bush doctrine of "freedom and democracy for all" sounds good from a podium. But Iraq is a good example of the costs when such words are put into deeds. To have tried to impose such a doctrine in Eastern Europe in 1945 would almost certainly have meant war with the Soviets. No president of either party—for the next half century—considered that a viable option.

November 13, 2005

On History's Most Powerful Vice President

There was a portrait of Winston Churchill directly behind the desk of I. Lewis "Scooter" Libby, Vice President Dick Cheney's former chief of staff. As Scooter was indicted on five counts of perjury and obstruction of justice in the CIA identity leak case, he is no longer there in the Old Executive Office Building right next to the White House. But two months after 9/11, Libby pointed to the portrait and told *Newsweek* editor Evan Thomas that Churchill was his hero. According to Thomas' account of their conversation, Libby said, "He felt an enormous spiritual kinship with the small band of men around Churchill who warned in the 1930s about the gathering Nazi storm, who were ignored and shunned but then vindicated at England's finest hour. Libby compared Cheney to Churchill." To paraphrase Lloyd Benson when he put down Dan Quayle for comparing himself to John F. Kennedy in the vice presidential debate of 1988, I know quite a bit about Winston Churchill—and Dick Cheney is no Churchill.

As a young man, Churchill was so eager to see military service that he traveled to India by train and boat for five weeks, at his own expense, to get to the fighting front. It was in his account of the battle he joined near the Afghan border that Churchill coined the phrase quoted by nearly every young war reporter since (including this one), "Nothing in life is so exhilarating as to be shot at without result." After he was dismissed from his cabinet post in 1915 as a result of the fiasco in the Dardanelles, Churchill, at forty, asked for a military commission and went to Belgium, where he served six months in the trenches with front line British troops.

When the United States was at war in Vietnam in the early '60s, Cheney received four student draft deferments. When they ran out, he got married. When the war heated up in 1965, the Selective Service commission decided childless, married men could be drafted. Cheney's wife Lynne became pregnant. While she was still in her first trimester, Cheney applied for and received a new exemption for being married with a family. The child was born exactly nine months and two days after the rules had been changed to include married men without children.

In 1989 when Cheney appeared at Senate hearings to be confirmed as President George Bush the elder's secretary of defense, he was asked why he had failed to serve in the military. Cheney answered that he "would have obviously been happy to serve had I been called."

While apparently no one challenged him, seeking five deferments doesn't exactly imply being "happy" to serve. Later that year, with considerably more frankness, Cheney told the *Washington Post*, "I had other priorities in the '60s than military service."

And what priorities! While a political science graduate student in 1968, Cheney won a congressional scholarship with Bill Steiger, a Republican from Wisconsin. According to the *New Yorker* magazine, "One of Cheney's first assignments was to visit college campuses where anti-war protestors were disrupting classes." He was, in effect, spying for his congressman and a few others who were trying to make a case for cutting off federal funding to campuses where violent protests had broken out. In the 1980s, Cheney was himself elected to the House where his record included the following votes: against abortion rights; against the Equal Rights Amendment; against the funding of Head Start and the creation of the Department of Education; against the imposition of sanctions against the apartheid regime in South Africa; against the ban on armor-piercing bullets, the so-called cop killers; against the ban on plastic guns that could escape detection in airport security systems (one of only four members against a ban even the National Rifle Association did not oppose); against refunding of the Clean Water Act; and against legislation to require oil and chemical industries to make public records of emissions known to have caused cancer, birth defects, and other chronic diseases.

As defense secretary, Cheney's most significant achievement was to lay the groundwork for the "privatization" of the military—what could also be called the outsourcing of planning and providing support for military operations abroad, including food preparation, laundry service, and latrine duty. The company that was paid nearly ten million dollars to do a study on the feasibility of such operations, and then given a five-year contract to perform the role it was paid to define, was Halliburton.

A great deal has been written about Halliburton—the world's largest oil and gas services company and now the biggest private contractor for American forces—of which Cheney was CEO before becoming vice president. The definitive article, by Jane Mayer, appeared in the *New Yorker* magazine a year and a half ago. These are just a few of the highlights:

- Cheney earned $44 million during his tenure at Halliburton.
- Although he claims to have "severed all my ties with the company," he gets deferred compensation of about $150,000 per year

and has stock options worth $18 million.

- Halliburton's 2002 annual report describes counter-terrorism as offering "growth opportunities."
- In 2003 the company got a non-competitive contract for up to $7 billion to rebuild Iraq's oil operation in a decision the *New York Times* reported was authorized at the "highest levels of the administration."
- Private companies are insulated from direct congressional oversight and government ethics rules.
- It's too easy to go to war when you can hire people to do it. Without private contractors there would be nearly three times as many soldiers in Iraq, which would make it far harder to obtain and keep congressional and public support.

I am not suggesting that Cheney strongly advocated the invasion of Iraq simply to line the pockets of his many business friends, although that has certainly been a consequence of the war. But it can be argued that Cheney was motivated by more than terrorism and weapons of mass destruction. Former Secretary of the Treasury Paul O'Neill has charged that Cheney agitated for intervention in Iraq well before the terrorist attacks on 9/11. It is also a fact that before the invasion, neo-conservatives with Cheney-ties were pushing the notion that control of Iraqi oil would make it possible to marginalize OPEC. At the time of the invasion, Cheney himself was quoted as saying that Iraq would be producing three million barrels of oil a day by the end of that year. (It's still fewer than two million, the pre-war level.)

Could it be that in Cheney's secret meetings with energy industry executives to formulate a new Bush energy policy (well before 9/11), taking over Iraq's oil was considered a strategic option? We don't know. But we do know the White House went to the Supreme Court to keep those discussions secret.

And to top it off, Cheney has become, as the *Washington Post* said an editorial, "Mr. Torture." Ninety senators, led by Republican John McCain, who knows a lot about what it's like to be tortured as a prisoner of war, want this country to accept international norms in its treatment of prisoners. But Cheney is fighting tenaciously to exempt the CIA from such rules. As he put it in 2001 on *Meet The Press*, the government might have to go to "the dark side" adding, "It's going to be vital for us to use any means at our disposal." Cheney's record may give you the chills. But it will never be confused with being Churchillian.

April 22, 2007

Where's the Outrage—Vermont?

"Am I the only guy in this country who's fed up with what's happening? Where the hell is our outrage? We should be screaming bloody murder. We've got a gang of clueless bozos steering our ship of state right over a cliff, we've got corporate gangsters stealing us blind, and we can't even clean up after a hurricane much less build a hybrid car. But instead of getting mad, everyone sits around and nods their heads when the politicians say, 'Stay the course.' Stay the course? You've got to be kidding. This is America, not the damned Titanic."

So writes Lee Iacocca, who was head of the Chrysler Corporation in the 1980s when he was not only saving his company from bankruptcy but appearing in its TV commercials. At the time, he was the most famous CEO in America, if not the world. That quote is just a tiny taste of his new book, *Where Have All the Leaders Gone?* It is a nonpartisan screed, as Iacocca is an equal opportunity critic—the Bush administration, the Congress, corporate America, and the news media are all targets of his outrage.

Another sample: "I hardly recognize this country anymore. The president of the United States is given a free pass to ignore the Constitution, tap our phones and lead us to war on a pack of lies. Congress responds to record deficits by passing huge tax cuts for the wealthy (thanks, but I don't need it). The most famous business leaders are not the innovators but the guys in handcuffs. And while we're fiddling in Iraq, the Middle East is burning and nobody seems to know what to do. And the press is waving pom-poms instead of asking hard questions...I've had enough. How about you?"

Iacocca no longer carries the clout he once did. I suspect very few people in their twenties or thirties have ever heard of him. Still, his new offering was given prominence among new arrivals at a national chain bookstore I visited this past week. And even if Iacocca no longer has the power to influence public opinion, I think his new book is noteworthy because his outrage may well be symptomatic of the feelings we saw in the results of the November elections, and which may be continuing to grow.

The strongest indication of the depth of public anger over the country's leadership would be a successful grassroots movement resulting in the impeachment of the president. I have to confess that I have never taken such calls very seriously, as they seemed to be coming only from the extreme fringe of the political spectrum and therefore had zero possibility to succeed. I still believe the chances that President George W. Bush will be impeached are extremely slim to none. But I no longer dismiss those calling for impeachment as "wing-nuts." In fact, they appear to represent the growing outrage among concerned citizens for the way America is being led. And it would seem that more than a few Vermonters are in the vanguard of this movement.

This past week, leaders of the Impeach George W. Bush movement met with senior Democrats of the Vermont legislature in Montpelier to once again press for a resolution to censure the president. They claim their mandate from the nearly forty Vermont towns that voted for an impeachment resolution during the last Town Meeting Day. In a recent article in the newsweekly *Seven Days*, columnist Peter Freyne quotes state Senate leader Peter Shumlin in a meeting of the Vermont Democratic State Committee, "The president deserves to have impeachment hearings. He lied about the war, lied about why he was going there, lied about 9/11 and Iraqis involvement, lied at every level. He made America the laughing stock of the world." Pretty strong stuff, and evidently most Democrats at the meeting agreed and voted overwhelmingly for an impeachment resolution.

In his column headlined, "Vermont's Impeachment Cry Gets National Attention," Freyne also noted that Pulitzer Prize-winning cartoonist Garry Trudeau had taken his *Doonesbury* strip to Vermont, where his intrepid reporter Roland Hedley posed the questions, "Who are these rebels? What drives them to give comfort to America's enemies by tearing down her commander in chief?" Thus readers of the 1,400 American newspapers that carry *Doonesbury* have been made aware of the Vermont impeachment movement. What Trudeau seems to be telling his readers in his amusing but ironic way is that at first glance this impeachment business may seem silly, but maybe it isn't.

Senate Leader Shumlin and House Speaker Gaye Symington don't think it's silly, but neither do they want to get trapped into forcing the issue in Montpelier. The speaker claims the House doesn't have the time to handle this issue, and Shumlin wants to pass it off to Vermont's congressional delegation. His message last week was, let Messrs. Leahy, Sanders, and Welch deal with this hot potato. My guess is this trio will not welcome that prospect, although not because they doubt Bush has committed impeachable offenses. If Bill Clinton could be impeached for lying about his sex life, how much more impeachable is a president who lied about the reasons for embarking on a disastrous war—not to mention a host of other possible violations of the Constitution?

But—and this is the real issue for Democrats in whatever legislatures they may be serving—do they want to press for impeachment and so forego all else in their current legislative sessions? Because that is what would happen. Republicans will unite, dig in their heels, and fight ferociously to head off any impeachment proceedings. And in Washington they probably have enough votes to prevent a conviction. In the meantime, the country would become even more bitterly divided, and much other legislative work, including the effort to try to end the war in Iraq, would be stymied.

So, while I think it is all to the good that growing numbers of Americans are so outraged by the performance of the Bush administration that they would like to see the president stand trial in the Senate, the political price the whole country would have to pay to accomplish that end is too high. Better to channel all that outrage into making sure profound political change is achieved in 2008. As for Bush, I predict future historians will do the job of exposing his presidency for what is: the worst in the last hundred years and, very likely, in the history of the Republic.

September 7, 2008

Pitch for a Made-for-TV Movie

Synopsis: just two months after his inauguration, the president collapses during a prime-time Oval Office news conference. All hell breaks loose. There are calls by White House aides to respect the president's privacy, but no network is going to go off the air under such circumstances, so the frantic scenes around his desk are transmitted instantly around the world. Medical people arrive quickly, but as he is wheeled out on a stretcher the president is evidently comatose. He is pronounced dead on arrival at George Washington Hospital.

The vice president (perhaps played by Sally Field) is a former mayor of a small town and for less than two years, the governor of a small state. She is energetic and vivacious and believed to have played a major role in the president's election. In the confusion around the president's seizure, we see her looking stunned, being hurried away by Secret Service agents and her top aide. When we next see her, several hours have passed since the president's death and she has been sworn in. She seems apprehensive as she is briefed by her national security adviser (perhaps played by Fred Thompson) and the White House chief of staff. Her full National Security Council, including the CIA, NSA and national intelligence directors, the Joint Chiefs of Staff, the secretaries of state and defense, plus their aides, are gathering for a meeting with her in the Cabinet Room.

The NSC adviser brings her up to date:

- Since the president's death, the NSA and the CIA have been swamped with signals indicating a new Al Qaeda terrorist threat may be in the making. The so-called "chatter" is at a higher level than at any time since 9/11.
- The Russians have mobilized large forces near the border with Ukraine.
- In Iraq, fighting has broken out on major fronts between Shiites and Sunnis, and the Kurds may be about to declare their independence.
- Communications have come from Jerusalem that Israel has decided to take out Iran's nuclear sites and that the attack could come at any time.
- He tells her that analysts for each of these areas believe that these crises are being deliberately provoked as a test of the new American leadership. He also tells her that the heads of every European

country and the UN secretary general have been calling frantically to speak to her as soon as possible. He suggests she take no such calls for now. They go into the Cabinet Room.

Her national security team is initially very deferential. But when it comes to drawing up a strategy for dealing with all these threats, each with major consequences of its own, she gets highly conflicting advice. She feels overwhelmed but stays calm. She finally says she wants to think about things and will get back to them, and retreats to her smallish White House West Wing office with two or three of her closest advisers (including Thompson). Each issue is complex, but after hearing their various proposals she decides to go with her intuition and to be assertive and not be cowed. After all, that's what she has always done and it has worked. This turns out to be a winning formula and by the movie's end, all the crises have simmered down. The new president has won her foreign policy stripes and the country lives happily ever after.

The End

This would make a great made-for-TV movie. It's a wonderful story and most people would eat it up. But it is absolute fiction. The crises themselves may be real, but the notion that Al Qaeda, the Russians, or even the Israelis are going to roll over because the president of the United States is "tough" does not conform in any way to the real world and the dangers out there lurking for the next president of the United States. Yet, in a sense, that is the story John McCain and the Republicans are trying to sell the American people regarding his selection of Governor Sarah Palin as his vice presidential running mate. McCain is seventy-two years old, and as all of us even near to that age know, our days are numbered. It seems to me almost unconscionable to suggest that she is qualified to be president. If that is true, literally thousands of men and women in this country are so qualified, and I adamantly do not believe that to be the case.

All other issues with Palin pale in comparison to her total lack of knowledge and experience to deal with the demands of the presidency, specifically on the issues of national security. Please don't tell me that being mayor of a small town and governor of Alaska for less than two years gives her more "executive experience" than Barack Obama. Using those criteria she has more experience than McCain, too, which is absurd.

I keep coming back to the new book on the Cuban missile crisis, *One Minute to Midnight* by Michael Dobbs, because it is so relevant to this whole issue of presidential decision-making at a time of ultimate survival. In October 1962, if anyone else but John Kennedy had been president, the United States would have attacked the Russian missiles in Cuba, almost certainly setting off World War III. Virtually all of Kennedy's advisers argued for a tough line with the Russians, and at the beginning of the crisis, Kennedy himself leaned toward taking out the missiles. He was angry that Khrushchev had lied to him, and he wanted to demonstrate that the United States and President John F. Kennedy could not be pushed around by a bunch of Russian Communists.

But fortunately Kennedy had time to reconsider his options. In those days there were no 24/7 cable news channels nor hundreds of highly opinionated-but-short-on-knowledge bloggers, beating the drums of war. Kennedy understood war, having lived in Europe during Hitler's rise; having lost a brother during the war and almost dying himself when his PT boat was rammed by a Japanese destroyer. He understood the American political scene as well as anyone, having been raised in a political household with a highly controversial father and having served in both the House and the Senate. He also had learned the essential lesson in dealing with the balance of nuclear terror: one must always try to see any crisis from the perspective of the adversary on the grounds that he or she most probably doesn't want to blow up the world either. (This would apply to Iranians as well as Russians.)

I firmly believe the Cuban missile crisis teaches us that crucial decisions, on which the survival of the human species depends, dare not be decided by one's "gut." That's the way the current president says he makes such decisions, which should be seen as a cautionary tale given the debacle of his presidency. McCain has also boasted that he too, operates on a gut level. This is one of the reasons he worries me because "gut," which may be translated as a synonym for "high testosterone level," has been responsible for far more of history's wars than firm, reasoned analysis and diplomacy.

Given what McCain has said about Palin, he would appear to believe that she too would bring a similar visceral approach to decision-making. And I can't think of anything more dangerous than a totally inexperienced person believing his or her "manhood" is being challenged and making decisions that could represent the difference between the life and death of this planet.

Palin was a huge success at the Republican National Convention.

The delegates and most of the news media loved her speech—much of which was devoted to heaping scorn on the "elite" media with its liberal bias (that Republicans so love to hate even though that same group of elitists loved Ronald Reagan, initially quite liked George W. Bush, and by his own description were John McCain's "base" for most of the past eight years).

No one can challenge that Palin is a sparkling, attractive personality with a compelling personal narrative. And with her convention speech she effectively met her first challenge, although by the McCain campaign's own admission, it wrote most of the speech for her, including, one assumes, her snappy lines denigrating Obama's experience and life accomplishments.

But my bottom line remains. By no conceivable stretch is Palin qualified to be president of the United States. And in this day and age, especially if the president is seventy-two when he takes office, that is the prime requirement of the vice president.

April 5, 2009

On Traveling with Presidents Abroad

President Barack Obama is well into his first presidential overseas trip—one with serious implications for the current global economic crisis. However, as I write, it is only just beginning, so the full post-mortem will have to come later. Before the trip began, pundits were pretty much unanimous that Obama would be running into a buzz saw at the Group of Twenty Nations meeting in London—and that his former status as celebrity rock star wouldn't be of much help. Without knowing the outcome of the London conference, I would still speculate that Obama critics have exaggerated the rift between America and the rest of the world over the size of each government's economic stimulation package. To be sure, there are differences. But the money most European governments already allocate to universal health care and employment benefits far exceeds the funds the American government contributes in normal times, so the actual differences between what each government is doing to stimulate its economy are not that significant.

As to his rock-star status, remember that this title was bestowed on Obama last summer by John McCain and was not meant to be a compliment. Actually, the adoring crowds of Europeans who greeted Obama last summer were as much motivated by their total disdain for the "cowboy" who had occupied the White House for the past two terms as by affection for his possible successor. And I would bet that just as polls on the eve of his trip showed that some two-thirds of Americans still strongly supported their new president, most Europeans will also be prepared to give him more time before casting judgment.

That said, a new presidential overseas adventure got me thinking about the many such trips I had taken—some notable, some not. My first such excursion was with President Lyndon Johnson to Mexico City in April 1966. The world little-noted nor long remembered the reason for the trip: to dedicate a statue of Abraham Lincoln. But I was captivated to see firsthand the high-level intensity that goes with any presidential visit abroad. As for reporting, I mainly remember explaining on live television why the Secret Service agents who were running alongside the president's limo had to be continually given oxygen. (It was to help them cope with Mexico City's altitude—7,400 feet or nearly a mile and a half. Heavy stuff.)

Although this was a minor presidential trip and I a very minor player, something did occur that for me at least was of special note. As a member of the ABC News team, I was invited to a small gathering in the hotel suite of James Hagerty, once famous as President Dwight Eisenhower's White House press secretary and at that time, a senior corporate ABC executive. He wanted to give us the real news of the day—he had just negotiated the deal giving ABC the rights to televise the 1968 Mexico City Olympics. Little did I imagine that this would begin decades of ABC's summer and winter Olympics dominance. This niche would have a highly positive impact on the network, its news division, and thus my career—which was about to enter its foreign correspondent phase.

Over the next ten years, at least half of my time would be spent covering the wars and occasional diplomacy of the Middle East. In 1974, I was assigned to President Richard Nixon's visit to Egypt, Syria, and Israel. In my mind, two aspects of that trip stand out. First: it really was significant because it re-established diplomatic talks and a wide range of business and cultural relations between America and most of the Arab world—ties that had been angrily severed by the Arabs in the aftermath of their humiliation by Israel in the June 1967 War. But second: as far as the American news media were concerned, this presidential trip (which began with a Summit in Moscow) was merely an exercise in self-aggrandizement by Nixon to escape the ever-looming finale of the Watergate crisis. If so, it didn't work, and in a matter of weeks he was forced to resign, thus negating the questionable axiom that foreign policy success can obscure domestic problems.

Still, President Jimmy Carter capitalized on the genuine success of the Nixon-Kissinger Middle East diplomacy by devoting a vast amount of energy to an Israeli-Egyptian peace agreement. He came close at Camp David in 1978. And in March 1979, Carter went to the region try to resolve the final differences. However, as we left Israel after many hours of intense negotiations with Prime Minister Menachem Begin and his cabinet, there was still no deal and those of us on the White House press plane began to polish up our reports on reasons Carter had failed. We TV guys planned to broadcast our conclusions during a brief stop at Cairo airport where Egyptian President Anwar Sadat was to meet Carter to say sorry and goodbye—or so we thought. In fact, Carter had Israeli agreement to a deal that Sadat quickly accepted. So Carter would come home with the most significant Middle East peace agreement ever achieved. It meant that Israel's largest and most powerful Arab adversary was no longer a threat to Israel's long-term security. And of perhaps greater significance, with long time Soviet client Egypt now firmly in America's camp in the Cold War, the Middle East would no longer be the tinder-box likely to ignite World War III.

But the Cold War would continue for more than another decade. In the early years of President Ronald Reagan's presidency, his policies and overseas visits to China and West Germany even seemed to heat it up. But in later summits I would witness in Geneva, Reykjavik, Washington, and Moscow, Reagan and Soviet leader Mikhail Gorbachev eventually broke down many of the barriers of forty years of mistrust. Yet by the summer of 1988, as a smiling Reagan strolled through Moscow's Red Square with Gorbachev, I held my breath as my colleague Sam Donaldson reminded Reagan of his once harsh words about the Soviet Union. "Do you still think you're in an evil empire?" Sam asked the president. Reagan answered without hesitation, "No, I was talking about another time and another era." With that, Reagan effectively ended the fears of nuclear holocaust so long associated with the U.S.-Soviet confrontation. A little more than a year later, the Berlin Wall came down and the Cold War was over, thanks largely to the courage of Reagan and Gorbachev to seriously negotiate with their once-mortal enemy.

Since World War I, the United States has been a major player in world affairs. But in this century, American foreign policy significantly damaged this country's once esteemed position among nations—so Obama faces real challenges. His first performance on the world stage is being intensely watched by critical eyes at home and abroad to find faults or cracks in the new president's façade. But, whatever happens on this trip, I am encouraged that Barack Obama understands the truly global nature of the world's most vexing problems; that he wants to lead multi-lateral efforts to resolve them; and that he does not appear to be afraid to talk or negotiate with anyone.

April 19, 2009

On Good Luck and Smart Policy

Last Sunday, on the first playoff hole to determine the winner of this year's Masters golf tournament, Angel Cabrera sliced his drive deep into the trees where he seemingly had no way out. His second shot could be heard ricocheting off one of many large trees in the grove. If his ball had bounced over to the right he was finished. But it went left and miraculously ended up safely in the fairway, from which he made a par. On the next hole, Cabrera won the tournament.

On that same Sunday afternoon, three Navy Seal snipers found the three pirates holding Captain Richard Philips in their gun sights, and with three deadly shots ended the hostage drama that had been playing out for several days on the high seas off the coast of Somalia. In the White House, President Barack Obama, who had authorized the use of lethal force if Philips' life was in imminent danger, would have felt great joy—because among other things, the president himself had just dodged a bullet.

These two Easter Sunday events support the old adage, "Sometimes it's better to be lucky than to be good." Call it luck, call it fate, or divine intervention; there are times in life when things happen which are out of one's control that end up determining the positive or negative outcome of some important event. I mentioned above that with the Navy snipers' success, Obama himself had escaped major political damage. Just think what might have happened if one of the snipers had missed and the third pirate had killed Captain Philips. This would not have been Obama's fault, but nevertheless he would have been widely blamed for what he did or didn't do. That's what happened to President Jimmy Carter in 1980, when six months into the Iranian hostage crisis, he authorized a large commando-style raid to rescue the fifty-two American hostages being held in Tehran. That effort had to be aborted because of a desert sandstorm and a collision between two American aircraft that killed eight servicemen. Neither the storm nor the crash could be properly blamed on Carter. But that failed rescue attempt was seen at home and abroad as an example of American impotence and of Carter's hapless leadership. And it certainly contributed to his loss of a second presidential term. For its part, Iran later claimed the American debacle in the Iranian desert was divine intervention on behalf of Islam.

There have been signs along the way that Obama is lucky. As we look at all the problems he and this country face, we want to hope so. But good fortune can only take one so far. As golfer Ben Hogan was fond of saying, "The more I practice, the luckier I get." By that he meant what some critics dismiss as "dumb luck" can often be attributed to good preparation and hard work. Or in the case of our leaders, good luck may flow from essentially smart policies.

Even before Captain Philips was rescued, I felt that by laying low and not making public statements, President Obama was doing the right thing. This was a lesson I learned during my deep involvement in reporting the Iran hostage story. As some of you may recall, the crisis spawned a new ABC News program titled *America Held Hostage* (which later became *Nightline*). Ted Koppel was the principal anchor and for most of the 444 days that the fifty-two American diplomats were being held in Tehran, I was that program's primary Washington correspondent. Almost every night I would report on what the United States government was saying and doing in its efforts to free the hostages. I got much inside information from a senior member of then-Secretary of State Cyrus Vance's staff. I would later learn that Vance himself had told this aide, "If Dunsmore is going to be doing this every night he might as well get it right." I wasn't told everything, but I was told a lot. What I learned each day certainly kept me busy and—here is the real point—it kept *America Held Hostage* on the air. After the fact, it was generally agreed among thoughtful people both in government and in the news media that keeping the hostage crisis on the front burner every night served neither the best interests of the Carter administration nor of the hostages themselves. By allowing the hostage story to dominate nearly every daily news briefing at the White House and the State Department for more than a year, the administration itself unwittingly escalated the hostage problem into a full-blown foreign policy crisis. For the new revolutionary regime in Iran, all that attention increased the hostages' propaganda value and therefore the price for their release kept going up.

In contrast to the way the Carter administration dealt with its hostage crisis, not so many years earlier there was a somewhat similar incident that created only a relatively minor stir. In January of 1968, North Korea seized the U.S.S. Pueblo, an American intelligence gathering ship trolling just outside North Korea's territorial waters. The eighty-plus crewmen were taken ashore and kept as prisoners for eleven months. Admittedly, the Vietnam War was raging and that was the year both Martin Luther King, Jr. and Bobby Kennedy were assassinated. But to my mind, one of the more remarkable aspects of the Pueblo incident is that it never really became a major story in the national or international news media—this in spite of the fact that eighty American servicemen were being starved and occasionally tortured for nearly a year by a brutal Communist regime with which the United States was not at war. One apparent reason was that the Johnson administration didn't talk about the Pueblo very much.

I now believe that perhaps a week or two after the Iranian hostage crisis began, President Carter should have simply declared that he was going to do all he could to get the hostages free but neither he nor any department of his administration would discuss it in public any further. I know that for another week or so there would have been major grumbling among working reporters like me—and high dudgeon expressed on the nation's editorial pages. But I am quite certain that public interest in the story would have waned and without real news from Washington, I know a program such as *America Held Hostage* could not have been sustained.

Given this history, in any story involving American hostages the news media will now always be clamoring to know what the president is thinking or doing about it. But a president simply cannot allow himself to be seen as totally invested in any situation over which he may have little or no control. I hope that has been a lesson learned by the new White House, because given the chaotic situation in Somalia, it is quite possible that other American ships will be captured by pirates and other Americans taken hostage. The next time, Obama may not be so lucky. But if he follows a policy of not allowing himself to be consumed by such an event, he will have a much better chance to resolve it if he deals with it as he did this first time: firmly but quietly.

December 12, 2010
Defending Obama's Bipartisan Tax Cut Legislation

In just two years, Barack Obama has gone from being compared to Abraham Lincoln and Franklin Roosevelt (first and third in most historians' presidential rankings) to being labeled another Jimmy Carter (eleventh worst), if not James Buchanan (bottom of the presidential barrel). The Carter comparison is the unkindest cut of all. Buchanan only ushered in the Civil War. Carter is widely considered to be that most demeaning of any name an American president can be called—a wimp. By the way, these are the views being expressed this past week, not by Obama's Republican opponents, but by the progressive/liberal wing of the Democratic Party.

These Democrats are furious with Obama for having caved, capitulated, and wimped out in his negotiations with Republicans over extension of the Bush tax cuts. They are bitter that he did not draw a line in the sand, or stand and fight over the principle that the richest 2 percent of Americans did not deserve a tax break which would add $700 billion to the national debt over the next decade. And they've been arguing vociferously that it would have been better to have to let all the tax cuts expire, even those for the other 98 percent of the country, and then lay the blame on those responsible for this outrage: the Republican Party. It seems to me this view is not without merit. But let's back up for a moment to examine this liberal anger.

From the day of his election, most thoughtful people knew Obama would almost certainly have a problem with the outsized expectations of his presidency. And to date, it's the liberals who have been the most disappointed because of his centrist tendencies. The initial comparisons of Obama to Lincoln were overwrought. As the first black president, there was a historical connection with Lincoln, but America was hardly on the brink of another Civil War. The FDR analogy, as it related to the Great Depression, was more valid, but there were important differences.

Indeed, on Obama's inauguration day this country was teetering on the brink of a depression. But remember when FDR took the oath in March of 1933, the United States had already been in the full throes of a depression for more than three years. Unemployment had reached the upper double digits; breadlines were widespread; banks by the hundreds had defaulted; and the world's economic engines had shut down. So when he assumed command, Roosevelt had a virtual carte-blanche to create the New Deal.

In contrast, the worst effects of the current recession, for which he had no responsibility, had not yet set in when Obama took office. Unemployment was at 7.6 percent, not the 10 percent it would eventually become. Obama did take steps to mitigate the impact of the recession—which nonpartisan analysts such as the Congressional Budget Office credit as having prevented a much worse recession or even depression. But after two years, when the economy did not substantially turn around, inevitably Obama was saddled with the blame.

Obama's ability to deal with the recession was significantly impeded by the strategy of Republicans in Congress to reject nearly anything he proposed. To accomplish this, they shattered historical records in the frequency of their use of the Senate filibuster—an anti-democratic procedural tactic that results in minority rule because it requires sixty votes to get anything passed. This political reality, more than any other single fact, is why most Americans have concluded that the United States' government seems to be dysfunctional. When a minority can use the filibuster to block every important piece of legislation, it certainly is. A perfect example: last weekend, two different Senate resolutions that would have effectively raised taxes on the super-rich were supported by more than fifty Democratic senators. But all Republicans and a few Democrats voted against any tax hikes so that each bill fell short of the sixty votes needed under the filibuster rule.

This put the president in an untenable position. He could have allowed all the tax cuts to expire on December 31, which many on the left have urged. But doing so would have had the following consequences:

- It would have resulted in significant tax increases for middle class families.
- It would have eliminated the possibility of extending unemployment benefits for another year for at least two million families.
- It would have precluded or ended additional middle class tax breaks that could add up to several thousand dollars per household. Some important tax incentives for small businesses would also be lost.
- To take all this money out of the economy at this time could very well have hurt the current weak recovery and cost many more jobs.
- Finally, when the new Congress convenes in January, the Republicans, with control of the House and increased power in the

Senate, were certainly going to reinstate all the tax cuts, probably permanently. Obama could, of course, veto any such bill, but that would result in negative political consequences, with none of the economic benefits (effectively another stimulus package of about $900 billion) that make up the latest compromise.

In the past week's searing debate among Democrats, ironically set off by what may turn out to be Obama's first truly bipartisan piece of major legislation, he finally lost his famous cool with his liberal critics. His voice dripping with sarcasm he accused them of preferring ideological purity over benefits for the American people. House Democrats defiantly responded by refusing to put the tax compromise to a vote, even though failure to pass it in this session would practically guarantee that when Republicans take over the House next month, they will ram through something much less attractive.

I would remind my progressive friends that there will soon be other, bigger political wars to be waged—such as saving the new health care bill from the Tea Partyers. This means Obama still has about two more years to demonstrate the courage of his convictions. Think Sarah Palin—and allow him to do so.

August 7th, 2011

Debt Ceiling Debate Debacle

For a while at least, anyone with any sense does not want to read another word about debt ceilings, defaults, or dysfunctional government. Yet the recent near-calamity was an event of great significance and its fallout is hard to ignore.

I have been taken by the extreme bitterness of so many Democrats, especially Progressives, toward President Barack Obama. These people apparently see him as an abject failure—a weak-kneed, hapless negotiator who was rolled by the terrorist tactics of the Tea Party and outsmarted by the smooth-talking Senate Minority Leader Mitch McConnell. In this version of history, Obama first gave away the store and then helped the crooks load up their trucks. Or as columnist Paul Krugman wrote in the *New York Times*, Obama recognized he was being held hostage and was merely negotiating the terms of his ransom. Such contempt toward this president is commonplace from the right. But when his natural supporters cut him no slack for the unprecedented nature of the dilemma he faced—that's news.

I share the deep disappointment people have in the process of the recent default debate and in many aspects of its outcome. While I am greatly relieved that there was no default, I do worry that the country has been damaged at home and abroad by a wholly unnecessary crisis—and that the terms of the deal are likely to come back to haunt us. That said, what to do now?

The sage of the *New York Times'* Op-Ed page Tom Friedman, has been writing about a third party. He suggests there is little hope the existing parties will ever be able to work together to deal with the country's problems. So a way out of this partisan gridlock may be a new third party, with new people and new ideas untainted by the incompetence and corruption attached to the current crowd in power. This theme has been picked up by other media pundits who continue to be mesmerized by that great ideological "center" of America—those independents who are said to feel ignored by the two major parties and their increasingly dominant extremist wings.

I've seen this movie before and I know how it ends.

During the 2000 presidential election campaign, the mainstream media decided they didn't like Al Gore. They ridiculed him for his brown suits; for supposedly claiming to have invented the Internet; for saying he was a model for the male character in the book and movie *Love Story*. It's hard to believe now but "Gore's Lies" became a significant part of the campaign narrative. I have deconstructed these so-called Gore lies in previous columns. To save space, please trust me. They are simply not true. Nevertheless, in contrast to Gore's negatives, his political opponent George W. Bush was portrayed as a good ol' boy from Texas whom every reporter on the campaign apparently wanted to have a beer with. Meantime there were increasing numbers on the left who decided that Gore wasn't liberal enough. They began eyeing Ralph Nader and the Green Party as a way to offer a protest vote against some of the centrist policies of the Clinton administration, particularly welfare reform. According to these folks, and Nader, there was no real difference between Gore and Bush.

Even considering the media disdain and a substantial Progressive defection, Gore actually won the popular vote in the 2000 election. But he didn't win Florida. Now I recognize there were numerous persuasive reasons for Gore's defeat in Florida. And as we all remember, after a month of vote counting and court challenges the Supreme Court stopped the recount and decided that Bush had won the election. It was one of the greatest electoral fiascos—and injustices—in American history.

But these are also the facts. Ralph Nader received 97,421 votes in Florida in 2000. Nader himself says exit polls reported that 25 percent of his voters would have voted for Bush, 38 percent for Gore and the rest wouldn't have voted at all. But that would still have given Gore a 13 percent advantage over Bush, meaning 12,655 votes. Ultimately, Gore lost Florida, and therefore the presidency, by 537 votes.

Think how different this country and the world would be if Al Gore had become president in 2000. No Iraq War. No massive tax cuts for the rich. Serious national and global efforts to deal with climate change. A balanced budget. It's enough to take your breath away. There is hardly a more compelling illustration to prove that elections do have consequences, sometimes extraordinary ones. So with another crucial election set for November 2012, it is important to consider the consequences if the Tea Party remains in power in the House and if Republicans were to win the Senate, the White House, or both.

In the final count down to Default Day, Democrats quite rightly were pointing out that their opponents' refusal to compromise was putting the entire global economy at risk. As many of us commentators argued, democracy cannot function without compromise. Especially in a political system based on checks and balances, compromise is the lubricant without which the system becomes totally paralyzed.

However, that spirit of compromise also needs to be applied when making choices about which party and which candidates to support. When it comes to presidents, some are clearly better than others—but there have been no perfect ones. For those who truly care about the future of the country, this is no time for despondency or capitulation. This is the time to recognize those who most closely reflect your values, to make your priorities known to them, and then do everything possible to get them elected. Forget about the seductive mirage of a third party presidential candidate. In some countries, that may work. But the way the American political system has evolved, when you vote third party, there is a very good chance you will be indirectly electing the candidate you like the least.

Cultural Commentary

March 21, 2004
Fundamental Anger

Could it be that Vermonters have acquired an acute case of the rage that so infected Howard Dean? In this place where political discourse has always seemed so civil, in the weeks since Howard Dean's demise, I sense a remarkable level of anger. It's almost as though Dean's penetrating scream has somehow shattered the veneer of gentility that kept real and raw emotions under control. Nowadays, following the example of their former governor, many Vermont constituents are strident and fighting mad. Among the issues that feed this anger are mostly those you'd expect: the Bush administration's policies on Iraq, terrorism, the environment, jobs, and healthcare.

But there's another subject that is also stirring people up. During my career as a foreign correspondent I found it *the* most divisive issue in most of the world's trouble spots. Until recently, I wouldn't have considered it a serious problem in this country, but that may be changing. I'm referring to religion, specifically fundamentalism.

One of the side effects of Mel Gibson's movie *The Passion of the Christ* is that it has provoked a great deal of thought and comment, some of it informed, much of it not, about Christianity. I have recently found myself in dinner table discussions about the secrets hidden in the Gnostic Gospels or the relative political power of Pontius Pilate, with people who previously wouldn't have given the time of day to such topics. But they, as I, have been caught up in the controversy over Gibson's interpretation of the New Testament's account of Jesus' crucifixion.

While the film has been widely criticized for being anti-Semitic and for its bloody, unrelenting sadism, it has now earned $350 million to become the most successful R-rated film ever made. Deliberately or not, Gibson has tapped into a huge audience in this country—the people who believe that the Bible is the literal truth. This is fundamentalism.

What the success of this movie underscores is the growing power in this country of the fundamentalists, without whose support George W. Bush would not have been elected president. And whether it is the appointment of federal judges who oppose abortion, the limitations on stem-cell research, the proposed constitutional amendment against gay marriage, or unquestioned support for Israel, Bush's White House goes out of its way to pursue and promote the fundamentalist agenda.

The pro-Israel part of that agenda escapes many people, but it goes like this: according to the Biblical prophesies of the Book of Revelation, the Jewish people must be in control of the land of Israel before the second coming of the Messiah can take place. His coming sets the stage for the ultimate contest between good and evil—the battle of Armageddon.

If the United States were to pressure Israel to give up substantial territory to the Palestinians, the so-called Christian Zionists believe that would interfere with the scripture's predictions. The fact that Bush has pretty much abandoned evenhandedness in the Israeli-Palestinian dispute suggests the views of the Christian right now trump America's longstanding policy to act as peacemaker in the region.

One does not have to be a bigot or an atheist to be concerned about the extent to which fundamentalism is shaping events in the world these days, whether it's the Islamic, Jewish, or the Christian variety. I find it ironic that just when modern science is opening up some of the secrets of the universe, our little planet's political agenda is being driven by people who believe God made that universe in a week, about five thousand years ago.

December 26, 2004

Truths about "Big Pharma"

Billy must have had a great Christmas. He just got this new job. For the first year, all he has to do is pal around with his old buddies—probably play some golf, go to their parties, and give them money on behalf of his new employer. Best of all, he's going to make more than two million dollars a year. And it's all legal.

The Billy in question is William Joseph Tauzin, a sixty-one-year-old Republican from Louisiana who is retiring after twenty-four years in Congress. His new job is president of Pharmaceutical Research and Manufacturers of America—the major lobbying group for brand-name drug companies. It is not unusual for former members of Congress to join lobbying firms when they step down. But what makes this case particularly outlandish is that Representative Tauzin was the principal author of the Medicare prescription drug benefits law passed last year. As chairman of the House Energy and Commerce Committee, he wrote major parts of the new law, one of the main features of which explicitly forbids the government from negotiating with drug manufacturers to secure lower prices for Medicare beneficiaries—in other words, the government can't negotiate a bulk discount the way HMOs and the Veterans Administration are able to do.

So the guy who wrote the bill that provides an enormous windfall—tens of billions—for the drug companies is now going to become their chief lobbyist. Federal law prohibits former members from lobbying Congress for a one-year cooling-off period. But during that year Tauzin will be able to interact socially with them, as well as make campaign contributions, attend fund raisers, and tell other people how to lobby.

In what struck me as one of the more ironic quotes of the week, Tauzin told the *New York Times*, "This industry has a problem. It has to earn the trust and confidence of consumers again." One could certainly not quarrel with that statement, but it's rather hard to see how Tauzin's great career move is going to fill us with more trust and confidence in our friendly drug company.

Something else that was not a trust-builder was last week's latest drug scare. In a national drug trial, Celebrex, the huge-selling painkiller made by Pfizer, more than tripled the risk of heart attacks and strokes among those taking high doses. Coming on the heels of similar problems with Vioxx and Bextra, all members of a class of drugs known as COX-2 inhibitors used to treat a wide range of aches and pains; it was bad news for drug company stocks, which were pummeled by investors. But please forgive me if I do not shed a tear over a dip in the value of pharmaceuticals. For the past two decades this industry has been far and away the most profitable industry in the United States.

Drug safety experts said the latest news about Celebrex demonstrated that the Federal Food and Drug Administration's systems for uncovering the dangers of drugs need to be fixed. True. But that is by no means the only thing that needs to be fixed. Evidence is now coming into the public domain—supporting suspicions many consumers have had for some time—that the pharmaceutical industry has been corrupted by success. One of the latest books to provide such evidence is titled *The Truth About the Drug Companies: How They Deceive Us and What To Do About It.* This is not a book by some low-life reporter skulking around drug company garbage cans trying to discover marginal malpractices. The author is Marcia Angell, a doctor trained in internal medicine, who for two decades worked for and eventually became editor-in-chief of the *New England Journal of Medicine.* She is now at Harvard Medical School and is a nationally recognized authority in the field of health policy and medical ethics. *Time* magazine named her as one of the twenty-five most influential people in America.

Here are a few of the things the publisher Random House says about Angell's book:

"Dr. Angell had a front-row seat to the growing corruption of the pharmaceutical industry....She saw them gain nearly limitless influence over medical research, education and how doctors do their jobs....Angell powerfully demonstrates claims that high drug prices are necessary to fund research and development are unfounded. The truth is that drug companies funnel the bulk of their resources into the marketing of products of dubious benefit. Meantime, as their profits soar, the companies brazenly use their wealth and power to push their agenda through Congress, the FDA, and academic medical centers."

Having read the book, I can tell you that Dr. Angell delivers the goods. For instance, did you know that:

- Basic research—where studies are done to determine the nature of the disease you want to treat and then, at the molecular level, look for a drug that will safely and effectively treat it—is almost always carried out at universities or government research labs. In this country, most of this research is conducted or financed by the National Institutes of Health; in other words, it's paid for by your tax dollars and mine.

• While "big pharma" (Angell's name for the major drug companies) claims the average cost of developing a new drug is $800 million, the actual cost after taxes could be less than $100 million.

• The marketing costs for most big drug companies are more than twice what is spent on research and development, even if we accept their R&D figures, which Angell claims are highly inflated. Among those marketing costs are billions in advertising for cures for "diseases" that a few years ago we didn't even know existed (and most of us still don't, though the TV pitchman is constantly at us to "ask your doctor if [drug X] is right for you.").

• Most new drugs being marketed are not new, but are simply copycats or me-too drugs that are perhaps one molecule different from the original. That's why we have six statins to lower cholesterol, three erectile dysfunction treatments, and countless acid reflux pills. Having so many choices adds nothing at all to the state of American health but certainly adds to overall costs of health care—not to mention drug company profits.

That's just a small part of the case against big pharma, as made by Dr. Angell.

Her book also points out that the United States is the only developed country that does not regulate drug prices. Each of the other Western countries may have a different way to regulate, but whatever the system, their costs of prescription drugs end up much lower than ours. For those who argue that the free market must be allowed to prevail, Dr. Angell has this answer: "The [pharmaceutical] industry is hardly a model of free enterprise. To be sure, it is free to decide which drugs to develop (me-too drugs instead of innovative ones, for instance), and it is free to price them as high as the traffic will bear, [but] instead of being a free market success story, it lives off government-funded research and [government-granted] monopoly rights."

And, she might have said, had she known soon-to-be-former Congressman Billy Tauzin would be the next president of the country's largest drug lobby, the pharmaceutical industry has also been free to apparently buy important members of the United States Congress.

February 6, 2005

Football in the Genes?

So today's the day, Super Bowl Sunday—a day which has actually eclipsed New Year's Eve as America's favorite party occasion. It's now a secular holiday when half of the people of this country will watch at least part of the game, eat more, drink more, and flush more toilets during the commercials than any other day of the year. And as a serious sports fan, I will certainly be among those eager to see the New England Patriots nail down their right to be known as a football dynasty.

But how has all this happened? How is it that half the country is attracted to a football game? Why has football become the favorite sport? These are interesting questions on which most of us have an opinion but, in truth, we don't really know the answer. And so I am pleased to report that there is a source you can go to which offers some very plausible—if not necessarily definitive—answers to those questions and more. It's a recent book titled *The Meaning of Sports: Why Americans Watch Baseball, Football and Basketball and What They See When They Do.* It's written by Michael Mandelbaum, a self-confessed avid sports fan. However, Mandelbaum is also a professor at Johns Hopkins University and one of this country's leading authorities on American foreign policy and international relations. In this book, he looks at sports from the perspective of anthropology, history, and literature. But Mandelbaum is no dilettante. He also knows a lot about these sports and can argue the relative merits of the designated hitter rule, the full court press, or the two minute drill with the best of the games' analysts.

Mandelbaum begins by explaining how and why team sports evolved. For example: how laws prohibiting child labor created time, between birth and work, for children to play; how the nineteenth century creation of the public school provided the setting and space for organized games; how the industrial revolution spurred the growth of cities from which large pools of players and spectators could be drawn; how modern methods of transportation like the railroads made it possible for teams to travel from one place to another to compete.

As to why games developed, Mandelbaum theorizes that team sports may be satisfying human needs which previously we got from religion. He writes, "Team sports provide three satisfactions of life to twenty-first century Americans that before the modern age only religion offered: a welcome diversion from the routines of daily life; a model of coherence and clarity; and heroic examples to admire and emulate."

But it's the author's ideas about football and why it appeals to so many Americans that are relevant on this Super Sunday. After having noted that football is the game most closely attuned to an industrial society because it's played by the clock, under externally imposed deadlines, Mandelbaum makes his main point, "A football game is like a war."

In summary, this is the professor's case for looking at football as a metaphor for war:

- War involves the organized deliberate use of force to attain a goal, often the control of territory. Football teams seek to conquer and defend territory.
- War has battles. Football has plays that correspond to small-scale battles.
- Seen from a distance, a football play looks like a pre-modern battle: uniformed, padded men, swarming together in a tangled melee of pushing, pounding, and grabbing bodies.
- Tactics such as concentrating power on one spot in the line, or trying to turn the opponents flank, go back to the days of the armies of Alexander the Great.
- Linemen are the equivalent of the infantry. Running backs function as the cavalry—highly mobile agents of swift advance. The forward pass is the artillery, attacking the foe through the air.
- Armies and football teams spend far more time in training than in actual combat. Preparations and plans involve the coaching staff which is akin to the general staff of an army, which draws up war plans for special circumstances. The coach is clearly the commanding general.
- Football has a vernacular borrowed from armed conflict. The pass down the field is a "long bomb." The offensive and defensive lines are like the infantry of World War I—"in the trenches." The quarterback is the "field general," while the all-out assault on the quarterback is called a "blitz"—taken from the German World War II tactic known as the blitzkrieg or lighting war.
- A most important common feature: war and football are dangerous. Deaths in football are rare, although certainly not unknown. But serious injuries are commonplace, and major, career-ending injuries not at all rare.

• Victory on the fields of battle or football requires physical courage, but it also requires discipline—the absolute need to carry out the orders of the commanders/coaching staff. And in carrying out those orders, football players, like soldiers, are expected to fulfill their assignments, even when exhausted or injured.

Thus football can be seen as the "moral equivalent of war," meaning something "that incorporates the desirable features of armed conflict, such as courage, discipline and camaraderie, without the destruction that war brings."

In his concluding chapter, Mandelbaum makes the point that there has been a declining tolerance for violence in recent decades, linked, he believes, to the rise in the status of women. "Women are less likely than men to engage in violent behavior but are just as likely to be the victims of violence. Tellingly, of the three major American team sports, football is the only one that lacks a version widely played by girls and women."

But going back to the days of the Roman emperors who gave the masses bread and circuses with gladiators who fought to the death and Christians who were fed to the lions, violence has always drawn spectators. In the eighteenth century the crowds came to public hangings in England and to the guillotine in France. And even in this country, only a hundred or so years ago mobs gathered to watch, if not participate in, vigilante-style lynchings. Some anthropologists believe that Homo sapiens were actually hardwired for violence as something necessary for the species' survival. So if we have reached the point of decreasing acceptability of violence, football might actually serve a useful purpose.

As Mandelbaum put it in an interview broadcast last week on North Country Public Radio, "There might be something almost genetic about the appeal of football, combined with the fact that while football does have at its core violence, it's controlled violence, it's non-lethal violence. So it may be a way of domesticating something that's both fascinating and inevitable, and making it palatable in our twenty-first century American society."

And so, fellow football fans, there it is: a reason, in case you needed one, to watch the Super Bowl today. It seems we can't help ourselves. Apparently, it's in our genes.

April 7, 2010

Can Tiger Still Play?

The return of Tiger Woods to the Professional Golf Association Tour has been making headlines this week. In addressing the question of how well Tiger will play, I admit I am not a golf expert—but I do know something about human nature. I do not condone what Tiger Woods has done to his wife and family. Yet it's a historical fact that compared to the personal behavior of more than a few entertainment stars, professional athletes, business titans, and politicians, Tiger's antics are not particularly notable. And so, my interest is focused on one thing only: can Tiger still play?

I seem to be among only a few who believe that Tiger will not win the Masters championship. I think he may not even make the cut to play the weekend.

Let me explain.

In almost all professional sports, the skill levels of the top 200 players do not vary that greatly. What separates average players from champions are intangibles. These are given different names: mental toughness, killer instinct, clutch, and attitude. Call it what you will, after many years of watching people perform at the highest levels in many fields, I have concluded that there is one factor that consistently separates the best from the rest, and that is self-confidence. Show me men or women who have reached the pinnacle of success, and I will show you people who believe they are invincible. What is equally true, if they lose that sense of invincibility, they no longer remain at the top.

Case in point. Why do most older golfers move from the regular PGA tour to the Senior Tour, which includes golfers aged fifty and over? It is not because they can't hit the ball as far as they could when they were in their twenties. The problem is that old men can't putt. When they stand over a four-foot putt for a championship or a lot of money they start thinking about all the putts they've missed and what can go wrong—and much more often than when they were young, they miss.

Which brings me to Tiger Woods. His skill levels are among the very best. But what Tiger has had on the golf course for his entire life is extreme self-confidence. Some would say arrogance. In countless situations this supreme faith in himself helped him pull off shots the very best of his opponents would hesitate to even try. That also had the added effect of making those he is playing against begin to doubt themselves.

However, if nothing else, events of the past few months must have shaken Tiger's confidence that he was bulletproof. And I predict that will negatively affect his game. It will also give new hope to some of professional golf's other top players.

Will Tiger ever again play at that level so rarely achieved? I don't know. In one sense, I hope he does, because he has given me and millions of others genuine pleasure in seeing one of the best golfers ever. But as a professional people-watcher, I certainly do not expect Tiger Woods to win the Masters this week, or very much of anything else for some time.

May 30, 2010

Who's in Charge Here?

Too many Greek men are sitting around in cafés drinking ouzo and dreaming of retirement at age fifty-two. If you believe what passes for analysis on the financial pages and the cable TV business shows, that's why what's left of my retirement funds are now once again on the skids. For most of this month, "investors are nervous" has been the cliché of the day. Investors are said to fear Greek government debt, contagion of debt problems to Spain, Portugal, Ireland, and Italy, the falling value of the euro, and how all of this will thwart global economic recovery. Those fears have driven world markets down about 10 percent and wiped out all of the stock market gains of 2010.

Even as a modest investor I have been nervous. But what I truly fear is not lazy Greek workers, or, even more relevant to the debt issue, the well-heeled Greeks, Italians, and Spaniards for whom tax evasion is the real national pastime. What I dread are the giant hedge funds and currency speculators who wield trillions of dollars in assets with which to drive a country—or an entire continent—into financial ruin. Using the same instruments that greatly exacerbated the crash of 2008—"naked shorts" and "credit default swaps"—these people have been systematically driving down the value of the euro and making all of us tiny investors poorer while they make a killing.

Without going into the weeds to explain these instruments, trust me when I say they make it possible for large speculators to bet against any currency they decide to attack at very little risk to themselves. It's like placing bets at the roulette table when you pretty much control the wheel. These financial behemoths of various nationalities truly are a world, and a power, unto themselves.

This is not meant to be a screed against the rich. (I would like very much to be rich myself.) I also concede that Europe has real sovereign debt issues. But these problems are being greatly aggravated by unelected currency speculators and hedge fund managers whose sole motive is quick and massive profit, no matter the costs to society. Yet I regret to report that in my geezerdom, one of things that has become clear to me is that presidential or prime ministerial power, and/or governmental power generally, is increasingly limited. The real power seems to be in the world's financial markets and the mega multinational corporations that effectively control them.

Perhaps the best illustration of the markets' power is that when greed and corruption threatened to bring the whole system down in 2008, governments around the world threw all caution to the wind and stepped in to prevent global economic collapse (which for all of our sakes was absolutely necessary). But within a year the same banks and financial institutions—that were saved by us taxpayers—again began rewarding themselves with obscene bonuses on grounds that their companies had made billions in 2009. (If I could have obtained virtually free money from the government and could loan unlimited amounts out at 4–6 percent, I would have had a good year, too.)

In spite of whatever gets passed in terms of new financial reform, I can't escape the anxiety that we have permanently entered the territory where profits are privatized but losses are socialized. It's not just that several major American financial institutions are too big to fail. It's that far too many international corporations are too big and powerful to effectively regulate. I'm thinking particularly of Big Oil.

During Bush II, we had both a president and vice president who had become wealthy through their ties to the oil business. It's now known that at some point during Dick Cheney's secret consultations with the oil companies to remake energy policy, the oil folks complained that the government's proposed acoustic blow-out preventers, at half a million dollars each, were too expensive. They claimed this was a waste of money, as drilling off-shore was perfectly safe and such a device would never be needed. Cheney and Bush gave them a pass.

It's long been known that the Department of the Interior has been co-opted by Big Oil. Gale Norton, Bush's Interior secretary for six years, has been under investigation by the Justice Department for allegedly using her position to further the interests of Royal Dutch Shell—a company she joined as legal counsel just a few months after she left her government job.

Another real mess at the Interior has been in the Mineral Management Services, the office charged with collecting the royalties, conducting the inspections, and enforcing the regulations for off-shore drillings. A series of investigations by the department's inspector general have found major ethical lapses on the part of numerous MMS employees. In return for lax enforcement of regulations, they received everything from sex, drugs, and alcohol, to free tickets to major sporting events and offers of employment. Much of this has been known since 2007. Obama's Interior Secretary Ken Salazar claims he has been trying to change that corruptive culture since he took over, but without apparent success, based on the latest inspector general findings that came out just this past week.

Both political parties have been infected by the toxic tentacles of Big Oil. And you don't have to look far to see how this shapes the political debate. In theory, BP should be stuck with the full tab of the Gulf of Mexico catastrophe. But there is a law on the books which conceivably could limit certain liabilities to just $75 million. So far, the efforts in the Senate to boost that limitation into the billions have been blocked by two Republican senators from oil states: Lisa Murkowski of Alaska and James Inhofe of Oklahoma (he who famously said in a Senate speech that global warming was the "greatest hoax ever perpetrated on the American people"). In fact, the greatest hoax may be the quaint notion that in a democracy, the elected representatives of the people are actually in control.

May 2, 2010

Whistling a Different Tune

Which of these two songs of the Great Depression best describes your mood these days?

Once I built a railroad, made it run, made it race against time.
Once I built a railroad, now it's done. Brother can you spare a dime?
Once I built a tower up to the sun, brick and rivet and lime.
Once I built a tower, now it's done. Brother can you spare a dime.
(Lyrics by Yip Harburg, 1932)

We're in the money, we're in the money,
We've got a lot of what it takes to get along!
We're in the money, come on my honey,
Let's lend it, spend it, send it rolling along.
(Lyrics by Al Dubin, 1933)

Just a guess, but if you live on Main Street (particularly if you're unemployed), Harburg's lyrics are probably most apt. If you work on Wall Street (particularly if you're an executive at Goldman Sachs), Dubin's words likely say it best. This past week, as I watched senators trying unsuccessfully to pry a shred of contrition out of Goldman Sachs' upper echelon, the words of these songs and a few others ("Pennies from Heaven," "Sunny Side of the Street," "Life is Just a Bowl of Cherries") began drifting through my mind.

I was born at the end of the Depression, but my parents had lived through the teeth of it and carried its scars for the rest of their lives. Still, they also had absorbed the music and culture of the 1930s, which is what I mostly grew up on. The many people like my parents, who were desperately fighting to survive with almost no social safety net in place, were by no means Pollyannas. Actually they were realists. Yet they responded positively to the culture of the era—the radio programs, the movies, and the songs—most of which tended to be upbeat. Cynics have claimed that this feel-good cultural food for the masses was an establishment plot to stave off a revolution. I am not that cynical. But what I do know is that the culture of hope helped millions of working and middle-class people cope with the cruelty and despair that they faced nearly every day for an entire decade.

Contrast that hope with the political and social cultures of the early twenty-first century. There may be some minor exceptions, but from what I see and hear there is nothing but gloom and doom in our movies, books, and television programs—and especially in our news media, where the political debate has become as toxic as in the Congress. The Republican Party's unprecedented threat to filibuster virtually every piece of legislation that can't attract sixty votes has made the Senate, and thus the government, seem nearly dysfunctional.

Sometimes it seems that the stars themselves are aligned against us. One week it's an Icelandic volcano eruption closing down the international air transport system. The next week it's an off-shore oil rig blowing up and spewing some 200,000 gallons of oil a day into the Gulf of Mexico and on to the coast lines of all the southern states. Meanwhile, stock markets everywhere dropped last week for fear of a financial collapse in Greece that could spread to Spain, Portugal, and Ireland. That would be a huge blow to the European Union and the shaky global economy still recovering from the crash of 2008.

And by the way, there are still two wars going on involving about a quarter of a million American troops suffering daily casualties. Iraq is politically paralyzed by the lack of a clear outcome to its most recent and most important election. And in Afghanistan, a major new military offensive into the province of Kandahar, which is the stronghold of the Taliban, is about to be launched. This new offensive is absolutely crucial to America's Afghanistan strategy, but every day we are being fed a heavy diet of commentary, especially on cable television, telling us there is no way the United States is going to prevail in this battle. And in case you weren't paying attention, the whole idea of a two-state solution of the Israeli-Palestinian dispute is being abandoned by some of its once-strongest supporters in Palestine, Israel, and even here in America. And Iran continues to thumb its nose at the international demand that it give up its nuclear ambitions—a standoff that could quite possibly end badly for us all. Is it, therefore, any wonder that the American people feel as negatively as they apparently do toward nearly every institution in this country?

I don't pretend to have a solution to all or any of these problems. To keep myself from falling victim to hopelessness, what I try to do is what I did throughout my life as a foreign and diplomatic correspondent: put things into perspective. As bad as things may now appear, during the recently-ended twentieth century this country and the world faced far greater threats to humanity's very existence than we face today. Our problems abroad are very serious, but we will survive them. Our economic crises are not over, but we just got through the worst of a very, very bad one, and we can and will learn some important lessons from it. Climate change is our biggest challenge, but I am confident that we will ultimately summon up the will and the way to deal with it, although it may take a catastrophe or two before that happens.

I am not suggesting that to improve our moods we fix up the barn, gather our friends, and put on our tap shoes for a rousing performance of "We're in the Money"—even though that might be fun. On the other hand, if I could get Goldman Sachs CEO Lloyd Blankfein to do a chorus of "Brother Can You Spare a Dime," that would certainly raise a lot of spirits.

January 23, 2011

Gun Control after Tucson

There is much that is notable in the aftermath of the Tucson tragedy. As I've watched events and interviews with those directly involved, I've been taken not just by the courage, but the basic decency of those involved and how they have come together in their support for each other, and in their devotion to Congresswoman Gabrielle Giffords, who was perilously close to death for several days and now faces months—if not years—of intense rehabilitation. Capped off by President Barack Obama's thoughtful speech which effectively calmed troubled waters, the Tucson tragedy has increasingly been presented as a feel-good story. Nothing wrong with that, except for the fact that six people died violently that day, including the lovely nine-year-old Christina Green. (We learned this past week that Christina's corneas have been transplanted to restore the sight of two other youngsters. That may be some solace to her parents, but hardly enough to ease the pain they will feel for the rest of their lives.)

It is unlikely that any of the families of the dead or the living victims are anywhere near closure—the favorite media word to describe the supposed goal of those whose lives have been completely overturned by violent forces not of their making and beyond their control. Yet two weeks after Tucson, people in the rest of the country, especially including their political leaders, appear to have reached a kind of collective closure and are getting on with their lives as though nothing can be done to prevent such tragedies from happening again and again and again.

While working abroad, I reported on the aftermath of the assassinations of John Kennedy, Robert Kennedy, and Martin Luther King, Jr. I was covering the State Department in Washington during the two attempts on Gerald Ford's life and was very much involved in the follow-up coverage of Ronald Reagan's near-assassination. Let me stress that the only thing all this makes me an expert in is the shock and pain I shared with millions of others on those occasions. But having had those life experiences does make me soundly reject one troubling idea: the notion that mental cases with access to guns are simply the price that must be paid for living in a free and democratic society.

For the moment, I choose not to engage in the argument over the potential consequences of the toxic political debate that has become the norm in the last two decades and has become demonstrably worse in the two years since a black man was elected president.

I also see no point in trying to re-litigate the 2008 and 2010 Supreme Court rulings on the Second Amendment, which reversed a century of case law and extended gun rights to individuals (also apparently giving the NRA a clear-cut victory in its decades-long fight against gun control). Since 2008 no major Democratic leaders, including the one now occupying the White House, have allowed the words "gun control" to escape their lips. This may represent a pragmatic concession to prevailing political winds, but it is hardly a profile in political courage.

Yet, if the six deaths in Tucson, the thirty-two at Virginia Tech, and all those others who have died at the hands of murderous people with far-too-easy access to deadly weapons are to have any meaning at all, it is going to take some form of courage to address this scourge. For far too long this has been an issue that has divided the left and the right—with the result that extremists have been able to have their way to the detriment of us all. I am not interested in taking people's guns away. As it happens, I do not hunt, but I respect the right of hunters to own guns, especially in a place like Vermont. I understand that hunting is very much of part of the American culture—as having guns for personal security is for some. So I am hoping that perhaps now that the fundamental right to own a gun has been settled by the Supreme Court, liberals and conservatives might be able to come together on some common-sense rules governing such ownership.

A good start would be a discussion on the reinstatement of the ban on assault weapons, which was allowed to lapse in 2004. Does anyone truly believe that the framers of the Constitution, wise and worldly men like Jefferson, Adams, Madison, and Hamilton, would have thought it was a good idea that more than two-thirds of its citizens (there are 240 million guns for the just over 300 million of today's Americans) have weapons that are capable of wiping out an entire regiment of Washington's Continental Army in less than a minute? Would erudite men, who could read history in the original Greek and Latin and were legal scholars of their day, think it prudent that concealed weapons be legal in schools, workplaces, parks, churches, taverns, sporting events, and on the floor of the United States House of Representatives?

With gun ownership now an established personal right, given the lethal nature of guns, should it not be possible for reasonable people to agree that this right should come with responsible licensing for owners and enforced regulations that make a serious effort to keep weapons out of the hands of the incompetent or mentally ill? How many more Tucsons, or Virginia Techs, or Kennedys, or Kings will it take? This is why I respectfully but strongly disagree with the palliative nature of the news coverage of these tragedies. I'm not looking for feel-good stories of the redeeming nature of humankind, and I don't want closure. That mindset only leads to passive acquiescence in an unacceptable status quo. I want remedial action. I want to see America try to correct a societal sickness that does it no honor while causing so much pain. If not now, ever?

September 25, 2008

Speech: **Race in the Presidential Campaign—**
Transcendent or Still Toxic?

Thank you. First, I'd like to address a question that may have crossed some of your minds. What does this old white geezer who lived most of his life in foreign countries know about race and American politics?

That's a fair question. Let me answer it by admitting at the outset that I do not pretend to be an expert on the subject. I suspect there are numerous people in this room who know a lot more about it than I do. But what I am kind of an expert in is looking at a complex issue, identifying its major elements, providing a historical context with detail that people may not be aware of, adding current contemporary aspects of the issue, and objectively tying that all together in an way that I hope makes our topic this evening more comprehensible to all of us.

That is the work that I have done now for nearly fifty years. Most of my life, I dealt with complicated world problems such as the Cold War, nuclear arms control, and the Middle East. The part of the United States story that I focused on most of the time dealt with its foreign policy and its relationships with the world. Therefore, much of my effort was devoted to an understanding of the history, people, and politics of Russia, Eastern and Western Europe, Israel, and the Arab countries of the Middle East. Of course, I also had to know and understand America's historical and contemporary interests as they intersected with these countries. But two unexpected moments early in my retirement made me realize there was a gap in my understanding of the history of United States—notably on the subject of race.

My first year of retirement I spent as a fellow at the Kennedy School of Government at Harvard. My main project at Harvard was to conduct a study on the potential consequences of live television coverage of war. As part of that study, I did lengthy interviews with all the network anchors and top executives in network news; with senior officials at the White House, State Department, and the civilian side of the Pentagon; and with the generals who had commanded and been victorious in the then-recent Gulf War.

One of those I talked to at length, and exchanged letters and phone calls with, was former Chairman of the Joint Chiefs of Staff General Colin Powell. This was early in 1996, and you may remember that at that time he was considered a very possible presidential candidate for the Republican Party. I kidded him about that several times, but I couldn't tell which way he would jump. It did seem to me that he wanted to run, although I could sense he really was struggling with the decision.

I later learned from someone who knew Powell well that the principal reason he decided not to seek the nomination was his wife Alma's fear that as a black man, he would become an assassin's target.

I am confident that given his combat experience Powell himself did not harbor such fears, and I initially thought it was touching that he was not prepared to put his wife through such anguish. But on further reflection, I was troubled because Powell's decision not to run meant that at least on some level, he was validating his wife's dread. If this could happen to a brave soldier who had broken most of his country's color barriers at the highest levels, then it suggested that race remained a more powerful force in American politics than I had realized.

My other unexpected post-retirement moment came after Harvard published my study on war and live television. That got me an invitation from the then-Chief of Staff of the Army, General Dennis Reimer, to join him and his senior staff for a meeting with a few other war correspondents at the Army War College in Carlisle, Pennsylvania. The purpose of this small conference was to discuss past and future relations between the military and the media. I don't think anything remarkable came out of that conference, but a side trip we took that weekend left a lasting impression on me.

Our small group of generals and reporters, about a dozen in all, was treated to a day-long tour of the nearby Gettysburg battlefields. Our guides were the War College commandant and its historian. After visiting the sites and hearing the stories of the first two days of the fighting, we walked side by side onto the once-bloody field of Pickett's Charge—the decisive engagement of the battle of Gettysburg and the turning point of the Civil War. Along the way, our guides shouted out to us from either side of our line, telling us what would have been happening at that moment on that July day in 1863: where Lee's generals would have been, what barriers we would have to cross, and what kind of fire we would have been under. This went on for about an hour as we briskly marched toward what had been the Union lines at the top of Cemetery Ridge. In this setting, one could truly visualize the carnage of thousands of soldiers being killed and wounded in such a short time on that very ground. I have to say that of all the world's famous historical sites I have been privileged to visit, this may have been the most moving.

Until that moment, I had never been as interested in the Civil War as the wars of the twentieth century. But for the next decade I would read extensively on the subject as I came to appreciate that you cannot truly understand this country until you recognize just how profound the impact of the Civil War has been on American history and on the American psyche, and how a large portion of the population has never fully stopped fighting or accepted the outcome of that war. The Civil War, unfortunately, was probably inevitable after its seeds were sown at the very creation of the Republic. And it is at the creation that the story of race and politics in America does indeed begin.

"We hold these truths to be self-evident, that all men are created equal ... " So reads one of the best-known phrases of the Declaration of Independence. It was inspired by the writings of Thomas Hobbes and John Locke, two English political philosophers of the seventeenth century. They had advocated societies and governments based on the proposition that all men were created equal. Their ideas were incorporated into the Declaration by Thomas Jefferson, who essentially used the British crown's failure to treat its American colonists as equals as justification for those colonies to declare their independence. After some editing of Jefferson's draft, the Second Continental Congress in Philadelphia concurred, and approved the Declaration of Independence on July 4, 1776.

For Americans of color, that phrase that all men are created equal is heavily ironic, especially since by 1776 black slavery was an accepted fact of life throughout all of the thirteen colonies. As David McCullough wrote in his biography of John Adams, "Of a total population in the colonies of nearly 2,500,000 people in 1776, approximately one in five were slaves, some 500,000 men, women and children. In Virginia alone, which had the most slaves by far, they numbered more than 200,000. There was no member of the Virginia delegation who did not own slaves, and of all the members of Congress at least a third owned or had owned slaves. The total of Thomas Jefferson's slaves in 1776 was about 200, which was also the approximate number owned by George Washington."

The founding fathers were not unaware of that irony embedded in the Declaration. Mostly, they chose to suppress it. In laying out the bill of particulars against King George III in his draft of the Declaration,

Jefferson actually blamed the British for bringing the horrors of the slave trade to America. McCullough writes, "As emphatic a passage as any, this on the slave trade was to be the ringing climax of all the charges." But as we now know that passage did not make the cut. It was removed in its entirety, according to Jefferson himself, because South Carolina and Georgia objected to any mention of slavery. This was not the first concession made to the slave-holding states as the American Republic came into being, and most certainly would not be the last.

Slavery was also a significant factor in the next major event in American history—the Constitutional Convention, presided over by George Washington that took place in Philadelphia between May and September of 1787. The product of this convention was the United States Constitution, which nearly all Americans know begins with these words: "We the People of the United States, in Order to form a more perfect Union, establish Justice, insure domestic Tranquility, provide for the common defense, promote the general Welfare, and secure the Blessings of Liberty to ourselves and our Posterity, do ordain and establish this Constitution for the United States of America."

As wholly admirable as this sentiment was, history would conclude that this extraordinary document, out of which the United States of America was born, contained the stain Barack Obama and others have described as the "original sin" of racism. Given the political realities of the day, based on the fundamental split between slaveholding and non-slaveholding states, the result could hardly have been otherwise. Quite simply, if they could not get major concessions on the question of slavery, the slaveholding states would refuse to join the Union.

One of those concessions would be enshrined as Article 1, Section 2, paragraph 3 of the Constitution. It is known as the Three-Fifths Compromise. The issue was how slaves were to be counted in establishing the official populations of the respective states. This was important for two reasons. First: total population would determine the number of members each state would have in the new House of Representatives and how many votes it would get in the electoral college to choose the president. Second: if the federal government were to levy taxes on the states, it would be according to their population.

The slaveholding states wanted their slaves to be fully counted for political purposes, but not at all when it came to taxes. The compromise reached was that slaves would be counted as three-fifths of a person for both political and tax purposes. As the political question was of much greater importance to the southern states, they accepted the deal.

That paid off very well for them. The three-fifths ratio had a major effect on pre-Civil War political affairs due to the disproportionate representation of slaveholding states. For example, in 1793, slave states would have been apportioned 33 seats in the House of Representatives had the seats been assigned based on the free population; instead they were apportioned 47. In 1812, slaveholding states had 76 instead of 59; in 1833, 98 instead of 73. As a result, southerners dominated the presidency, the speakership of the House, and the Supreme Court in all the years right up to the Civil War. Historian Garry Wills has argued that among other things, without the additional slave votes, Jefferson would have lost the presidential election of 1800.

The other compromise reached at the Constitutional Convention concerned the slave trade itself. Ten states had already made it illegal. Many delegates strongly denounced it. But three states—both Carolinas and Georgia, where the slave trade still flourished—threatened to leave the Convention if such trade were banned. Ultimately, the delegates to the Convention did not want their efforts to fail because of the conflict over slavery. Therefore, a special commission worked out another deal whereby Congress would have the power to ban the slave trade, but only after at least twenty years had passed—meaning not until at least 1808.

Benjamin Franklin, who had owned one or two household slaves during much of his life, was generally opposed to slavery. He had stated his views publicly, and in 1787 accepted the presidency of the Pennsylvania Society for Promoting the Abolition of Slavery. The group tried to get him to present a petition against slavery to the Constitutional Convention, but knowing the delicate compromises then being negotiated between North and South, he kept silent on the issue.

In his 2003 biography *Benjamin Franklin: An American Life*, author Walter Isaacson says that Franklin considered the compromises on race to have been absolutely essential to the achievement of the new constitution. In what he calls Franklin's "remarkable closing address," Isaacson writes, "The speech was a testament to the virtue of intellectual tolerance and to the evil of presumed infallibility, and it proclaimed for the ages the enlightened creed that became central to American freedom. They were the most eloquent words Franklin ever wrote."

These are some of the words Franklin spoke at the end of the Constitutional Convention:

"I confess that I do not entirely approve this Constitution, but sir, I am not sure I shall never approve it....

I agree to this Constitution with all its faults—if they are such—because I think a general government necessary for us....

I doubt too, whether any other convention we can obtain, may be able to make a better Constitution; for when you assemble a number of men, to have the advantage of their joint wisdom, you inevitably assemble with those men, all their prejudices, their passions, their errors of opinion, their local interests and their selfish views. From such an assembly can a perfect production be expected? It therefore astonishes me to find this system approaching so near to perfection as it does."

Belatedly, on behalf of the abolition society of which he was president, Franklin presented a formal abolition petition to Congress in February 1790. It declared, "Mankind are all formed by the same Almighty Being, alike objects in His care and equally designed for the enjoyment of happiness." The petition went on to note that it was the duty of Congress to secure "the blessings of liberty to the People of the United States," and that this should be done "without distinction of color." Franklin and his petition were ignored by Congress and denounced by those members who remained steadfast defenders of slavery.

Some of you may be gazing at your watches and thinking, "Nearly halfway done, and he's only just through the Revolutionary War." I promise you this is not going to be a full history of race in America. My intention is to present fragments of this story—the highlights, or in most cases, more properly described as the lowlights. And as much is so often made about the "imperfect Union," I thought it important to focus on those crucial early political decisions.

The Civil War is of course the next major historical event, but I suspect there may not be much about that subject that most of you don't already know. But I would like to address what I find intriguing about the Civil War: that in spite of the incredible trauma that was inflicted upon this country by one of the bloodiest civil wars in world history, it actually settled so little of the issue over which it was fought, namely slavery.

I was surprised to learn just this year that more than 3,000 African Americans and their white allies were killed by terrorist organizations in the South in the decade between 1866 and 1876. (As a percentage of the population, that would be about 20,000 today, or more than six times the death toll of 9/11.) That is just one of the disturbing assertions in a book published this past spring, *The Bloody Shirt: Terror after Appomattox* by Stephen Budiansky. Budiansky is a military historian who concludes that while the North won the Civil War, it was the South that ultimately won the peace. The book focuses on five courageous men who tried to stop the violence and to support the dream of freedom.

I was interested to discover that one of those five was General James Longstreet, the man known as General Robert E. Lee's most trusted lieutenant. If Lee had followed Longstreet's advice on the third day at Gettysburg to turn the Union's left with a flanking maneuver, instead of the full frontal assault now known as Pickett's Charge, the Confederate Army might have won the battle of Gettysburg, and the war may well have ended differently.

Longstreet later admitted that the third day at Gettysburg was the saddest day of his life, but he remained loyal to Lee. That was not true of Pickett. According to Budiansky, "The romantic haze of Southern chivalry that soon enveloped Pickett's hopeless charge left Pickett unmoved." Said Pickett, "That old man [meaning Lee] had my division massacred."

Longstreet's story is too complicated to detail here, but basically he ran into trouble by trying to accommodate Reconstruction efforts in the South, and by reminding his fellow Southerners what the surrender at Appomattox meant; namely, an end to the Confederacy and an end to the South's total domination over its sizeable black population. In Longstreet's words, "The political questions of the war should have been buried upon the fields that marked their end." For this he was vilified, and went from being a giant in the pantheon of Confederate war heroes to something closer to a traitor to the Southern cause.

In *The Bloody Shirt*, we also learn about a state judge in North Carolina who had fearlessly defended the rights of the common man, whether white or black, defied the threats of the Ku Klux Klan when he put blacks on juries, and fined attorneys for using the "N" word in his courtroom. However, by 1879 the judge was exhausted and dispirited and told the *New York Tribune*, "In all except the actual results of the physical struggle, I consider the South to have been the real victors of the war. I am filled with admiration and amazement at the masterly way in which they have brought about these results. The way in which they have neutralized the results of the war and reversed the verdict of Appomattox is the grandest thing in American politics."

The Thirteenth Amendment to the Constitution did ban slavery. The Fourteenth Amendment required states to provide equal protection under the law to all of their citizens and the Fifteenth Amendment banned race-based voting qualifications. These are the Civil War Reconstruction Amendments that were designed to secure the rights of former slaves.

But the Reconstruction of the South ended with another notorious compromise—the one which followed the contested presidential election of 1876. Republican candidate Rutherford B. Hayes lost the popular vote, but his opponent fell one vote short in the Electoral College as four states' delegations were in dispute. Three of those disputes were in Southern states still occupied by the Union Army. When a committee of Congress was set up to elect the president, a deal was struck whereby Southerners on the committee agreed to vote for Hayes in return for his commitment to withdraw the remnants of the Federal army from their states.

Not only was that the end of Reconstruction, it marked the beginning of the Jim Crow era—the time when state and local laws were enacted in the South and border states to mandate a "separate but equal" status for black Americans. That meant public schools, public places, and public transportation became separate, that there would be separate toilets and restaurants and water fountains, and almost always the blacks' facilities were inferior. Meantime, the Fifteenth Amendment passed in 1870, and which granted the newly freed blacks full voting rights, was negated by a web of insidious laws and regulations that throughout the South effectively blocked black participation in the political process. That situation would prevail for about another ninety years.

Throughout this long dark period for African Americans, successive Democratic and Republican administrations in Washington, at a minimum, were complicit in allowing this blatant discrimination to continue. I remember feeling great sadness a few years ago when I first read details of how the likes of President Franklin D. Roosevelt had capitulated to racist southern Democrats who had a stranglehold in Congress. As they usually faced no political opposition in their home states, and therefore were repeatedly re-elected, the seniority system allowed southern Democrats to rise to the chairmanships of many of the key committees of Congress.

In his biography of the economist John Kenneth Galbraith, author Richard Parker recounts how during Roosevelt's first term, the newly created Agriculture Adjustment Administration put together a complex system of farm subsidies to try to mitigate the effects of the Depression and successive droughts in the West. But under the original plan, in the South much of the federal help ended up going to large-scale cotton plantations and not to those who really needed it: the sharecroppers and tenant farmers.

So it was decided to try to get funds directly to this mainly black and particularly vulnerable group. As Parker writes, "One young AAA lawyer recalled what happened when Senator Ellison DuRant Smith of South Carolina discovered the AAA had begun sending allotment checks to the sharecroppers. 'Cotton Ed' was chairman of the powerful Agriculture Committee and a major cotton grower himself. [He was] massively rotund, with thinning gray hair and a walrus mustache stained by a lifetime of chewing tobacco. Senator Smith went to the young lawyer's office when he heard the allotment checks were going out to the tenants … he said, 'Young fella, you can't do this to my niggers, paying checks to them. They don't know what to do with the money. The money should come to me. I'll take care of them. They're mine.'"

During that summer, the tensions between the AAA and the plantation owners continued to build. Finally, with his entire legislative agenda suddenly at risk through defections by southern Democrats who controlled Agriculture, Appropriations, and Rules Committees, Roosevelt ordered his Secretary of Agriculture and the AAA to surrender. Direct payments to sharecroppers ended and within the next year more than 700,000 southern tenant farmers and their families were evicted and left homeless.

For African Americans, some things finally began to change for the better after World War II. In 1947, when Jackie Robinson took the field for the Brooklyn Dodgers he became the first African American to play major league baseball, which had been segregated for eighty years. This breakthrough transcended baseball and made a major impact on society at all levels.

In 1948, President Harry Truman signed an executive order designed to desegregate the U.S. military by providing for equal treatment and opportunity for African American servicemen. The order had little immediate effect, and it would take another six years before all the services were completely integrated. Nevertheless, Truman's decision was an important milestone.

Truman was rewarded for that decision and for the civil rights platform of the Democratic Party at its 1948 convention. It was because of that platform that South Carolina Senator Strom Thurmond stormed out of the convention and formed the Dixiecrat Party. At the time, this made many Democrats very nervous and contributed to the fear among them that Truman would lose to Dewey in November.

But as we know, Truman astounded nearly everyone by winning the election, with almost 50 percent of the popular vote, while the Dixiecrats picked up just over 2 percent. But very significantly, African Americans in the North and Midwest voted overwhelmingly for Truman. This was clearly a determining factor in Ohio and Illinois, where he won by less than 1 percent, and without which he would have been defeated.

Finally, the event which marked the beginning of the end of official segregation was the Supreme Court decision of 1954—Brown v. the Board of Education of Topeka, Kansas.

In a unanimous decision, the court of Chief Justice Earl Warren ruled that "separate educational facilities are inherently unequal." This decision paved the way for the civil rights movement of the 1960s, which resulted in the ground-breaking Civil Rights and Voting Rights Acts of 1964 and '65. For those laws, we owe an enormous debt to Martin Luther King, Jr. and the thousands of brave black and white people who marched with him—but also to Lyndon Johnson who used all of his persuasive skills to get the legislation passed—and to John Kennedy, who not too long before he was assassinated, decided to proceed with significant civil rights legislation even though he believed it might cost him the 1964 election.

The new Civil Rights Acts profoundly changed the political and personal situations of millions of African Americans, but did not take race out of politics. Southern Democrats were fuming that it was their party that had passed the legislation that effectively put an end to the Jim Crow era. Richard Nixon responded with a southern strategy that amounted to exploiting racial tensions for political gain. By appealing to segregationist Democrats, Nixon hastened the transformation from Democratic to Republican of much of the South—where virtually no members of the party of Lincoln had been elected to national office for almost a century.

Because of the Civil Rights laws, racism in American politics is no longer as overt as it once was. But it is evident nonetheless. Forced busing to integrate schools and, later, affirmative action, were seized upon as wedge issues by Republicans, who just like the southern Democrats of the Jim Crow era, used working class whites' fear of blacks to gain political advantage—more often than not to the detriment of working class whites.

Fear of blacks was the subliminal message in the infamous television commercial during the 1988 presidential campaign, when the Republicans portrayed Democratic candidate Michael Dukakis as soft on crime. They did so by exploiting the fact that a black convict named Willy Horton had committed murder while on a weekend prison furlough, a program approved by Dukakis when he was governor of Massachusetts. The Willy Horton story wasn't the sole reason Dukakis was defeated, but it certainly contributed to that loss.

As most African Americans vote Democratic, one of the most common examples of the modern Republicans' use of the race card is in suppression of the black vote. There are numerous ways this can be done. One way is the official publishing of lists of convicted felons near election time, which include many common black surnames but often omit full first or middle names, ages, or addresses. In a state such as Florida where convicted felons were banned from voting for life, that could mean that every black G. Washington in the state would be challenged when they went to cast their ballots. Considering how close things were in 2000, this was not insignificant. For their part, Republicans regularly make the claim that there are threats of massive voter fraud throughout the country. And so in recent decades, Democratic Party efforts to increase voter registration are inevitably met by Republican Party counter-moves to purge the voter lists of people who they claim for one reason or another are not eligible.

These struggles are ongoing now in several battleground states, most recently including Wisconsin. I can't speak to the merits of the arguments of either side in these particular disputes. But history suggests that when southern Democrats in the past, or Republicans more recently, have wanted to cull the voter lists because of alleged registration fraud, their real motivation has usually been to keep black people from voting.

Still another recent problem became evident when we learned that the Bush administration apparently gutted the Civil Rights Division of the Justice Department. This, after all, is the division charged, among other things, with enforcing the Civil Rights and Voting

Rights Acts. And if violations of these laws aren't prosecuted, one can only assume that attempts to suppress the black vote will again become more overt. This particular problem remains unresolved while official investigations are underway to look into credible reports about how Bush political appointees interfered with, and in some cases forced out, professional civil rights lawyers working in the Justice Department.

McCain campaign officials adamantly deny any suggestion that they might be using the race card, even covertly. I do not know what is in their hearts, but when they run an advertising campaign which depicts a man with very humble origins as an elitist out of touch with common people, when they suggest he is nothing more than a vapid celebrity and is full of himself with his big speeches, the message I am receiving is that Obama is an "uppity black."

I was happy to be joined in that analysis by David Gergen, who has worked at the White House for Bill Clinton but before that for Ronald Reagan and George Bush, Sr. Gergen said the portrayal of Obama in those McCain campaign ads is indeed code for "uppity black." And as we know, that is not a term of endearment. It is a phrase used historically by whites to describe blacks who sought to be treated as equals. They were called uppity because they did not know their place—which used to be the back of the bus only—and most certainly cannot possibly be the Oval Office.

A postscript to this matter: according to the Capitol Hill newspaper *The Hill*, during the Republican National Convention, Republican Congressman Lynn Westmoreland of Georgia publicly let slip that he thought both Obama and his wife Michelle were "uppity." I guess Westmoreland got the message.

But finally, the question before us now is whether it can be said that the nomination of Barack Obama to be the Democratic Party's presidential candidate means that we are actually going beyond the issue of race in American politics—that race as a political issue is being or has been transcended. Never before has an African American reached such a lofty position in the political pecking order. In a matter of weeks he might well be elected president. Surely this must indicate a profound change in American attitudes—doesn't it?

One person who has chosen to argue that there has been a profound change is Barack Obama himself. As a central part of his campaign strategy, he has gone out of his way not to be seen as an "angry black," or even as the black candidate. He does not play the victim, and he discourages other black people from doing so. Rather than decrying this country's imperfections, he works at ways to make it a more perfect union. This is a strategy that makes a virtue out of necessity, because the only way a black man can win an election of this magnitude is to persuade a majority of whites that he can be trusted—that they don't have to be afraid of him.

Here I must be emphatic: in terms of historical accomplishment, that Obama has come so far represents major progress in race relations in this country. This would have been absolutely impossible for the first 200 years of the Republic. It couldn't have happened even twenty years ago. Conceivably, Colin Powell might have been nominated by the Republicans in 1996 had he decided to run—there is no real way of knowing.

But it is also a fact that Obama is still having problems attracting support among working-class whites, especially in small towns and rural areas, many of whom voted for Hillary Clinton during the primaries and some of whom are now flocking to Sarah Palin. I would love to believe that Obama's nomination does mean that the issue of race is no longer determinant in this country's presidential politics. But I think we cannot make that assertion until we see the results of the election. Given all the disadvantages the Republicans are facing due to their dismal record of the past eight years; given that eight out of ten Americans believe the country is moving in the wrong direction, logically it would seem that Obama should be way ahead in the polls. He is not. The race remains basically tied.

So what if Obama loses? Was he just a weak candidate who ran a bad campaign—was he too liberal—or is there something else at work here? Throughout the campaign so far, a substantial majority has supported Democratic rather than Republican policies. So, if not issues, what? Even through extensive exit polls it may be very hard to determine exactly why he lost, the reality is that very few people who will not vote for a black presidential candidate are willing to admit their prejudices in public or to pollsters—basically because they are ashamed. If Obama loses in a close election—and very close is what the current polls predict—I for one will find it hard not to conclude that his color was ultimately what kept him from closing the deal with a majority of the American people. By that I don't mean to imply that everyone who voted against him is a racist, or to suggest that working class whites are racist, or that Republicans are racist. But if he loses, I believe it will be because a small number of whites—I don't know what percentage, perhaps 2–3 percent—voted against him because he was black. I cannot prove it, but that is my considered opinion. And if that is so, for me it will mean the toxicity of race has not yet been entirely cleansed from the American body politic.

However, if Obama should win, it will be possible to argue that the issue of race has been transcended because the biggest taboo in American politics will have been broken. Race won't cease to be a factor in presidential politics, but it will no longer be a dominant one. And let there be no doubt—that will be a monumental event in the history of this country.

Editor's note: The above speech was presented to an audience in Montpelier, Vermont in the fall of 2008 as part of an effort to raise funds for Central Vermont Anti-Racism Study Circles.

Journalism & the Mainstream Media

THE MEDIA: Media Matters

The news media are, of course, a large part of America's political life and its culture. I have given this subject its own chapter because of my own direct connection and frequent commentaries about it.

As I left ABC News after thirty years, I was certainly aware of how much what we now call the mainstream media had changed during the course of my career. The greatest innovation was the communication satellite that made it possible to report live from most parts of the globe. Just as the invention of the telegraph in the nineteenth century made same-day news possible for newspapers, thereby changing them dramatically, the satellite would bring the sights and sounds of major world events into people's homes, even as these events were actually happening. This was huge. But even with that technological revolution, little did I realize that in another decade or so, journalism as I once knew it would become almost unrecognizable, due in large measure to the exponential growth of the Internet and its social networks.

I had made a vow to myself when I retired that I was not going to become one of those geezers obsessed with the past. My day had been very good for me, but that didn't mean it was better than the present. I confess, it has been difficult to keep that vow. But in a series of lectures in 2010 to the journalism classes of Vermont's St. Michael's College, I was able to refrain from directly comparing my era to today's journalism. Only half jokingly, I suggested the students look at me as archeologists might examine a discovery from a new dig—a well preserved, completely intact relic of the past from which some useful things might be learned.

The columns and comments that follow are a sampling of media matters over the past decade on which I had something I wanted to say. Like most people who were, or still are, a part of American journalism, I have little idea where things are headed. If a new business model for the news business is not soon found, it is hard to imagine in what form most newspapers and news magazines—not to mention the network news divisions—are going to survive. I do know this: American democracy, at its core, cannot function without a relatively well-informed electorate. Yet in spite of, or perhaps because of, the surfeit of information from so many platforms and sources, the electorate may actually be less informed today than at other important times in American history.

September 20, 2009

Crisis of Confidence in the News Media

Old-fartitis (my definition): condition peculiar to males that becomes apparent near the end of their careers. Its most common symptom is the repeated assertion that nothing in their previous business or profession is as good today as it was when they were in their prime.

Long before my retirement, I swore to myself that I would not be like those geezers I had had to deal with when I was young and eager. I knew there would be many more changes in journalism. But most of the younger reporters I knew were as dedicated and actually better educated than much of my generation. And the explosion of advanced communication technologies promised both new challenges and greater opportunities for reporting the news. So as I saw it a decade ago, the news media of the future would be different, but no worse than their predecessors. But alas, I confess I have been overtaken by an acute case of the dreaded old man's disease as defined above. As I have watched the profound changes in journalism in recent years, I have come to fear that where once the news media were part of the solution to the country's problems (the news coverage of the civil rights battles of the 1960s being the best example), they have become part of the problem. In fairness, it's not necessarily the fault of today's journalists. It's what the news media business has become.

A couple of weeks ago, President Barack Obama spoke at the memorial service of the late CBS News anchorman Walter Cronkite, the man the pollsters of his day identified as "The Most Trusted Man in America." The president raised some interesting questions. "Would [Walter] have been able to cut through the murky noise and the blogs and the tweets and the sound bites to shine a bright light on substance? Would he still offer the perspective that we value? Would he have been able to remain a singular figure in an age of dwindling attention spans and omnipresent media?" To all of those questions the president answered, "Yes." With great respect to President Obama and Walter Cronkite, I disagree. The question is not what Walter would do in this era, it is what would he be allowed to do? In fact, Cronkite was replaced by CBS News before he needed to be and then wandered about in the journalistic wilderness for nearly a quarter of a century after that. Even back then, that was a business/ratings decision.

Cronkite and those of us from that generation had the good fortune to start working in network television news when it was not solely driven by ratings. For many years, the networks' news divisions operated at a financial loss. This was not out of altruism but to keep the Federal Communications Commission happy and so ensure network licensing renewals. Today's problems for network news really started when it went from being a loss leader to a cash cow—that is, when the news divisions started making big money. That made the networks themselves targets for large corporate takeovers and that's when ratings—the basis on which network advertising revenues are set and depend—started to significantly shape news broadcasts just as they did the entertainment programs.

Now, let me be clear. I am not against making money. And the fact is that right now American journalism is being threatened because newspapers of all sizes are teetering on the brink of bankruptcy due to advertising revenues lost to the Internet. That is a very important part of what is happening to the news media today (and a subject that deserves greater attention at another time).

But I believe that what is actually causing the crisis in confidence in the news media of today is that there is now too much "news"— news that bombards us from all directions and media platforms, that comes at us unedited and without grownup supervision. This is a consequence of that explosion of technologies which completely revolutionized the communications industry—a revolution to which both broadcast news and newspapers were very slow to adapt. Nowadays, with 24/7 cable news programs; with the Internet and its plethora of blogs and social networks; with "citizen" reporters armed with cell-phone cameras, our world is inundated with cascades of images and cacophonies of voices. The loudest and most extreme opinions are what all-news cable channels choose to offer with virtually no regard or weight given to that which is true and that which is clearly false. Conflict, it seems, is good for ratings. Quiet, reasoned discourse is largely seen and heard only on public broadcasting, which critics deride as "lefty elitist." Meanwhile, the PBS-antithesis FOX network was the only major network not to carry the president's prime time news conference on health care or his speech to a joint meeting of Congress. That matters because FOX viewers are the ones who are angriest about everything, and might have learned something from hearing the president in his own words rather than getting a twisted version of his speech from right-wing commentators who now openly call him a Nazi, a Communist, and a racist.

In such a media landscape, deciding who or what to believe

becomes a major challenge even for the most discerning citizens. As my friend Ted Koppel wrote in an email exchange we had recently on this subject, "What is particularly troublesome about the decline of public confidence in the mainstream media lies in the field of breaking national crises, to wit: if there were a biological terrorist attack in one city, with the attendant threat of a second, third, or fourth attack in other cities around the country. The nation is now wired so that every rumor is amplified a million times or more, while the networks (which could in earlier times have been counted upon to disseminate the best information and instructions available) are now routinely dismissed as propaganda outlets for the government." That's how the right wing views them, while to many on the left the networks are simply corporate apologists. In either case it would seem the mainstream media are basically no longer trusted. And one day, many more than just us old reporters may greatly mourn that loss.

August 11, 2005

Remembering Peter Jennings

Peter never tired of teasing me about how I got my job with ABC in 1965, by waylaying him in a hotel parking lot in Toronto and thrusting my audition tape into his car as he was racing for a plane to New York. Like all such stories, it's basically true—but short on some important details. One: he had asked for the tape. We had worked together for the CTV network in Canada before he went to the United States, and ABC was looking for young reporters. And two: the reason he was in Toronto was to host the Miss Canada Pageant, where he had to sing and dance. As I often reminded him, he was no Bert Parks.

Through wars, summit meetings, marriages, and divorces, Peter and I shared hotel rooms, apartments, and television studios around the world. Everyone in the business agreed that nobody was better in front of a television camera. But of course there was very much more to the man than that.

Peter could be a nitpicker. I mean that both figuratively and literally. I'd be all dressed up, ready to go and he would come up to me and flick some imaginary piece of dust or hair from my lapel and straighten my tie. I would sometimes wonder if he was trying to remind me of my flaws, or if he really just wanted me to look perfect. I think it was probably a bit of both—for one of the things about Peter Jennings was that he was never satisfied. He always wanted to know more, to travel more, to meet new people, and to get more airtime to report on the world that so captivated him.

Peter could be a harsh critic of other peoples' work, including that of his friends. But he was even harsher on himself. It was this relentless drive for perfection that propelled him to the very top of a field not known for its shrinking violets.

But one of his more endearing qualities was the way he treated people outside the business. He would give due deference to both the prince and the pauper—but showed more interest in the pauper. When we worked and lived together in Rome and Beirut, Peter would go out of his way to get to know everybody in the neighborhood—the flower sellers, the waiters, or the street sweepers. He had this unique ability to give them his full attention and make them feel he was truly interested in them—which indeed for that moment, he was. This quality of caring was evident as he calmly talked millions of

Americans through every major news event of the past twenty years.

There will be time later to discuss Peter's legacy and the implications of his passing on the future of television news. But for now, it's enough to note that many millions of people apparently share some of my sadness of having lost a dear friend.

June 12, 2011

On Friends in High Places

I got to know and traveled extensively with eight U.S. Secretaries of State, including Lawrence S. Eagleburger. Considering the normal tension between major public figures and the reporters who cover them, we were usually friendly. Journalists must never confuse proximity to power with their own importance. But that said, for many years I have been proud to call Eagleburger my friend. Larry, as his many journalist and professional friends knew him—though his wife Marlene always called him Lawrence—died June 4 at the age of eighty.

I am saddened by his death. But in some respects it is amazing he lived so long. As the obit writers all noted, he had chronic asthma and always carried inhalators with him while continuing to smoke heavily. He had a knee injury and muscle disorders that forced him to use a cane. In his later years he had heart problems and was considerably overweight. Yet in many ways, these physical ailments and the stoic way he coped with them endeared him even to opponents. In a sense, this vulnerability had a way of smoothing over the rough edges of the often gruff and caustic manner of one of this country's finest and most respected diplomats.

Although a Republican and a Henry Kissinger protégé, Eagleburger was named ambassador to Yugoslavia by President Jimmy Carter during the final days of the Tito regime. Among his qualifications, was the fact that he spoke Serbo-Croatian from his years in the Belgrade embassy in the 1960s. After Ronald Reagan was elected in 1980, Eagleburger returned to Washington to become Secretary of State Alexander Haig's assistant secretary for Europe. In December 1981, a major crisis erupted when hard-line Polish Communists, pressed by Moscow, cracked down on the Solidarity movement, imprisoned its leaders, and imposed martial law. This not only created dangerous new tensions between Moscow and Washington, it put significant strains on the NATO alliance as the new Reagan administration wanted to be much tougher in its response than most of the Europeans. Haig and Eagleburger, both having served in NATO, privately contained the hawks, so preventing a larger crisis.

During that time I began meeting fairly regularly with Eagleburger. I would go to his office, often on Saturday mornings, without a tape recorder and with my notebook in my pocket, and we would just talk. He knew I would not be quoting him, but we both knew that what he told me would inform my reporting. We would discuss the issues of the day or week, strategies and tactics for dealing with them, pending trips, personalities, and of course, Washington gossip.

In 1982, with a relationship of mutual trust now established, Larry invited me to have Christmas dinner with him and his family. At that time they lived in a modest town house in Arlington, Virginia. This was a far cry from the forty acre estate he would purchase in his retirement outside Charlottesville, Virginia, with the millions he earned between 1984 and 1988 as president of Kissinger's high-powered foreign policy consultancy. In '84 I went back overseas, and in '86 Larry did me a big a personal favor. He spent an hour briefing my then fiancée Whitney Taylor (now my wife of twenty-four years) on the 1981 Polish crisis and its impact on NATO, which by happenstance was the subject of her Master's thesis at the London School of Economics.

I can see this raising alarm bells among journalism ethicists around the country but I am deliberately going public with this information because I wish to make a larger point. There was a time in American journalism when people such as James "Scotty" Reston of the *New York Times* often had the kind of conversations I had with Eagleburger with presidents of the United States. I think this process can produce very useful, nuanced reporting that is generally lacking today. But this works only if neither source nor reporter forgets the true nature of their relationship, which I believe what follows will illustrate.

After another eight years abroad, I returned to Washington in early 1992 as diplomatic correspondent. Eagleburger had left Kissinger Associates when Secretary of State James Baker persuaded him to become his deputy secretary. He then became acting secretary when Baker reluctantly resigned to run President George H.W. Bush's sagging presidential re-election campaign. And finally after Bush's defeat, Larry was named secretary of state, the first career Foreign Service officer ever to earn that honor. Also that year, I resumed holding Saturday conversations with him as I had in the early '80s.

In December '92, Eagleburger went to Belgrade to try to get Serbia's Slobodan Milosevic to stop the repression of Albanians in Kosovo. I was among a few reporters who traveled with him. At a news conference in London, the British were skeptical about his mission. I suspected what they were getting at, so I asked him outright: "Mr. Secretary, what would you say to those who are worried about the baggage you may be carrying on this trip?"—a reference to his previous relationship with Milosevic, which some thought too cozy. He looked daggers at me, denied having any "baggage," and ended the news conference. A short time later he called and still angry, growled, "I thought you were my friend." I responded that I was his friend but that I was also a reporter and had to do my job. He mumbled something and hung up. The next day the new secretary of state held a failed meeting in Belgrade with Milosevic. On a stop in Brussels on our way home to Washington he gave me an exclusive on-camera television interview in which he denounced the Serbian dictator. I had done my job. He did his.

That was probably the last story I did with Secretary Eagleburger, but he and his wife attended my retirement dinner and we remained friends for many more years. We talked every few months, mostly about our health and families. We did discuss his membership in the Iraq Study Group, which was trying to find a way for America to get out of Iraq. With his usual candor, Eagleburger told me the Iraq War continued to be a disaster. I already knew as much, but as always, his wisdom brought clarity to my understanding of the complex issues of American foreign policy and, I believe, to my reporting of them.

May 29, 2005

Deceptions of the Echo Chamber

The "Echo Chamber" is once again at full reverberance. Right-wing pundits, politicians, PR men, and talk show prattlers are repeating and repeating the charge: the *Newsweek* story on American desecration of the Koran was much more than a journalistic blunder, it was part of the mainstream media's fundamental disrespect for America's military.

Washington Post media columnist Howard Kurtz gathered a collection of typical quotes from the Echo Chamber as it resonated and fumed about the *Newsweek* report.

The *Wall Street Journal* blames "a basic media mistrust of the military that goes back to Vietnam."

Rush Limbaugh says *Newsweek* "wanted the story to be true" because the media "have an adversarial relationship with America" and "end up siding with the bad guys."

Bill O'Reilly claims news outlets "magnify every mistake the military makes in order to hammer the Bush administration."

National Review editor Rich Lowry says there is a "media culture, set during Vietnam" aimed at "exposing wrongdoing and failures of the U.S. military. Instead of tending to give the military the benefit of the doubt, there is a tendency to believe the worst."

The Echo Chamber usually "echoes" the political spin it gets from Karl Rove, presidential adviser and master propagandist. He apparently wants people to believe that *Newsweek*'s report that American interrogators at Guantanamo Bay had flushed copies of the Koran down the toilet to intimidate Muslim prisoners is proof that the mainstream media hates the American military. This is nothing but a smokescreen to cover up the multitude of mistakes and misjudgments by the Bush administration in Iraq. But you can be sure that after listening to this Echo Chamber for a week or so, folks out there in the red states and probably lots in the blue states, too, will believe the media are out to get the military. Thus, the media are un-American.

Let me state emphatically: that is absolutely false.

I know this because I spent thirty years in the mainstream media. I covered the U.S. military all over the world: in Vietnam, in Gulf War One, and at the Pentagon. I know that the vast majority of the reporters, producers, and editors of America's national news organizations respect the military as an institution and recognize the sacrifices made by its men and women in uniform. I'll concede that most senior officers who served in Vietnam and most reporters who covered that war remain leery of each other for a lot of reasons. But few of those are now in active service—on either side.

After I retired from ABC News, as a fellow at the Kennedy School at Harvard, I conducted a research study about live TV coverage of war that focused extensively on the media/military relationship. Even back in 1995, a major poll by the Freedom Forum First Amendment Center showed how the scars of Vietnam were healing. The center surveyed 2,000 military officers and 351 selected media representatives who had been or were likely to be involved in covering military operations. Among its more encouraging findings: 82 percent of the military agreed with the statement, "The news media are just as necessary to maintaining U.S. freedom as the military." And 93 percent of the media *dis*agreed with the statement, "Members of the military are more interested in their own image than in the good of the country."

From the time of the Civil War there have always been tensions between these two institutions because they serve fundamentally different functions in our society. In time of war, those functions are often in conflict. Among other things, the media are constantly pushing to show and tell as much as they can about the war. And the military is concerned that revealing too much could threaten its operational security. But in the dozens of interviews I conducted with military and media members, including those at the very top, I found a remarkable level of mutual respect and understanding.

This positive attitude apparently carried over when plans were made for news coverage of the Iraq invasion. The use of embedded reporters gave viewers and readers a real front row seat to some of the action and reflected a new maturity in military and media relations. For the most part, that system served both sides well—as long as the news organization had people giving us the big picture while the embedded reporters provided flavor and detail.

So do not be deceived into thinking the media are undermining America in Iraq and elsewhere because of an inherent antipathy for the military.

The United States invaded a Muslim country. Many thousands of Iraqi Muslims have been killed and wounded. American jailers have mistreated and humiliated Muslim prisoners and the whole world has seen the pictures. For four years, this country sided almost exclusively with the Israelis in their conflict with the Palestinians, which is a major issue with most Muslims.

Against this backdrop, it is not credible to claim that a small item in *Newsweek* was responsible for a wave of anti-Americanism throughout the Islamic world. If Muslims of the world do not respect or trust the United States it is in large part because of this country's policies—the policies of civilians in Bush's White House and Pentagon. The Oval Office is supposed to be where the buck stops—not where the Echo Chamber of deceit gets its inspiration.

September 8, 2005
Hurricane Katrina's Effect on the Media

Reporters working for the so-called mainstream media come in many political stripes. But there are times when a major event can, in a sense, bring them together. The Vietnam War and Watergate made most reporters of the day much more skeptical and less willing to accept the Nixon White House version of events. As we soon learned, such skepticism was justified. In the years that followed, the relationship between administrations and the reporters who covered them was increasingly adversarial, reaching a climax with the Clinton-Lewinsky scandal and subsequent impeachment hearings.

George W. Bush had a longer than usual honeymoon period in his first term—and then came 9/11. With the country reeling from the most deadly attack on its soil since Pearl Harbor, news organizations and their reporters became as patriotic as the rest of the country. While not all the news people wore flags the way FOX News anchors and reporters did, there was clearly an effort not to appear to be so critical of government policy that it could be interpreted as being disloyal. With some exceptions, this attitude carried through the invasion of Iraq and for much of what followed there. The once-esteemed White House press corps, which had led the charge against Nixon and Clinton, instead was now being parodied on late night TV shows for its cowardly performance.

Katrina appears to have changed all that. The *New York Times* television critic Alessandra Stanley put it this way: "After spending time with storm refugees in the Superdome and Convention Center, normally poised and placid TV reporters now openly deplore the government's failure to help the victims adequately, and their outrage [is] illustrated with hauntingly edited montages of weeping mothers, sickly children, and dead bodies rotting on the street."

Television was by no means alone in challenging the administration. National Public Radio did an extraordinary job in covering the event and had no qualms about placing blame where blame was due. Most of the country's print media has been highly critical of the president's own personal performance—which *Time* magazine described as "tone-deaf and flat footed." The vaunted White House propaganda machine run by Karl Rove tried to have it both ways by condemning the "blame game" even as it pointed fingers at state and local authorities. But the newly aroused White House reporters were having none of that. As one of them snapped at the president's spokesman, "It's not a blame game. It's accountability." The *Washington Post*'s media columnist Howard Kurtz wrote, "This kind of activist stance, which would have drawn flak had it come from American reporters in Iraq, seemed utterly appropriate when applied to the yawning gap between mounting casualties and the administration's reassuring rhetoric."

I believe BBC commentator Matt Wells had it about right when he said, "Good reporting lies at the heart of what is changing…. Amidst the horror, American broadcast journalism just might have grown its spine back."

October 30, 2005

On Spurious Cases for War

"The first casualty when war comes is truth." Senator Hiram Johnson, who was Teddy Roosevelt's running mate in 1912, coined that phrase during a Senate debate in 1917 over the wisdom of America's involvement in World War I.

War and truth are very often incompatible—especially when it comes to the pretexts for war. Down through the ages many more wars have been fought under false pretenses than for noble reasons.

The classic way to mobilize public support for going to war is to make naked appeals to patriotism while creating a climate of fear—the potent mix of jingoism and xenophobia. Dictatorships have the additional weapon of intimidation. It is more difficult to stir up war fever in democracies because as a general rule, free people are less eager to fight.

Early in World War II, President Franklin Roosevelt believed that protecting America's security would ultimately require the nation to join Europe in the fight against Germany. But it wasn't until the Japanese attack on Pearl Harbor two years into the war that he had enough public and political support to do so. To this day, there are those who believe Roosevelt knew of the Japanese attack before it took place but allowed it to happen to provide the "casus belli" to justify American entry into the war. While there is no hard evidence to support this theory, given the growing hostility between the United States and Japan in that period, the attack cannot have been a total surprise to FDR and his inner circle.

The justifications offered for other American wars have not held up well under postwar scrutiny. "Remember the Maine!" was the slogan of the Spanish-American War, based on the sinking of the battleship of that name in Havana harbor in 1898, supposedly by the Spanish. But while the incident ignited the war, historians have long believed that the explosion was most probably the result of an accident.

The Gulf of Tonkin incident in 1964 prompted Congress to pass a resolution giving President Lyndon Johnson a blank check to escalate the war in Vietnam. But the attack on U.S. ships by North Vietnamese gunboats may not have really happened, and whatever did occur was certainly not as threatening as the American people were told at the time.

And then there was the invasion of Iraq in 2003 to rid the world of the tyrant Saddam Hussein and his weapons of mass destruction.

As I write, special prosecutor Patrick Fitzgerald has made no announcements regarding his nearly two-year investigation into the leak of the identity of CIA operative Valerie Plame. She just happened to be the wife of former Ambassador Joseph Wilson who had publicly accused the White House of "twisting" the facts to justify the war in Iraq. But quite apart from whether there are any indictments, this case has brought into sharp focus many of the critical details of how the war was "sold" to the Congress and the American people.

Many skeptics (including yours truly) were finally persuaded that going to war was justified because Saddam Hussein had weapons of mass destruction and as such was a menace to the world. We were told that categorically by senior members of the Bush administration, especially Vice President Dick Cheney, who time and again raised the specter of a nuclear attack on this country or its allies.

But in addition to this public campaign we now know there was a more subtle and secret effort to make the case for war. It involved leaking selective intelligence to prestigious news outlets such as the *New York Times* (which has enormous impact on thousands of newsrooms throughout the country). These leaks of course supported the administration's claims that Iraq had chemical and biological weapons and was developing a nuclear capability.

We have known for more than two years that those stories in the *Times* by reporter Judith Miller were wrong. But only recently we learned through Fitzgerald's investigation, that one of Miller's key sources was Lewis "Scooter" Libby, Dick Cheney's chief of staff. It was to avoid revealing this source that Miller went to jail for eighty-five days and finally agreed to testify to the grand jury, after getting Libby's personal blessing to do so.

In the controversy that has followed Miller's grand jury appearances we have also learned some extraordinary things: 1) That two years ago the *Times* executive editor Bill Keller had actually banned Miller from writing anything further about Iraq and weapons of mass destruction. 2) That Miller had misled the paper's Washington bureau chief about her conversations with Libby. 3) That a reporter with whom she had collaborated on the WMD stories told editors he would not work with Miller anymore because he did not trust her judgment and because she was an "advocate." I take that to mean she had become a true believer in WMD and was no longer objective on the issue.

In defending herself from the criticisms of her WMD reporting, Miller wrote, "I got it totally wrong. If your sources are wrong, you are wrong." But as the *Times* columnist Maureen Dowd wrote (in one of the nastiest hatchet jobs of a supposed colleague I have ever seen), "investigative reporting is not stenography." In other words, investigative reporters have an obligation to do more than just to write down and report as fact what officials sources tell them. There of course is an equal obligation for editors to make sure such stories are balanced and in this case, the editors clearly failed to fulfill that duty.

Not to put too fine a point on it, most of the news media were very skillfully manipulated in the run up to the war. But in the last analysis, it is not Judy Miller or the *New York Times,* nor the American news media that took us to war in Iraq. It was an administration that was determined to take out Saddam Hussein as part of a grand neoconservative pipedream to democratize the Middle East, make the neighborhood safe for Israel, and use Iraqi oil as a lever against OPEC and Saudi Arabia. If these goals had been offered up as the reasons for war, I have no doubt the American people would have soundly rejected such a notion. But when weapons of mass destruction were put at the top of the list, that completely changed the equation.

And so whatever the special prosecutor decides, we should not lose sigt of the fact that when the CIA operative's identity was revealed by senior White House officials in apparent retaliation against her war-critic husband, this was not just some politics-as-usual dirty trick. No matter how it ultimately turns out, the Fitzgerald investigation has been of great significance because it has blown the cover off the covert campaign to justify the Iraq war—a war that an ever-increasing number of Americans, both liberal and conservative, now firmly believe was a major strategic blunder.

December 25, 2005

America's Precious but Fragile Gift

This season of reflecting upon the blessings of life is a good time for renewed appreciation for one of the greatest gifts ever bestowed upon any nation: the United States Bill of Rights. These amendments to the Constitution contain the guarantees of civil liberties that for more than two centuries have made America "the symbol of the free." But as many generations of Americans have discovered, this extraordinary gift of freedom is something that cannot be taken for granted.

This comes to mind, of course, with the contentious arguments over renewal of the Patriot Act and other government actions related to the War on Terror—among them, the confinement of enemy combatants and terrorist suspects without charge or trial; the use of torture and harsh treatment of prisoners and detainees; and, as we have learned in recent days, the electronic eavesdropping on Americans in their own country and in their own homes by the National Security Agency without judicial warrant. At a minimum, whether these practices do or do not violate established laws is a matter of intense nonpartisan debate.

As it happens, the subject is especially on my mind because I am about to teach a course at Middlebury College during the winter term on War and the First Amendment—particularly freedom of speech and freedom of the press. As a reporter who covered numerous wars, I have some firsthand experience on the subject. But in preparing for the course I have become reacquainted with the sometimes egregious threats to civil liberties which regularly have taken place in this country in time of war, going back to the early days of the republic.

I have decided to use as the primary textbook for this course a recent book titled *Perilous Times: Free Speech in Wartime*, by Geoffrey R. Stone. Professor Stone is a former dean of the University of Chicago Law School and is considered one of the country's leading First Amendment scholars.

As Stone writes in his introduction, "War excites great passions. Thousands, perhaps millions of lives are at risk. The nation itself may be at risk. If there ever is a time to pull out all the stops, it is surely in wartime. In war, the government may conscript soldiers, commandeer property, control prices, ration food, raise taxes, and freeze wages. May it also limit the freedom of speech?"

In the broadest interpretation of the First Amendment, the answer to that question would seem to be no. But no freedom is absolute—as the old saw goes, you can't yell "Fire!" in a crowded theater when there is no fire. And it is this ambiguity about freedom of speech that has been exposed and exploited in wartime. According to Stone, "The United States has a long and unfortunate history of overreacting to the perceived dangers of wartime. Time and again, Americans have allowed fear and fury to get the better of them. Time and again Americans have suppressed dissent, imprisoned and deported dissenters, and then—later—regretted their actions."

Perilous Times documents six episodes in American history when the United States has attempted to punish individuals for criticizing government officials or their policies.

- In the very early years, when the United States was on the verge of war with France, Congress passed the Sedition Act of 1798. Strongly supported by President John Adams and the Federalist Party and opposed by Thomas Jefferson and his Republicans, the act made it a crime to publish or utter any disloyal statement against the government, the Congress, or the president. (The first person to be indicted under this law was Matthew Lyon, congressman from Vermont.)

- During the Civil War, President Lincoln suspended the writ of habeas corpus—the procedure by which an accused can appeal to a judge to determine the legality of his detention by the government. The national leader of a significant Northern political party known as the Copperheads was arrested and brought before a military tribunal because he publicly condemned the president, the war, and the freeing of the slaves. He was convicted, jailed, and then exiled to the South.

- During World War I, the Espionage Act of 1917 and the Sedition Act of 1918 were used to prosecute some 2,000 people for their opposition to the war and the military draft. Under President Wilson, debate about the war was squelched and those convicted were routinely sent to prison for ten to twenty years.

- In World War II the major civil liberties issue was the internment of 120,000 people of Japanese descent. But President Roosevelt also attempted to stifle criticism by prosecuting or deporting those who questioned the war, especially American Fascists.

- The Cold War, which immediately followed World War II, was marked by anti-Communist "witch hunts." While no one would deny the reality of the Communist external threat, the internal threat was never more than marginal. But the excesses of the House Un-American Activities Committee followed by Senator Joseph McCarthy's reckless crusade to expose so-called Communists in the government and the army turned this era into perhaps the most repressive period in American history. On this issue, neither President Truman nor President Eisenhower was a profile in courage.

• In the 1960s and '70s came the war in Vietnam. Massive anti-war demonstrations, widespread acts of civil disobedience, and instances of serious political violence were often met with pro-vocative actions by the police and sometimes the National Guard. In 1970 at Kent State University, four student protesters were shot and killed by guardsmen. Meantime under Presidents Johnson and Nixon, the FBI carried out far-reaching programs to "expose, disrupt, and otherwise neutralize" dissident activities while anti-war protestors were prosecuted for desecrating the flag and burning their draft cards.

"In each of these episodes," writes Professor Stone, "the nation faced extraordinary pressures—and temptations—to suppress dissent. In some of these eras, national leaders cynically exploited public fears for partisan political gain; in some, they fomented public hysteria in an effort to unite the nation in common cause; and in others they simply caved in to public demands for the repression of 'disloyal' individuals."

In wartime, as we have seen, the line between disloyalty and dissent is elusive and often ignored. There are plenty of examples of that in our public discourse today. At the same time, I think it is fair to conclude that while the current threats to civil liberties are real, they may not yet have reached the magnitude of some of the six historical eras mentioned above.

But that does not mean they are insignificant. On the contrary, it is imperative to challenge governmental authorities every time they take actions which appear to violate the Bill of Rights, or more recently, established civil liberties. For if that extraordinary gift is to survive another 200 years it must be vigorously defended by each and every successive generation—especially in wartime—because that is when the country's most precious freedoms are most likely to be in peril.

March 12, 2006

History's Lessons Unlearned

On Dec. 7, 1941, Japanese forces attacked Pearl Harbor killing more than 2,000 people and destroying much of the U.S. Pacific fleet. On Feb. 19, 1942, President Franklin Roosevelt signed executive order no. 9066.

Over the next eight months, 120,000 individuals of Japanese descent were ordered to leave their homes in California, Washington, Oregon, and Arizona. Two thirds were American citizens representing almost 90 percent of all Japanese Americans. No charges were brought against these individuals; there were no judicial hearings.

After being temporarily held in detention camps set up in converted race tracks and fairgrounds, the internees were transported to concentration camps in the deserts and swamplands of the Southwest. There they were kept in overcrowded rooms with no furniture other than cots, surrounded by barbed wire and military police. There they remained for three years. As Geoffrey Stone writes in *Perilous Times: Free Speech in Wartime:* "All this was done even though there was not a single documented act of espionage, sabotage, or treasonable activity committed by an American citizen of Japanese descent or by a Japanese national residing on the West Coast."

Why did this happen? In a word: fear. But it was a fear that was incited, encouraged, and exploited by political players of many stripes. In the weeks that followed the attack on Pearl Harbor, California was teeming with rumors of sabotage and espionage. The mayor of Los Angeles, Fletcher Bowron, spread the story that Japanese fishermen and farmers had been seen mysteriously waving lights along the shoreline. The top American military commander for the region General John DeWitt reported as true rumors that enemy airplanes had passed over California—and claimed that 20,000 Japanese were about to stage an uprising in San Francisco. All of these stories were false.

The news media also did its share of rumor-mongering. The *Hearst* columnist Damon Runyon erroneously reported that a radio transmitter had been discovered in a rooming house that catered to Japanese residents. Even the respected national columnist Walter Lippmann warned of a likely major act of sabotage by ethnic Japanese. It would not be long before virtually all West Coast newspapers, the American Legion, the L.A. Chamber of Commerce, a host of other business and fraternal organizations, in addition to the area's top political and military leaders were demanding that all persons of Japanese ancestry be removed from the West Coast. Many of these demands were overtly racist, such as that of the attorney general of Idaho who proclaimed all Japanese should "be put in concentration camps for the remainder of the war...we want to keep this a white man's country."

Still, President Roosevelt was not being pushed by his own advisors to sign the order for the internment. Attorney General Francis Biddle strongly opposed it. FBI Director J. Edgar Hoover concluded that the demand for mass evacuation was based on "public hysteria." Secretary of War Henry Stimson thought internment was a "tragedy" that was almost certainly unconstitutional. But Roosevelt was evidently determined to proceed. Professor Stone writes, "Although Roosevelt explained the order in terms of military necessity, there is little doubt that domestic politics played a role in his thinking, particularly since 1942 was an election year." But, of course, it must be remembered the United States had been attacked and was now involved in another world war.

Those civil libertarians who opposed the internment and thought the Supreme Court would ultimately reverse Roosevelt's order would be disappointed. Two related cases finally reached the Court and in both, the convictions were upheld.

It was only after many years had passed that some of those involved would publicly express regret for their decisions in these cases. The famously liberal Justice William O. Douglas would later confess, "I have always regretted that I bowed to my elders." The also notably liberal Chief Justice Earl Warren, who played a pivotal role in the process as California's attorney general, wrote in his memoirs in 1974 that the internment "was not in keeping with our American concept of freedom and the rights of citizens."

On Feb. 19, 1976, as part of the bicentennial of the Constitution, President Gerald Ford issued a proclamation noting that the anniversary of Roosevelt's internment order was "a sad day in American history." Ford observed, "We now know what we should have known then," that the internment of Japanese American citizens was "wrong." He concluded by calling "upon the American people to affirm with me this American promise: that we have learned from the tragedy of that long-ago experience" and "resolve that this kind of action shall never again be repeated."

And what, you may ask, is the purpose of recounting this

regrettable chapter in American history? Actually, I have several reasons for doing so.

- The Japanese internment is a significant example of how in time of war, the president, be he a Democrat or a Republican, is almost certainly more interested in the war and the politics of the war than he is with civil liberties.
- It is an example of how citizens, be they conservative or liberal, can rather quickly begin to demonize their enemies—and that the demonization becomes easier when there are racial or ethnic differences.
- It tells us that especially in time of war, what we are told by our political and military leaders is not necessarily the truth, and what we read, hear, or see in the news media shouldn't be trusted blindly.
- It shows us that we should not expect that the Supreme Court will save us from ourselves, because in spite of its denials, the Court, too, gets caught up in the politics of the day. And the Court is always going to be reluctant to challenge the president and the executive branch when military and security issues appear to be involved.
- Finally, the Japanese internment case is a reminder that as much as we feel that this country is essentially a good and decent one, it is capable of pursuing policies that are neither. When one looks at the present policy of rounding up so many hundreds of mainly Muslims as "enemy combatants" and holding them for several years without charges or trials, there is reason to believe that what President Ford said "should never be repeated" is actually happening once again.

June 4, 2006
On Reporting From the Battlefield

The war in Iraq has been the most deadly in the history of war reporting. The deaths of two members of a CBS crew last week brought to seventy-one the number of journalists killed while covering that war. Others have been critically injured, including CBS correspondent Kimberly Dozier, who suffered severe injuries in last week's incident and Bob Woodruff, the ABC News anchorman whose career and quality of life remain in limbo since he suffered multiple head wounds there in January. I have had some experience in covering wars, but as I have written here in the past, nothing in that experience was ever as unrelentingly dangerous as the current war.

However, when we in the news media focus on the dangers faced by our journalistic brethren, many people are quick to point out that things are a lot worse for the troops there, not to mention for Iraqi civilians. That may be true. Although I suspect a calculation of the number of reporters killed compared to the total number of reporters working there might well yield a higher fatality percentage than that suffered by troops or civilians. However, I am not a statistician and my purpose here is not to make such quibbles. Today I come not to praise war correspondents—nor to bury them—but to discuss their history and to assess their role in democratic societies.

The advent of the war correspondent in the Western world can be traced to the middle of the nineteenth century and the Crimean War a war involving Britain, France, and Turkey against Russia. It was a war of minor historical significance, except for three memorable things:

- It was the site of the infamous Charge of the Light Brigade immortalized in the Tennyson poem by that name.
- It marked the beginning of nursing as a profession when the British nurse Florence Nightingale was sent to Turkey in response to newspaper reports that wounded soldiers were suffering horribly from lack of any medical treatment.
- Those stories about the wounded became public knowledge because for the first time, British newspapers had begun to publish news from the battlefront from their own on-scene civilian reporters. Previously, war news appeared haphazardly, usually based on letters sent by junior officers.

Among the first and certainly the most famous war correspondent of the time was an Irishman named William Howard Russell of the *London Times*. According to Phillip Knightley, in his definitive history of war reporting, *The First Casualty*, Russell's reporting was closer to the truth than anything the public had previously been permitted to learn. Words such as "folly," "ignorance," "mistakes," "blunders" became commonplace in the reports of the day, which for the British Army confirmed its worst fears about the nature of the press. Queen Victoria let it be known she was displeased with the *Times*. Her consort Prince Albert called Russell, "That miserable scribbler." And a former secretary of war wrote, "I trust the army will lynch the *Times* correspondent."

There were many other claims that the work of the *Times* and Russell was little short of treason. Knightley sums it up, "It is clear that before the Crimean War ended, the Army realized it had made a mistake tolerating Russell and his colleagues but by then it was too late. The war correspondent had arrived and when the American Civil War broke out five years later, five hundred of them turned out to report the conflict on the Northern Side alone."

As important as the Civil War was in the history of this country, so was its significance as a milestone in the history of war reporting. It was the first American war to be reported by civilians for the mass civilian population. And it was the first war in which technology played a key role in how it was reported. As the war began, almost 50,000 miles of telegraph lines were in use in the eastern United States. "By Telegraph" became a common sub-heading on newspaper stories much the way in which "Via Satellite" appeared on television screens in the 1970s and 1980s. With the telegraph, or "the lightning," as the reporters called it, for the first time it was possible for the public to read what had happened yesterday rather than last week. Unfortunately, then as today, getting it fast sometimes precluded getting it right. Because of early deadlines, many of the reports of the first major engagement of the war, the Battle of Bull Run, had the Union victorious. In fact the tide had turned later in the day and the battle ended in an embarrassing Union defeat.

As is the case with many aspects of the Civil War, its war correspondents have been romanticized into legend. As Knightley writes in his history, "The legend overlooks the fact that the majority of the Northern correspondents were ignorant, dishonest and unethical. And the dispatches they wrote were frequently inaccurate, often invented, partisan and inflammatory."

The Civil War was also one in which journalists had virtually unfettered access to the battlefield. But in the major wars that followed (two World Wars, Korea, and Vietnam) governments would use a variety of ploys, regulations, and censorship in an attempt to control what the media reported, and therefore what the people were allowed to know about the war their country was fighting. World War I had by far the most restrictions, Vietnam the least.

In the case of World War I, it can be argued that if the European and American people had been made fully aware of the futility of that war, it would have ended sooner, perhaps saving millions of lives. Among those who take that view is Senator John McCain (R–Ariz.) who said several years ago, "I still believe World War I wouldn't have lasted three months if people had known what was going on in that conflict."

On the other end of the spectrum, the freewheeling behavior of the media in Vietnam is frequently cited as the main reason that war was lost. I personally believe it was the unpopularity of the military draft and of course the 55,000 body bags that ultimately turned the American people against the war. Still, it would be silly to argue that news coverage of history's first TV war did not help to shape American public opinion about it.

It is clear that the historical record of war correspondents is a mixed bag. Still, the war correspondent came into being largely because civilians on the home front increasingly didn't believe they were getting the full truth from the country's leaders about what was actually happening on the battlefield. War reporting evolved over the next century and a half—usually at odds with the powers-that-be in government and the military who inevitably claimed they, not the people, knew what was best for the country.

But if history teaches us anything, it is that all governments need to be held accountable. Otherwise bad things very often happen. So for all the shortcomings of the news media's war reporting, who among us today would want to depend solely on the word of the government and/or the military for all of our news from the battlefield? In my view, only those who do not wish to know what their government is doing in their name. That, by the way, was the prevailing attitude of the German people during World War II.

April 23, 2006
A Rich Dinner Conversation

Normally, I would not write about a journalism awards dinner. The notion of reporters gathering to celebrate one another's work would seem to a lot of readers like a mafia meeting in praise of family values. But recently, I attended such a dinner in Washington, D.C., and because it was so relevant to the issues of the day, my journalist gene compels me to share some of it with you.

This was not a splashy affair with television cameras, limos, and a red carpet. In fact, the annual presentation of the Weintal Awards is a very modest event, held at Georgetown University where its School of Foreign Service recognizes the work of journalists who cover diplomacy and foreign affairs. The awards are named for Edward Weintal, a Polish diplomat whose career ended when the Germans invaded his country in 1939. He turned to journalism and went on to become a distinguished diplomatic correspondent for *Newsweek* magazine. Each year since 1975, two or three national journalists from print or broadcasting have received the Weintal Prize. You've undoubtedly read, seen, or heard their work but except for a few television anchors, most of the recipients have not been household names. They are, however, well known by those who closely follow international affairs and they have our gratitude for skillfully serving as this country's eyes and ears on the world, sometimes at great personal peril.

That is certainly the case with this year's winners: Anne Garrels of National Public Radio, George Packer of the *New Yorker,* and Christiane Amanpour of CNN. Each was cited for distinguished reporting out of Iraq before, during, and since the American invasion. As I listened to their stories it underscored my feelings that no war in the past century has been more difficult for journalists to cover, nor more dangerous. In Baghdad, you never feel safe—certainly not on the streets but not in your office, apartment, or hotel room, either. Each recipient told of how local Iraqis in their news bureaus have been performing heroically and of how there would be very little news out of Iraq without them. But as the sectarian violence continues to increase, those Iraqis are being put under enormous pressure. And while no one would say this explicitly, I sensed a concern that these pressures might one day affect the Iraqis' dependability or even their loyalty if, for example, sectarian gunmen were to force them to choose between the safety of their own families or the Americans they worked for.

As for the broader picture, I won't put words in their mouths, but nothing I heard from these three veteran reporters who know the situation in Iraq very well gave me reason to be hopeful about the eventual outcome of this war.

There was another award presented on this occasion that gave many of us a unique perspective on an important aspect of the war. It was a special citation given to Garry Trudeau, creator of the comic strip *Doonesbury*.

Trudeau was chosen because his more than three decades of work, much of it dealing with the military from Vietnam to Iraq, has endeared him to the American soldier. Trudeau is a twenty-first century composite of the famed World War II journalists, reporter Ernie Pyle and cartoonist Bill Mauldin. Both men were loved by the troops because they did not glorify the war and told its story through the ordinary G.I. When jokes were made or fun was poked, it was almost always at the expense of the top brass.

Garry Trudeau, who follows that tradition, hardly needs another award. Thirty-one years ago he became the first comic strip artist to receive a Pulitzer Prize for editorial cartooning. Since then, Trudeau and his creations have won countless awards including an Oscar and an Emmy. He's received twenty-two honorary degrees, and a few years ago Vermont's own Ben & Jerry's Ice Cream even introduced a sorbet made with raspberries and blueberries which they dubbed "Doonesberry."

In his remarks, Trudeau told how during the first Gulf War, the Army began to take a positive interest in his work. He went to the Persian Gulf with the Army's blessing, and shortly after the 100-hour land war that drove the Iraqis out of Kuwait, was given a helicopter tour of the battlefield and then was introduced to many of those who fought that battle. As he put it, "... soldiers sat with me in their Bradleys and tanks and told me stories that were notable for their lack of triumphalism. They struck me as committed professionals who had seen awful things."

To deal with the latest Iraq war, Trudeau turned to what he called "a radical experiment in realism" by having his main character B.D. lose a leg in battle. This took the cartoon strip into what happens to soldiers when they return with grievous physical and psychological wounds. In dealing with these issues, Trudeau said he has received "the completely unfettered support of the United States military." After B.D. was wounded, the Defense Department almost immediately offered to help tell his story. This led to meetings with caregivers and patients at several different veterans' hospitals to make Trudeau familiar with the medical and social environment of amputees as well as those suffering from post-traumatic stress disorder.

On his first visit to Walter Reed Army hospital, he met a beautiful young soldier who had lost her hand and part of her forearm when she was struck by a rocket while defending the roof of an Iraqi police station. She recalled how her buddies had carried her down and placed her on the hood of a Humvee where medics worked to stop the bleeding. But her most vivid memory was that her sergeant and a platoon-mate went back up to the roof against orders, found her severed hand, removed her wedding ring and brought it back to her. "I could have bought another ring. But it meant the world to me that my guys would do that," the young woman told Trudeau. He continued, "And then she smiled. It was a tale of gratitude, not bitterness. These sorts of stories, told without self-pity or guile, can bring you to your knees."

It is this empathy with the victims of war that makes Trudeau a powerful storyteller. But he is evidently torn between his feelings for these people and his fundamental opposition to the war. As he said, "We have asked a lot of the young men and women who have been sent to fight in our name for a cause that is now in bitter dispute. They obviously deserve our compassion and respect upon their return, no matter what side we stand on [in] the divide that has opened up in this country."

Therefore it greatly troubles him when people question the sincerity of those who "walk the anxious line between hating the war and loving the warrior." He mentioned a sign outside a conservative district in Pennsylvania which reads, "Either you support the troops and their mission or you support the terrorists." With great frustration he asked, "Could there possibly be a better example of the false choices we've been presented with since 9/11?"

It is indeed a false choice. However, for the many millions of Americans who no longer believe the war in Iraq was worth the cost, but who truly support the troops, Garry Trudeau is demonstrating through his work that it is possible to walk that "anxious line."

Editor's note: Dunsmore won the Weintal Award himself in 1995.

May 16, 2010

Newsweek **For Sale**

In the context of the profound changes taking place in the news business, it wasn't exactly a huge surprise. Yet, hearing that *Newsweek* magazine had been put up for sale by its long-time owners, the Washington Post companies, left me numb. I've been reading *The Publisher,* Allen Brinkley's new biography of Henry Luce, the legendary founder of *Time/LIFE,* so I had already been musing on the rise and fall of the weekly news magazine. The *Newsweek* story drove home the reality that whether they survive or not, neither *Newsweek* nor *Time* will ever again approach the highly prominent role they once played in the culture of American life and journalism. And contemplating this fact has set off a torrent of memories for me.

In 1965, when young and green I went off to be a foreign correspondent, network television was emerging as a major news medium because of its coverage of the Kennedy assassination, the civil rights movement, and the Vietnam War. But the new generation of broadcast news journalists of which I was a part was often viewed with suspicion, if not derision, by many of the veteran reporters in the field. People such as myself and my colleagues Peter Jennings and Ted Koppel and a couple of dozen others at ABC, CBS, and NBC were expected to prove ourselves as foreign and war correspondents. On the whole, I think we did.

Still, looking back I realize I owe a debt to some of those at the top of the journalistic pecking order in those days—namely, the elitists at the weekly news magazines. I say elitist because more often than not they were highly educated, multilingual, impeccably dressed, and moved in the highest social circles of whatever country they were covering. They had fat expense accounts to travel and to wine and dine sources. And without exception they knew which fork to use and which expensive wines to order, usually in excellent French.

In 1968, I became ABC News' new Mediterranean bureau chief. I'd been sent to Rome from Paris, largely to cover the Middle East. As a lapsed Protestant, I knew little about the Vatican—nor was I expected to—until one Sunday that July when *Time* magazine scooped the world on Pope Paul VI's encyclical, "Humanae Vitae" (Of Human Life). This was a huge story because Vatican Council II had left open the possibility for change in the Roman Catholic Church's attitude toward birth control. This new encyclical slammed that door shut. The *Time* reporter on this blockbuster was goateed Louisianan Wilton Wynn. I had made a point to meet Wynn when I arrived in Rome, because he had taught at the American University of Cairo, had covered the Middle East for the AP, and had written a well-received book on then-President of Egypt Gamal Abdel Nasser. When I called him that Sunday for help on his big story, he could not have been more gracious. After briefing me on his report, he gave me the name and private phone number of an American priest at the Vatican he said might be helpful. Father Edward Heston, once of Notre Dame, was in fact invaluable in guiding me through the thickets of Vatican politics with remarkable frankness. He continued to be a valued news source and friend as he later was elevated to Archbishop and key Vatican spokesman.

When I reflect on the magazine writers I'm glad I have known, I immediately think of Arnaud de Borchgrave, for many years *Newsweek*'s chief correspondent. Known as "the Count" because his Belgian father had been one, Arnaud held court wherever he went, often in hotel bars such as the famous one at the elegant St. Georges Hotel in Beirut. Arnaud was a shameless namedropper, but he actually knew and interviewed the many famous and powerful people whose names he dropped. He was brave under fire, and generous with colleagues, even young TV reporters.

I think of William Tuohy of *Newsweek* and later the *Los Angeles Times*. Bill won a Pulitzer Prize for his reporting in Vietnam in 1968. He believed in traveling first class and in looking like you belonged up front and not in steerage. As we both had lived in Rome, we both wore Gucci loafers without apologies. Touhy wrote in his memoir, *Dangerous Company*, "One ought to dress as well as any ambassador one is interviewing. I've never seen the point of looking like a reject out of The Front Page." More seriously, he also wrote there was no glamour in war and that even though "war goes with the territory" for foreign correspondents, most of them were "horrified" by the carnage of modern warfare.

Between wars, a most unusual magazine writer looking to work in television came to see me. Prince Peter Dragadze was a Georgian aristocrat with a British passport, married to a once-famous Russian opera singer. Prince Peter specialized in insider stories on both European and Hollywood royalty for *LIFE* magazine. After King Constantine II went into exile in Rome when the colonels took over Greece in 1967, he told all to Peter. Not long before her death, Maria

Callas explained to Peter exactly why she could no longer sing. Peter got me onto the set of director Vittorio de Sica's last film, *The Voyage,* starring Sophia Loren and Richard Burton (when all three were Very Hot News). He also persuaded a flirtatious Gina Lollobrigida to work with me on a feature for a special late night ABC News program about historical ghosts. Gina and I walked through the actual sites of the story of the Renaissance Roman beauty Beatrice Cenci, who was beheaded for her part in the murder of her incestuous father and has forever since haunted Rome's Castel Sant'Angelo.

The following week I was in the Sinai desert covering the Israeli forces trying to repel the Egyptians who had crossed the Suez Canal at the beginning of the October 1973 Middle East War. My buddy Bill Touhy (sans Guccis) was with me.

May 21, 2010

From Facts to Opinions

Following Tuesday's primary results in Pennsylvania, Kentucky, and Arkansas, the most common word used to describe voters was "angry." I do not dispute the fact that there is some voter anger out there. And as might be expected, last Tuesday it was directed against incumbents and the establishment. But I have watched large Russian mobs tear down massive statues of Lenin with their bare hands as the Soviet Union was disintegrating in the early 1990s. I've seen thousands of British coal workers riot repeatedly against Prime Minister Margaret Thatcher's decision to close down many of their mines in the 1980s. And I was in Paris in May 1968 when French students, intellectuals, and workers battled on the streets against the establishment represented by then–President Charles de Gaulle. In each case there was seething, uncontrolled anger over fundamental political differences. People were killed and many more were injured as citizens fought with authorities over the future direction of their respective countries.

Which brings me to my own personal theory. I believe what we are seeing in American politics today is less anger than confusion.

I'm not trying to impugn the authenticity of Tea Party members. But it's a fact that they are not starving; very few are unemployed; their children are not being drafted to fight in unpopular wars; and income taxes are historically low. They claim to hate the federal government but also warn that government not to touch their Medicare or their Social Security. Yet, if enough Tea Party candidates, such as Kentucky Republican Senate nominee Rand Paul, were suddenly elected and quickly passed the balanced budget amendment that he promised, those are precisely the programs that would have to be seriously cut.

Likewise on the Democratic left there is anger at President Obama for giving up on a public option in the health care bill, for continuing the war in Afghanistan, and for not nominating a real liberal to the Supreme Court. But for all that unhappiness, do they really feel the country would be better off if Sarah Palin and the Tea Party were running it?

I believe there is a reason for the confusion demonstrated by the inherent contradictions in the goals of both the far left and far right. It is because in the past decade or so, we have gone from a fact-based news media to one based on opinions. I remember when someone might jokingly say, don't confuse me with the facts, my mind is made up. Today that's not a joke; it's a reality. People now watch only the cable news networks, listen only to the talk radio stations, and read only the publications and Internet blogs that conform to their political prejudices. In response to this demand, most news organizations now supply the most controversial or outrageous opinions—within which facts simply do not matter. Gone are the days when false assertions were automatically challenged by knowledgeable reporters.

That is why most people today no longer trust the news media. But it is also why far too many voters hold firm opinions that are mostly fact-free.

April 4, 2010

On Tea Parties, Past and Present

John Hancock, the founding father with the most identifiable signature, was one of the richest men in the thirteen American colonies. His wealth came from international shipping. Among the details that are often forgotten from that period is that when the British imposed the dreaded Tea Tax of 1773, they also began to ship East Indian tea directly from India to the American colonies, eliminating the London middlemen. As a result, even with the new tax, the price of East Indian tea in Massachusetts was lower than the price of the tea that Hancock and others were bringing in (some historical accounts say smuggling) from the Dutch East Indies.

So while he was not an active participant in the Boston Tea Party revolt, Hancock had a significant economic stake in it. We do know that Samuel Adams, who led those "Mohawks" who threw the British tea into Boston harbor, was a close ally of Hancock. As one source from that time put it, "Sam Adams writes the letters to the newspapers, John Hancock pays the postage."

The thought that this historical act of defiance by the colonists may have been inspired by the economic interests of one of the richest among them is an intriguing one—especially since a similar situation may be playing out again today in the case of the latest incarnation of the Tea Party.

It is not a stretch to say that the Tea Party of 2009–10 is largely the creation of FOX News. This is not to say that there was not an inchoate group of working and middle class white Americas, mostly without college degrees, who want to "take their country back" from African Americans and homosexuals and Hispanic immigrants and Harvard professors and the "socialist" Democrats in Congress and the White House. But without FOX News, this group would never have been able to so quickly grow and coalesce into the significant political player it has become.

From the spring of 2009, FOX began its aggressive campaign to organize and promote the Tea Party. All of its big names—Bill O'Reilly, Greta Van Susteren, Sean Hannity, and Glenn Beck—regularly devoted their programs to encouraging membership in, and hyping the activities of, this new phenomenon. Many FOX News stars offered themselves as special attractions at regional Tea Party meetings. Last summer when Tea Party members began disrupting political meetings in various parts of the country, FOX gave such ruckuses extravagant news coverage. The Tea Party convention and the so-called Tea Party Express have received countless hours of airtime and the attention normally given to truly major news events. And of course all of that coverage has been highly positive. I confess I have by no means seen it all, but from what I have seen or read, there has never been a discordant or critical note in any of the FOX News Tea Party "reporting."

And what's in it for FOX? The answer was on the front page of the business section of the *New York Times* last Tuesday under the headline, "CNN Fails To Stop Fall In Ratings." CNN's ratings are not just falling—they are collapsing. Its main hosts have lost almost half their viewers in the past year. Meantime FOX News enjoyed its best quarter ever, trouncing both CNN and MSNBC. Bill O'Reilly's numbers are up 28 percent; Glen Beck's, 50 percent. As it cannot be plausibly argued that CNN's anchors suddenly became tongue-tied or stupid, there must be something else going on—and there is. CNN has been victimized by Roger Ailes, the evil genius who created the monster of FOX News.

Ailes is responsible for the hyper-politicization and super-partisanship of cable television news. CNN has tried to play it straight, MSNBC has swung to the left—but to no avail for either. Especially since an African American became president, there are clearly far more angry, right wing conservatives watching cable news than there are liberals or independents. And FOX is cleaning up, as is Ailes. In a recent profile on Ailes, the *New York Times* reported that in early 2008, he went to his boss Rupert Murdoch to complain that he had heard Murdoch was going to endorse Obama for president—and also, that he'd been told Murdoch was sometimes embarrassed by FOX News. Ailes denies he threatened to resign but it's a fact that Murdoch's *New York Post* endorsed John McCain and Ailes got a fat new contract that now pays him $23 million a year.

I would have thought by now that FOX would have zero journalistic credibility. But that apparently isn't the case. In fact, CNN commentator David Gergen, a thoughtful man I know and like, who has worked in both Republican and Democratic administrations, has never cashed in to become a lobbyist, and now teaches at Harvard, claimed recently there was little difference between FOX News and National Public Radio—one leaned to the right, the other to the left. To me, that's like suggesting Martin Luther King, Jr. and Birmingham police chief Bull Connor each had ideologies that were equally valid and their only differences were tactical. By such faulty logic has FOX entered the mainstream.

Given all of the above, it's easy to despair about the direction of journalism and the country. But I also heard something on the radio the other day that reminded me of what could help to restore some balance here. I was listening to a BBC interview with a government official who first dissembled and then blamed public confusion about the subject on "media distortions." The BBC anchor fired back that the public's confusion was more likely the result of "your fatuous statements." This is the exactly kind of objectivity we desperately need—knowledgeable journalists with the courage to challenge Democrats, Republicans, or anyone else when they are clearly lying through their teeth. Perhaps when hell freezes over—or when FOX News dumps the Tea Party.

November 27, 2004

Drop the Hypocrisy

I was offended by the notion that 22 percent of voters apparently thought that I and many of those who supported John Kerry were somehow lacking in "moral values." Like the Democratic Party, I became defensive and began a self-analysis of what I was doing wrong and how I could become a better person—just as Democrats want to be a better party, namely not a losing one.

I don't know what the Democrats are going to do. But after a period of introspection, I have come up with a simple but radical notion that could cut to the heart of the moral values argument. All we need to do is rid ourselves of our most common and the most insidious character flaw—hypocrisy—defined by Webster as "pretending to be what one is not, or to feel what one does not feel, especially, a pretense of virtue."

Let me offer two cases in point.

A major item in the news this past week was a riot at an NBA basketball game in Detroit. Even staid news organizations like NPR and PBS devoted much time to it. The main feature of this riot was that some of the players ran into the stands and began fighting with the fans. No one was seriously injured, but it has provoked a storm of protest, soul-searching, and public angst about the future of basketball or organized sports or the American way. Needless to say, the NBA is concerned because it doesn't want to drive away those high rollers who pay $1,000 to sit court-side but who certainly don't want to get mugged by some seven foot point guard who doesn't like what they may be cheering or jeering.

For us as a society, the incident may be a wake-up call. But why do we need to be awakened? Because some fans are secretly jealous of the huge salaries being paid to professional athletes? Because white fans still harbor racist feelings toward African American players? Because the security procedures at games need to be greatly strengthened?

Maybe all of the above are true. But for me, the real message is that this is a natural progression in the glorification of violence in sports. Columnists and commentators will tut-tut about a dirty hit in football; will cry "foul" if a hockey player uses his stick to hit an opponent; or profess outrage if fans throw trash onto a baseball diamond. But those same people will celebrate rough play even when it breaks limbs, causes concussions, or puts somebody out for the season.

They will speak gushingly of the "intensity" of fans in various cities and give special attention to the most bizarre behavior or dress code.

Sports talk radio lives on churning up rivalries and fan anger. ABC, CBS, ESPN, and FOX Sports devote special programs to the big hits of the week and give annual awards to tough guys—the All-Madden Team for example.

Likewise the sports media pretend that modest, quiet, dedicated team players should be the role models for our children. But those who are rewarded with the most ink and airtime (which often tends to lead to the biggest contracts) are frequently those who are the biggest showboats.

And as athletic competition plays such a dominating role in shaping or reflecting our cultural values, I also take my second example of societal hypocrisy from the sports world. On the opening segment on Monday Night Football a couple of weeks ago, ABC produced a flagrant promo that posed as an opening for its new *Desperate Housewives* show. We see one of the show's stars, dressed only in a towel (but with her back to the camera), trying to seduce one of the players. In the end, she drops the towel, and jumps naked into the player's arms (he's in full uniform). The clamor that followed this incident was almost as great as the outcry over Janet Jackson's briefly bared breast at last year's Super Bowl.

Critics suggested it had racial stereotypical overtones because the woman was white and the player was black. Others gasped that this was highly inappropriate for children to see at the beginning of a "family" show. The NFL itself harrumphed about how outrageous ABC had been. Excuse me. This is the same NFL that allows extreme close-ups of cheerleaders' breasts, beer commercials that glorify "the twins" and other male fantasies, and an almost endless number of ads for medications for erectile dysfunction that may cause "erections that last four hours." Stadium tunnels and the stands are festooned with Levitra signs and when team rosters are shown on television they often carry the Cialis logo. Talk about saturation coverage. These days, commercial plugs for ED pills are literally all over the lot.

But it's not just NFL hypocrisy we're talking about here. Let's deconstruct the TV game coverage a little more. Many of the most sexist commercials are for a beer company whose owner recently ran for the Senate in Colorado as man of family values.

And what about the drug companies who say their products are so expensive because of all the money they spend on research. Did mankind really need three major pharmaceuticals to devote so much of their research time and money to come up with the cure for erectile dysfunction? And do we really need them to pollute the airwaves with hundreds of millions of dollars in ads to market a product that supposedly is for geezers like me but apparently is being used by much younger men who use it as protection against performance problems when they drink too much? Prejudiced I may be, but I'd rather see more cures for cancer and fewer designer drugs for illnesses of dubious urgency.

But hypocrisy is by no means the sole purview of organized sports—or the beer or drug companies for that matter. I use them as examples as they are easy targets. In fact, hypocrisy is universal. It is non-ideological. It's not exclusive to one race, one gender, one religion. Hypocrites can be liberal or conservative, smart or dumb, rich or poor, young or old.

And that's the real virtue of my idea to try to rid ourselves of this pervasive and hugely debilitating affliction. To stop being hypocrites, we don't have accept anyone else's value system or be for or against any idea or philosophy. There's no need to change political parties or move to another part of the country. We just have to be honest with ourselves.

October 17, 2010

Mainstream Media Malaise

The dramatic rescue of the thirty-three Chilean miners who had been trapped nearly half a mile below the surface for more than two months is certainly the feel-good story of the year. As many as 1,400 journalists, even North Koreans, covered this story. By comparison, in my day a major event such as a Reagan-Gorbachev summit would attract at most a few hundred reporters. Of course, times have changed. But at the risk of showing my age, I would argue that more journalists doesn't necessarily mean better journalism.

The wall-to-wall coverage around the world was focused almost exclusively on the human part of the story. That was appropriate. But for me, there was something missing in all that coverage—something I finally found buried deeply in a *New York Times* feature about the odd assortment of people who gathered at Camp Hope during the seventy-day drama. A local Chilean Roman Catholic priest named David Pauvif told the *Times* that many news organizations were glossing over the real story in favor of simpler tales. "These miners are being called heroes" said Father Paufit. "But they are, in reality, victims of a great injustice in work conditions."

The priest's words inspired me to look again at the Upper Big Branch tragedy that killed twenty-nine West Virginian miners last April. What I found was not comforting. Just last week the *Washington Post* ran a story with the headline, "Obama push to unclog backlog of contested mine safety citations has backfired."

According to this report, the administration has spent $23 million to reform the system and the Labor Department has issued hundreds of new citations for safety violations, which it called "significant and substantial." But, writes the *Post*, "the result is that instead of revolutionizing mine safety in the wake of the worst mining disaster in forty years, some experts said government officials have succeeded only in generating increased litigation." Apparently the backlog of 16,600 safety citations under appeal before the West Virginia disaster has now grown to 18,100. That's because most mine owners have decided it's cheaper to fight the government in court than to pay the fines and make their mines safer. Meantime, nine more men have died in American mines since April.

Rep. George Miller (D-Calif.) who sponsored the Miner Safety and Health Act that passed the House in July, told the *Post* that mining companies are not only clogging up the system but also using their influence to prevent meaningful reforms from getting through Congress. "Clearly the process in Congress has broken down in favor of the mine owners—the law breakers," said Miller.

If the news media would give even a small fraction of the time and space they devoted to the Chile rescue to following up what so often happens in the wake of these mining tragedies—usually, very little in terms of improved safety—we would be better served. But I see no evidence this will happen. On the contrary, whether reporting from Chile or this country, even the so-called liberal media can't seem to rise above the easy, obvious story or the conventional Washington wisdom. This mainstream media malaise has been particularly troubling in their casual indifference to the true meaning of the Supreme Court's decision last January (Citizens United v. Federal Election Commission) that gives corporations the same freedom of speech rights as individual citizens.

The real impact of this decision is now being felt as tens of millions of dollars or more are swamping the current mid-term election campaigns in the form of slash and burn television ads against President Obama, his policies, and Democratic candidates for Congress who are deemed vulnerable. Using newly created non-profits as fronts, oil companies, Wall Street banks, health insurance companies, quite possibly foreign companies or countries, and yes, coal mine owners, can now contribute unlimited and unregulated sums to get candidates sympathetic to their interests elected. And since campaign finance laws were gutted by the Court, the identity of these contributors need not be disclosed.

The U.S. Chamber of Commerce is in a category of its own. It does take money from foreign sources but claims such funds are not used to pay for the $75 million dollars the Chamber says it will spend in this election cycle—almost all on behalf of Republicans. But again, who the foreign entities are and how much they gave is something the Chamber is not obligated to make public under existing law.

This past week President Obama raised this issue in several campaign speeches. But on the reputed "liberal" cable channel MSNBC, the *Washington Post*'s Chris Cillizza (who writes the *Post*'s daily political column "The Fix" and so has a devoted following among political junkies) dismissed Obama's warning that special interests were now threatening the entire political system. Cillizza said this was a "process" argument that would be of no interest to average voters because the only thing they care about is "jobs." That vacuous analysis is stunning because the issue Obama is raising is ultimately all about jobs. The secret money inundating the system is not coming from corporations or countries interested in putting more Americans back to work. We may not know exactly who they are, but we can be virtually certain that what these undisclosed contributors expect to get for their money are members of Congress who will do their bidding—lower their taxes, de-regulate their businesses, plus act as Senate Republicans did six weeks ago when they blocked Democratic attempts to deny tax breaks to companies that ship jobs overseas.

Two weeks ago the *Washington Post* itself reported that $80 million had been spent under the now almost non-existent campaign finance rules—and that Republicans had a seven-to-one advantage in contributions. Since then, some of those involved with these shadowy non-profits (including Karl Rove) have been publicly promising that they'll be spending much, much more on the campaign between now and November 2. That's one promise you can believe.

July 26, 2009

The Golden Age of Television Anchormen

Golden ages, whether they be of ancient Greece, Renaissance Italy, or Broadway musicals, are inevitably a product of their times. They evolve from a unique set of circumstances and they pass when those circumstances are fundamentally changed. Walter Cronkite was the leading, although not the only, giant of the golden age of television anchormen. David Brinkley (NBC/ABC) and Howard K. Smith (CBS/ABC) were also titans of the age.

Cronkite's death marks the passing of a remarkable journalist and an iconic national treasure. However the era he came to personify has been effectively over for a quarter of a century. As a diplomatic and foreign correspondent for ABC News from 1965–95, I had the great good fortune to have been a part of that era.

The golden age of network television news ran from roughly the mid-fifties to the mid-eighties. Before the fragmentation of news that came with cable, satellites, and eventually the Internet, CBS, NBC, and ABC were indeed the windows on the world for the great majority of Americans. Each night, more than fifty million of them would gather in front of their TV sets at the dinner hour to watch the evening news. (Fewer than twenty million do so today. And while ABC was number three in the ratings race for many years, in the late sixties and seventies it actually had more viewers than it attracted in later years when it was number one.)

The newscasts were a shared national experience where people learned about the momentous events of their world, their nation, and their neighborhoods. And these were momentous times. The Vietnam War was raging, as were the anti-war protests. The Cold War was at its height and nuclear war was widely believed to be a real possibility. The Middle East seemed constantly in turmoil and had the potential to ignite a superpower confrontation. At home, a president, his brother, and the country's most prominent African American leader were assassinated. Below that seething surface, the country was in the throes of at least four ongoing and interlocking social revolutions over race, feminism, sexual freedom, and an array of new technologies. At such a moment, the newfound power of television could have become an instrument for division and extremism, as a free but irresponsible press had been in other times and places. It did not. Perhaps as much by accident as design, the television news broadcasts of that era were voices of moderation amid chaos. They reflected middle class values and essentially centrist politics, mainly because the people who produced and presented them were middle class and moderate.

As was noted in many of the Cronkite tributes, the assassination of President John Kennedy was a major watershed for television news. When tears welled up in Cronkite's eyes as he announced that Kennedy had died, he reflected an emotion almost universally shared by the American people. Television's three-day nonstop coverage of the aftermath of the event went a long way in calming a deeply shaken and, at the margin, almost paranoid population. It was crucially important at this time of high anxiety for the networks to conduct themselves responsibly. After all, just a year before, the United States and the Soviet Union had come to the brink of a nuclear war over the Cuban missile crisis. Were the Russians behind the assassination? Should we launch a pre-emptive nuclear strike against them if they were? These were questions hanging in the air at that moment. The TV networks firmly said "no" and "no" to both of them, and the country began to breathe easier. One can almost hear the breathless tones and purple prose of the cable news channels if, God forbid, something like a presidential assassination were to befall us today. But in November 1963, the networks and their anchors behaved with great seriousness and dignity, and in so doing achieved new levels of respect in the eyes of most Americans.

That credibility would serve them well in what I believe was one of the most important roles played by the networks during the golden age—their coverage of the civil rights movement of the 1960s. Remarkably, Cronkite, Brinkley, and Smith all grew up in the South, which turned out to be significant as they approached one of the major stories of their times. As young men, none of the three had been an activist for racial equality. In fact, in his autobiography Cronkite confesses that he lacked the courage to take issue with his high school friends (in Texas) when they made racist remarks. But all three future anchors had seen enough racism in the South to know it was morally wrong to perpetuate a system that enforced unequal treatment and protection under the law. This was a proposition that would eventually be accepted by the nation as a whole. But it took physical and moral courage by both reporters and anchormen to accomplish that acceptance. Brinkley was constantly bombarded by poisonous comments and death threats by mail and phone. Smith was fired for editorializing in a documentary he wrote and anchored on the savage beating of civil rights workers by the Ku Klux Klan in Birmingham, Alabama. Smith argued that the civil rights issue was not something over which reasonable minds might differ: one side was clearly justified by the Constitution, the other side clearly was not. CBS President William Paley told Smith if he believed that he should leave, and so he did, to the great benefit of ABC.

In the time of Cronkite, Brinkley, and Smith, network television news had its greatest influence because it rejected extremes, and had as its symbols men of unquestioned journalistic excellence and integrity. Dan Rather, Tom Brokaw, Peter Jennings, and Ted Koppel were worthy successors, but it was not within their power to repel the powerful forces of change which ultimately ended this golden age. (Cronkite himself would most probably not have been able to stem the tide of tabloidization of the news that came with the cable networks.) Among the young people who have taken over television news, the common metaphor for the first and second generation of anchors is that they were "dinosaurs." Probably so, but I believe in this case, we can genuinely regret their inevitable extinction.